Economic Interest, Militarism, and Foreign Policy

Economic Interest, Militarism, and Foreign Policy

ESSAYS ON GERMAN HISTORY

Eckart Kehr

Edited and with an Introduction by GORDON A. CRAIG

Translated by GRETE HEINZ

UNIVERSITY OF CALIFORNIA PRESS

Berkeley • Los Angeles • London

Translated from the German edition with permission:
Eckart Kehr, *Der Primat der Innenpolitik.*
Gesammelte Aufsätze zur preussisch-deutschen
Sozialgeschichte in 19. und 20. Jahrhundert.
Berlin: Walter de Gruyter & Co., 1970 (First edition, 1965)

University of California Press, Berkeley and Los Angeles, California
University of California Press, Ltd. London, England
Copyright© 1977 by The Regents of the University of California
ISBN 0-520-02880-5
Library of Congress Catalog Card Number: 74-22964
Printed in the United States of America

1 2 3 4 5 6 7 8 9 0

Contents

Acknowledgements

I wish to express my gratitude to my colleague Peter Paret of Stanford University, who first suggested that an English edition of Eckart Kehr's essays might be useful for students of history and the social sciences, and to Otto Büsch of the Historische Kommission zu Berlin and Hans-Ulrich Wehler of the University of Bielefeld, the editor of the excellent German edition of the essays, who actively encouraged the idea.

The text followed here is that of the German edition, published under the title *Der Primat der Innenpolitik,* as Volume 19 of the Veroffentlichungen der Historischen Kommission zu Berlin in 1965. A few of the more fragmentary pieces in that edition have been omitted here. Kehr's notes, which are indicated by arabic numerals, are to be found at the bottom of the pages, as in the German edition. To these have been added my own editorial notes, indicated by letters, which will be found at the end of the book.

G.A.C.

Editor's Introduction

In October 1931, *The New Republic* published an article by Charles A. Beard in which he alluded to the international conference on general disarmament that was expected to begin its work in the following year. Beard's view was pessimistic in the extreme. The intellectual preparations for a serious meeting had, in his opinion, been wholly inadequate. "In spite of the millions spent by peace societies for research and propaganda, there does not exist in any language a realistic description and analysis of all the forces now at work and all the fundamental problems at stake in armament rivalries. What is national interest? Who has the right to define it? What is adequate defense? Adequate to what and to whom? Why do armies and navies grow bigger and better? What is to be gained by war? Who gains by it, when, as and if? Do navalism and imperialism pay? Pay whom? The questions are not even asked officially and the materials for answering them are not yet assembled."[1]

Given the amount of ignorance that prevailed with respect to these basic issues of international relations, there was little likelihood, Beard intimated, that the democratic states would be able to meet the challenges that would almost certainly confront them in the years ahead. Yet no one seemed to be worried about this, and there was little indication that serious scholars were interested in pursuing the historical research that might suggest answers to the

1. Charles A. Beard, "Making a Bigger and Better Navy," *New Republic,* LXVIII, 223 (14 October 1931).

questions that Beard was asking. A happy exception was a young German historian named Eckart Kehr who, on the basis of extensive researches in the archives of the Ministry of Defense in Berlin, had recently published a study of German naval policy and party politics in the years 1894–1902. This provided "deep insight into the political, social and ideological presuppositions of German imperialism" before the war, demonstrated the considerable extent to which national policy had been manipulated by interest groups for their material or political advantage, and made it clear that "the naval armament struggle [was] a phase of the domestic social and economic conflict, mirrored in patriotic ideology." "It is now possible," Beard wrote, "for one nation on earth to know what went on behind its governmental facade during momentous years."[2]

This encomium of Kehr's work was entirely justified, but it found no echo among the people for whom the book was written and who might have been expected to be the principal beneficiaries of its revelations. The merits of the book on naval construction and the parties were, to be sure, proclaimed by a few distinguished German scholars—notably by Alfred Vagts, Beard's son-in-law, who had brought it to Beard's attention, and by Wilhelm Mommsen and George W.F. Hallgarten—but in the main the German professoriate either ignored it or dismissed it as "political," that is, one-sided and hence bereft of scholarly interest. Most journals of opinion that mentioned it at all vied with the publications of the armed services in accusing its author of an unpatriotic attempt to denigrate the motives of the men who, before 1914, had labored faithfully for the national interest.[3] After this hostile reception, the book was virtually ignored, and when Kehr died, not yet 31, during a visit to the United States in 1933, it must have been with a bitter sense of failure.

Kehr could not have guessed—the year 1933 was not a good year for Germans to make guesses of any kind—that his time would come, that in thirty years his reputation would have eclipsed that of most of his critics, and that his kind of history—that is, his choice of

2. *Ibid.* The Kehr volume was *Schlachtflottenbau und Parteipolitik, 1894–1902* (Berlin, 1930).
3. The critical response to Kehr's book is described in detail in the editorial introduction to Eckart Kehr, *Der Primat der Innenpolitik: Gesammelte Aufsätze zur preußisch-deutschen Sozialgeschichte im 19. und 20. Jahrhundert,* edited by Hans-Ulrich Wehler (Berlin, 1965).

subjects and his method of investigating them—would have become a source of inspiration to a new breed of German historians, some of whose leading members would describe their own work as a continuation of his.[4] Yet this is what has happened. In the last decade, the influence of Eckart Kehr has become perhaps the strongest reforming force in German historiography and the one that has been largely responsible for curing the myopia that affected its vision of the past.

1

Kehr may, indeed, be described as the father of modern German historical revisionism, the charter member of the school that is today graced with such members as Fritz Fischer, Helmuth Böhme, and Hans-Ulrich Wehler. This in itself poses a problem. If lineage and education were the chief determinants of careers, it would be difficult to explain why Kehr became such a dedicated antagonist of historical orthodoxy. His background was impeccably Prussian. He was descended on his mother's side from a long line of civil servants, jurists, and theologians. His father, himself the son of a pedagogue, was director of the Ritterakademie in Brandenburg an der Havel, a respected school for boys; his uncle, a distinguished medievalist, became general director of the Prussian state archives in 1915. When Eckart Kehr began his studies at the University of Berlin in 1921, his principal teachers—men like Hans Rothfels and Friedrich Meinecke—were admirers of the Prussian ideals and the Prussian leadership that had created and maintained the German Reich of 1871. One might have expected the young scholar to follow the example of his forebears and his professors and to nourish the tradition in which he had been raised.

That he did not take this route was due principally, as Hans-Ulrich Wehler has suggested,[5] to the war and the German collapse of 1918. While the great majority of Germans in public life and a distressingly high percentage of those in academic posts sought to deny any German responsibility for the debacle, preferring to blame

---

4. See, for example, the introduction to Helmut Böhme, *Deutschlands Weg zur Großmacht: Studien zum Verhältnis von Wirtschaft und Staat während der Reichsgründungszeit, 1848–1881* (Köln, 1966).

5. Wehler in *Der Primat der Innenpolitik*, p. 1.

it on foreign resentment and internal subversion, Kehr looked to German history for an explanation of what had happened to his country. Even before his apprenticeship was complete, he was turning a coldly critical eye upon those German policies which, by alienating the sympathies of powers that had once been friendly, had contributed to the coming of war in 1914. How had those policies been determined, he asked. By statesmen who were motivated by a rationally defensible concept of national interest, or by political forces that were responsive to the desires and anxieties of organized professional or economic interests? The more he thought about the question, the more convinced he became that the latter was the case, and that, indeed, the whole course of German history in the nineteenth century could be understood only if one turned one's attention to its economic and social development and studied the relationship between the strains caused within the structure of society by the progress of industrialization and the ways in which the government sought to cope with them. Might it not be true, for instance, that those aspects of German foreign policy that were most disruptive of good relations with the country's neighbors, and hence most dangerous to the international peace, were not reflexive actions caused by changes in the international political system but rather the result of domestic pressures that were strong enough to make a rational conduct of foreign relations impossible?

In beginning his studies with this hypothesis, Kehr was, to use the language of *Treasure Island,* tipping himself the black spot as far as his future career was concerned. Since the death of Gustav Schmoller in 1917, economic and social history had ceased to be respectable fields for investigation. As Kehr was to write later in his essay on German historiography, one was not supposed to assign a political role to economics or to believe that it influenced the policies of statesmen or the debates of parliaments. Indeed, anyone who persisted in attempting to demonstrate the influence of economics on the history of the modern period ran the risk of being considered oppositional in political attitude and hence beyond the social pale. As for social history, it was regarded as a disguised form of socialist propaganda, to be avoided at all costs by scholars who hoped for academic preferment. The fields in which careers were made were, first, the kind of national history once professed by Heinrich von

Treitschke and his followers, which, even in its modern forms, showed the profound influence of Hegelian *étatisme* and was not curious about the domestic origins of the State's activities, and, second, the kind of intellectual history made popular by Friedrich Meinecke and his school.

Kehr had little interest in these varieties of history. The first he regarded as superficial; the second seemed to him to be a form of culture fakery that discoursed of ideas without any close attention to their political and social context and was careful to avoid any discussion of movements like democracy and socialism that had demonstrable social consequences. The monopoly that they held in German academic life was, in his view, unwholesome and intolerable. It was a mirror image of the whole miserable history of the German bourgeoisie, which had acquiesced in the powerlessness to which it had been reduced by its defeats in 1848 and 1866 and had compensated for its loss by combining an uncritical nationalism, which in time of crisis degenerated into an unedifying *Hurrapatriotismus,* with an idealization of private and cultural values *(Innerlichkeit),* which it used as an excuse for its lack of any sense of political responsibility. Kehr believed that, if the new republic of Weimar was to survive, it would do so only with the help of a new kind of history that would face up to the political and economic realities of Germany's past and draw the proper lessons from them. Anything less than that would invite a recurrence of the tendencies that had led to the disaster of 1918.

Disregarding the doubts of some of his teachers and the open hostility of others, Kehr set out to demonstrate what a critical historical method could achieve. The first draft of his doctoral dissertation, which dealt with the early stages of Tirpitz's naval policy, was completed in 1926, and the finished work was accepted in the summer of 1927. But even before that happened, he had written the first of the essays that were to startle the scholarly world with their uncompromising iconaclasm, "The German Fleet in the Eighteen Nineties and the Politico-Military Dualism in the Empire" and "Anglophobia and *Weltpolitik,*" which were published in 1927–28; and before his dissertation appeared in book form, he had followed these up with others dealing with the social and financial foundations of Tirpitz's naval propaganda, the origins and significance of the Prussian Reserve Officer Corps, and the reform of the Prussian civil service by Robert von Puttkamer.

These articles are all included in this volume, and they should be allowed to speak for themselves. A few comments may be in order concerning their originality. At a time when thousands of Germans were alienated by the failures of leadership and the lack of direction in republican Germany and were turning yearning eyes to the past and to what they conceived to be the legitimacy and stability of the Bismarckian Reich, Kehr had the temerity to argue that the old Empire was anything but stable, that it was, indeed, an attempt to maintain an anachronistic political structure by expedients that became increasingly desperate and were ultimately disastrous. In place of the traditional view of Bismarck as the great statesman who stood above the passions of lesser men and who, as an honest broker, adjudicated the ugly disputes of the European powers with sovereign nonchalance and unfailing wisdom and so protected the security of his own country, he offered a picture of a conservative politician seeking to master the problems that confronted his new Reich in its first difficult decade by presiding over a *connubio* between the two strongest economic interests in the country, the East Elbian grain producers and heavy industry, and by cementing that union by state subventions in the form of tariffs and by an all-out attack on organized socialism. The Chancellor's inauguration of these policies in 1878–1879 was of more significance in German history than what had happened in the Hall of Mirrors at Versailles in 1871. It represented the *grosse Wendung* that determined "the Empire's political and social configuration until the collapse of 1918."[6]

Bismarck was not, however, content with these first steps. He believed that his new conservative system required safeguards against the possibility of dissidence within the state service or of a revitalization of political liberalism among the people of *Besitz und Bildung*. In essays that took him into areas that were *terra incognita* to German historians, Kehr demonstrated how the Chancellor obtained the reassurance he desired, thanks to Robert von Puttkamer's purge of the Prussian bureaucracy, which systematically eliminated potentially oppositional elements,[7] and to the skillful way in which

6. See below, Chapter VI.
7. *Ibid.*

the army, using reserve commissions in the officer corps as bait, appealed to the latent parvenuism of the wealthy middle class and, by doing so, feudalized their values and killed their political instincts.[8]

These expedients were successful, indeed disastrously so, when one considers the political inertness of the middle class in the last decades of the nineteenth century. Less effective was Bismarck's campaign against social democracy, whose defiant growth accounted for his increasingly erratic behavior in the first years of William II's reign and ultimately caused his dismissal from office, an event that did not, however, relieve the government's predicament. The Chancellor's successors were soon as alarmed as he had been about the socialist threat to the system, and their first impulse was to seek to contain it by more extreme forms of Bismarck's anti-socialist legislation. With the failure of the Subversion Bill of 1896, this tactic was abandoned in favor of the so-called *Sammlungspolitik* or Concentration Policy, which was the brainchild of Johannes Miquel in 1897. Based upon a reaffirmation of the social compact of 1879, this provided for a dynamic and aggressive foreign policy that would, it was hoped, divert the attention of the proletariat from domestic concerns and, by the psychic and material benefits that it would bring to them, convert them from socialism to nationalism. In his essay "Anglophobia and *Weltpolitik*,"[9] Kehr demonstrated triumphantly that historians who were trying to find the causes of the war of 1914 by reading diplomatic correspondence and government white papers would have to broaden their field of inquiry. Germany's first long stride toward war was the attempt by Bülow and Miquel to relieve their domestic dilemma by means of the *Sammlungspolitik*. Its first fruits, the supplementary naval construction law of 1900 and the agricultural tariff of 1902, redounded to the advantage of the social partners. They also led inevitably to the alienation of Great Britain and Russia, a dramatic shift in European diplomatic alignments, the growth of a feeling of encirclement in Germany, and the frantic attempts to break out of it that eventuated in war in 1914.

Kehr's essays on armament policy, on naval propaganda, and on the Anglo-German problem were remarkable performances. In

8. See below, Chapter V.
9. See below, Chapter II.

them, and in his dissertation, which was published in revised and expanded form in 1930, he provided a persuasive and well-documented account of how economic interest groups operated politically and how they brought their influence to bear upon the government's decision-making processes. Nothing like this had ever been done before. One can understand Charles Beard's enthusiasm, when he became aware of Kehr's revelations,[10] and that of Alfred Vagts, a long-time student of militarism in its varied forms, who must have felt that he had discovered a kindred spirit when he read Kehr's article "Class Struggle and Armament Policy."[11] In this provocative essay, Kehr pointed out—as Vagts was to do in his magisterial study of the subject[12]—that, in the last analysis, militarism was not a soldierly attitude but a civilian one, and that a militarized public opinion was capable of exerting its will even against the doubts and hesitations of the soldiers themselves. In Germany before 1914, the leaders of the military establishment feared that to expand the army beyond a certain point would destroy the social cohesiveness of the officer corps and threaten the army's effectiveness as a fighting force. "Yet the militarized bourgeoisie blithely demanded and approved an armament policy that was in no wise justified by the foreign-political situation and blindly waved aside the serious misgivings that the military had about the reliability of such mammoth armies."[13]

Kehr was not content to confine his researches to the Bismarckian and Wilhelmine periods. He was convinced that the history of Prussia in the years after 1807—the time of the reform of the Frederician state and the liberation of Germany from French domination—had been romanticized in the school books and needed to be reexamined by the methods that had been so successful in his work on the armament question. He began his researches in 1928 and three years later had finished a manuscript, "Economics and Politics in the Prussian Reform Period," which had as its central theme the relationship between the bureaucracy and the banking fraterni-

10. Arthur Lloyd Skop, "The Primacy of Domestic Politics: Eckart Kehr and the Intellectual Development of Charles A. Beard," *History and Theory,* XIII:2 (1974).
11. See below, Chapter III.
12. Alfred Vagts, *A History of Militarism: Romance and Realities of a Profession* (New York, 1937), pp. 11–15.
13. See below, Chapter III.

ty and was intended to demonstrate that an appreciation of the true nature of the economic and social forces that were at work in Prussia after Jena would dispel the notion that the period was one of unalloyed heroism and dedication to the state.

Unfortunately, no trace of this manuscript has survived, although we are able to derive some sense of its general approach and of Kehr's treatment of Baron Karl vom und zum Stein and his colleagues from his essay "The Genesis of the Prussian Bureaucracy and the *Rechtsstaat*" and the shorter piece "The Dictatorship of the Bureaucracy," which are included in this volume.[14] These indicate that he was not impressed by the idealistic preachments of the reformers, whom he regarded, indeed, as typical examples of the bureaucratic profession, motivated principally by the desire to acquire and exert influence. It is likely that the lost manuscript made this point more forcefully, and perhaps with even more immoderate language, than the essays that are reprinted in these pages. However that may be, when Kehr sought to persuade Hans Rothfels to accept the work as the basis for his habilitation, Rothfels, for reasons that are not entirely clear, refused.[15]

This was a blow to Kehr's academic prospects, and he reacted violently. In the fall of 1931, at the invitation of the Prussian State Archives, he had undertaken to prepare four volumes of documents on Prussian financial policy from 1806 to 1815; and he now plunged furiously into this task with a determination to produce "a sensation of the first magnitude" that would validate his views and confound his detractors.[16] This was not an approach likely to win the confidence of the historical profession, and although Kehr managed, in defiance of the deteriorating condition of his health, to put together the first two volumes of the projected edition in the course of 1932, they were not published by the Archives. Indeed, after the accession of the National Socialist regime, the director revoked Kehr's contract. By that time Kehr was traveling and pursuing his researches in

14. See below, Chapters VIII and IX.
15. See Hans-Ulrich Wehler, "Eckart Kehr" in *Deutsche Historiker* (4 vols., Göttingen, 1971–72), I, 104. Hermann Oncken thought that the refusal was politically motivated, but manuscripts are rejected for many reasons, and we have no reliable way of discovering in what shape Kehr's manuscript was when it was submitted. It had, after all, been written very quickly.
16. Wehler in *Primat der Innenpolitik*, p. 14.

the United States, whence he wrote ruefully to a friend that, given his reputation, it was possible that, when he returned, the rulers of the new "Swastika Reich" would hang him. If that should happen, he added, "be so kind as to write a few friendly lines in the HZ: 'He was, to be sure, a red, but, even so, a human being.'"[17]

When he wrote that letter, his controversial course was all but run. He died of heart failure three months later.

2

One does not have to be a specialist in German history to be impressed by the brilliance of Kehr's formulations and the incisiveness of his *aperçus*. He was not, to be sure, much of a stylist, neither possessing nor striving after the literary grace that characterized the work of many of the historians he attacked. His writing is often repetitious—indeed, there are times when he not only repeats himself in successive sentences, but uses the same words to do so—and his prose intermittently becomes so compressed as to resemble a kind of shorthand, or so convoluted that even readers who are patient with the German passion for dependent clauses are temporarily daunted. Yet, despite this, he was capable of a lapidary conciseness that enabled him to say volumes in sentences. Hermann Broch, in his novel *The Sleep Walkers*, repeatedly interrupted the narrative with ruminative essays in which he sought to define the style of the Wilhelmine era. Kehr needed only sixty words at the end of his essay on the Prussian reserve officer to fashion a striking and essentially fair characterization. "If," he wrote, "one identifies the period from 1890 to 1914, with some justice, as Wilhelmine, then this word signifies that inherently misguided outlook which, in its weakness, mistook bravado for an expression of strength, arrogance and conceit for a manifestation of dignity, and swagger for sensibility: in this life style William II was at one with his reserve officers."[18]

Less just, but no less striking, is his sardonic description of intellectual history and its practitioners. "In the long run, it is a dead end. But temporarily those who enter it are strengthened and ex-

17. Kehr to Dietrich Gerhard, from Chapel Hill, North Carolina, 10 February 1933. Professor Hans-Ulrich Wehler was kind enough to make this letter available to me and to give me permission to quote it.
18. See below, Chapter V.

alted. They feel as if they are on a high mountain from which they look down into a squalid valley where the mob, struggling for its daily bread, is penned in by the narrow horizon and cannot see the light beyond. The superiority complex of the mountain climber is highly developed in the intellectual historian."[19]

Kehr was fascinated by the problems of bureaucracy, to which his careful study of Max Weber had led him, and by the effect of bureaucratic affiliation upon individuals. At an early stage in his investigation of the arms race from the 1890's to the outbreak of the war, he became convinced of the importance of the *Apparat*, the agency, as a vital force in the policy-making process. He pointed out that, in matters of great moment, when decisions must be made, the government officials who assemble to make them rarely act as individuals, viewing the issues at stake objectively and making independent judgements; on the contrary, they find it impossible to detach themselves from the traditions and interests of their own departments, which inevitably color their views, and sometimes—particularly when interagency rivalry runs high—induce the kind of institutional loyalty that makes objective judgement impossible. "The problem of history," Kehr wrote, "is not the wilfulness of the human beings who appear to be directing these institutions but the fact that they are the captives of the laws that govern their institutions and their class and are subordinate to their interests without even being aware of their dependence."[20] Today no student of foreign policy would be much surprised by that statement; thanks to Graham Allison's analysis of the Cuban missile crisis of 1962[21] and Zara Steiner's study of the British Foreign Office before 1914,[22] we have been persuaded of the importance of institutional influence in the decision-making process. But Eckart Kehr deserves some credit for being one of the first scholars, not only to sense this, but to demonstrate how the influence was exerted: another indication of that originality of mind that was so unappreciated by his contemporaries.

19. See below, Chapter X.
20. See below, Chapter III.
21. Graham T. Allison, *Essence of Decision: Explaining the Cuban Missile Crisis* (Boston, 1971).
22. Zara S. Steiner, *The Foreign Office and Foreign Policy, 1898–1914* (Cambridge, 1969).

On at least one occasion, Kehr's ability to penetrate the ethos of institutions and to understand the common values and desires and frustrations that were shared by their members assumed an almost prophetic power. This was in his brief essay "The Sociology of the Reichswehr," written in 1930.[23] Kehr's entirely accurate prediction that the 100,000-man army permitted by the Versailles Treaty would, when the right time came, have no difficulty in expanding to a size equal to that of the forces of other major powers would have been enough in itself to make this a notable article; and the same could be said of his justifiable criticism of the Social Democratic party for its share in the responsibility for making the Reichswehr politically unreliable. The Socialist leader Julius Leber was to reach the same conclusion before he died for his part in the conspiracy against Hitler, and so, during his long years in the concentration camp, was Kurt Schumacher, who later insisted that the future of German democracy would depend upon his party's ability to free itself from the shibboleths of the past and to understand, instead of merely reprobating, militarism.

But by all odds the most remarkable aspect of Kehr's essay on the Reichswehr was his description of the alienation of the German officer corps from the society that supported it and his prevision of where this would lead. In his view, nothing illustrated the failure of German liberalism and democracy more clearly than the contrast between the civilian-dominated military establishments of Great Britain and the United States and the self-contained army of hirelings that existed in Germany, and it was one of the ironies of history that, at the precise moment when the Germans were most disposed to creating a true citizens army, in 1918–1919, they were prevented from doing so, and forced to do the opposite, by the victorious powers at Paris. Between the Reichswehr that was authorized by the Versailles Treaty and the democratic society of Weimar, there was no vital link, and the oath that the former had taken to defend the republic was worthless because praetorians don't understand allegiance to paper, but only to persons. At a time when many political pundits were writing confidently that the Reichswehr would never tolerate Adolf Hitler's assumption of power, Kehr sensed that the soldiers wanted a leader so badly that they

23. See below, Chapter VII.

would not hesitate to accept a dictator. On 2 August 1934 what he had foreseen came to pass, when the leaders of the armed forces and every officer and man in the Reichswehr made the fateful declaration: "I swear by God this sacred oath that I will yield unconditional obedience to the Fuehrer of the German Reich and *Volk*, Adolf Hitler, the Supreme Commander of the *Wehrmacht*, and, as a brave soldier, will be ready at any time to lay down my life for this oath."[24]

Kehr's judgment was not always as sound as it was in this admirable essay, and he had other faults that should be borne in mind by the prudent reader. He was often dogmatic, and this tendency led him to take insupportable or inherently contradictory positions. James Sheehan has pointed out that some of his sweeping generalizations in the essay "Class Struggle and Armament Policy" come close to being a parroting of vulgar Marxism and that they suggest a belief in the complete domination of the individual by impersonal social forces that is contradicted, elsewhere in the essays, by the importance that Kehr attributes to the achievements of single actors on the political stage, like Tirpitz, for example.[25] This is not the only inconsistency that can be found in the essays, and there is no doubt that Kehr's treatment of what Theodor Schieder has called the problem of structures and personality in history suffers from a methodological lack of precision.[26]

In addition, like many another revisionist historian, Kehr had a tendency to overstate his case, in order to make sure that his point was not missed, and to make deliberately outrageous statements because he liked to cock a snook at his more conservative professional colleagues. A good example of the overstretched bow is his argument that it was Great Britain's victory in South Africa that made the Prussian agriculturalists give up their anti-naval stance and throw their support behind what one of their spokesmen called "the horrible fleet." Kehr does not support this view with any convincing evidence, and his point—which is, in any case, not essential to his main argument—does not gain credibility from categorical statements like "The English victory over the Boers had the same

24. *Militärwochenblatt*, CXIX:8 (25 August 1934), 283–284.
25. James J. Sheehan, "The Primacy of Domestic Politics: Eckart Kehr's Essays on Modern German History," *Central European History*, I:2 (June 1968), 173.
26. Theodor Schieder, "Strukturen und Persönlichkeiten in der Geschichte," *Historische Zeitschrift*, CLXXXXV (1962), 265 ff.

internal political and social implications for the conservatives that Koniggratz had had for Napoleon III" or muddy ones like "The crushing defeat of Metternich's principle of intervention in South America was echoed by the English victory over the Boers at Kimberley and the Modder River."[27]

His exaggerations became more extreme whenever he found an opportunity to assault either the cherished orthodoxies of the older generation or a field of contemporary historical investigation of which he disapproved. It was, of course, not accurate to say, as he did say, that Robert von Puttkamer's influence on the shaping of the internal structure of the Second Empire was comparable with that of Bismarck;[28] nor was it, for that matter, true that all intellectual historians removed themselves as completely from the realities of everyday existence as Kehr implied in his metaphor of the mountain climber.[29] But he knew that these passages would annoy fellow scholars, and he always enjoyed doing this and imagining the people toward whom he adopted an adversary position "standing on their heads with rage" and "panting for revenge."[30]

One cannot refrain from feeling that this was self-indulgence and that it merely gave hostages to fortune. This is all too apparent in the essays on the reform period, where Kehr was so eager to have people believe that the reformers were a power-hungry clique who made "ruthlessly brutal and slanderous attacks" upon their enemies[31] that he failed to reflect that some of his readers might remember that those enemies were the cabinet councillors who had led Prussia to the disaster at Jena and that they might begin to question his sense of proportion. At the same time, the shrillness of his attacks upon Stein and the illogic and pettiness of some of his arguments (as in the case of his denial that Stein should be given any credit for promoting the cause of local self-government)[32] makes one suspect that Stein was not his real target at all but that, like other revisionists since his time, Kehr was striking out at his own teachers, who were admirers of the reformers and their work. Kehr was al-

27. See below, Chapter II.
28. See below, Chapter VI.
29. See below, Chapter X.
30. Quoted by Wehler in *Der Primat der Innenpolitik*, p. 5.
31. See below, Chapters VIII and IX.
32. See below, Chapter VIII.

ways polemically most excessive when he was discussing the work of those who taught him, and things like his charge that Hans Rothfels was an advocate of fascist historiography justify the late Klaus Epstein's warning that his work should be read with a decent amount of caution rather than with any preconception that it represents the new historical gospel.[33]

That having been said, one must immediately add that for the student of German history or for anyone with a serious interest in bureaucratic behavior patterns, in military politics, in the complexities of arms control, or in the decision-making process in the age of developed capitalism, Kehr's essays should be required reading. He studied the past, not for its own sake, but for the light that it could throw upon the perplexities of his own time. The questions he asked were the ones that should have been asked but rarely were, and he sought answers to them with shrewdness and pertinacity. It is this unceasing endeavor to get behind the appearances of things and to grapple with reality that makes the reading of an essay, or indeed a page, written by Eckart Kehr an exciting and rewarding experience.

G.A.C.

Stanford University

33. Klaus Epstein, *Geschichte und Geschichtswissenschaft im 20. Jahrhundert: Ein Leitfaden,* edited by Eberhard Pikart, Detlef Junker, and Gerhard Hufnagel (Frankfurt am Main, 1972), p. 21.

The German Fleet in the Eighteen Nineties and the Politico-Military Dualism in the Empire

The characteristic and distinctive feature of the Bismarckian Reich lies in the peculiar way in which the relationship between state and nation was arranged, the method of regulating relations between the federal states and the attribution of legal sovereignty to the *Bundesrat,* while real hegemony was reserved to the Emperor and Prussia.[1] It would be a mistake, however, to consider these the dominant problematic areas in the years following the establishment of the Reich, since their urgency had by then abated. In these later years, the most burning issues were no longer primarily repercussions of these conflicts (it is amazing how quickly the German Reich of 1871 became a matter of course and how soon its singularity and relative nature were forgotten); the central issues of that time were of a different kind. On the one hand, there was the class struggle of the proletariat and the defensive measures it entailed on the part of the state and the other classes, setting in motion a process that subverted domestic politics as a whole into a tool of class politics; on the other hand, there was an issue of secondary importance to people of that generation, but no less significant: the dualism between political and military power, that is, the dualism between the sector regulated by the constitution and a sector of the state that might be compared to the Old German Munt District or

1. The interpretations expressed in this study have not received any official endorsement and only represent the author's independent opinion.

the Russian Oprishchina in that it remained alien to the adjoining constitutional domain, to wit, the military sector.[a]

The hitherto available information on this dualism of military and political power, which will be our main concern in this essay, leaves much to be desired. Marschall von Bieberstein's work, *Responsibility and Counter-Signature in the Case of Orders of the Supreme War Lord*,[2] deals only with a special facet of the problem, though it does take a sweeping view of the subject.[b] It also suffers from the fact that it was written before the war, that is, in a period when it was difficult to view the problem from a politically unbiased angle, quite apart from the superficiality of the factual information then available. In his book on the constitutional position of the German General Staff published shortly after the war[3] Wohlers had some advantages over Marschall von Bieberstein. By then—in the wake of the sharp conflict that surfaced during the war between the Supreme Military Command on the one hand and the Reich government and the Reichstag on the other—everyone had come to recognize the politico-military dualism as a historical-political problem. Wohlers therefore paid special attention to the gradual disengagement of the General Staff from the political structure of the Reich and to its establishment as a separate military sector. However, nobody has as yet made an over-all study of this dualism in time of peace or investigated to what extent it overlaps the general historical evolution of the Reich.

To begin with, there were three sources—of very unequal weight —for the autonomy of the military. The residue of absolutism was one, with its strict separation of the different estates and their functions; this source of autonomy merged with Frederick William IV's principle of surrounding himself with ministers-at-large like Radowitz and Leopold von Gerlach in addition to the regular ministers.[c] Then there was the conflict between the Crown and parliament, the representative of the nation as a whole, in which the Crown relied on the army's support against its opponent. And finally there was the fact that unification had been the product of wars, as a result of which the strategist Moltke could carve out a separate sphere of in-

2. Berlin, 1911.
3. *Die staatsrechtliche Stellung des Generalstabs in Preussen und Deutschland* (Bonn, 1920).

2]

fluence, alongside Bismarck's political sphere, for the General Staff.[d]

These reasons for the genesis of military autonomy do not in themselves explain why this system, which split the state into a political and a military half, persisted in later years. When examining the relationship between the political and the military element in Germany, we are dealing with a difference in kind, in that all standing armies have special psychological attributes—which have been carefully analyzed by Lorenz von Stein[e]—so that the dualism must not be interpreted solely as an opposition between civilians and men in uniform but involves the coordination of two heterogeneous sectors of the state, whose mutual relations are comparable to those of autonomous states. German history has more than its share of dualisms: the religious cleavage, the Prussian-Austrian opposition, the conflict between state and nation, and the split between the bourgeois and proletarian classes. The relation between military and political power within the state assumes an equally dualistic form in Germany. Characteristically, when one manifestation of the dualism loses its vitality, a new one emerges to take its place. Leopold von Gerlach's death coincided with that of his king, but the dualism of the sixties rested on different foundations than that of the fifties. Besides, the preeminence of the General Staff was induced not so much by internal political factors as it was the result of military victories, which were, of course, closely connected with the internal political conflict, but which did not specifically aim to increase the power of the General Staff.

Hidden beneath these political and pragmatic factors, which first emerged when the facts were carefully examined, the decisive element was the pressure of the social situation. The absolutist governments, under the pressure of the bourgeoisie's demand for political and social power, were forced to rely on the military, who remained loyal to absolutism after the liberal interlude of Prussian reformism.[f] It was only in the wake of the French Revolution that this dualism arose and divided the German state into two parts which could no longer communicate with each other.

This dualism persisted during the time of the empire, when the opposition between state and nation had become less pronounced and been supplanted by the conflict between the bourgeois state and the proletariat. Its persistence can be explained by the fact that the bourgeoisie and the military now formed an alliance against the powers from the lower depths. And once more this social factor combined with other reasons that were partly social but also partly organizational and personal.

Moltke had trained a generation of outstanding officers, who accomplished great things in their special field. The peculiarity of military discipline shaped them into a tight hierarchy with similar attitudes in political and military matters. The Prussian General Staff had been converted into a homogeneous block, in which the decisive influence on each person's character was not his distinctive individuality but his integration into the group. The political leadership, on the other hand, both in the diplomatic service and in the domestic ministerial bureaucracy, could also count on a number of superior brains even after Bismarck's dismissal, but no collaboration between them seemed possible. The political leadership displayed marked diffuseness, a perpetual flux in its interpretation of the tasks and goals of foreign, social, and commercial policies. Not enough material has been collected as yet to reach a final verdict about the differences in level, but a preliminary judgment would be—purely on the basis of professional expertise—that the greatest number of good brains could be found in the growing economic realm, the next largest number among the military, and the smallest number in the political bureaucracy.

But even this intrinsic preponderance of militarism over the political leadership would not have sufficed to make this dualism endure, had the whole system of government not gradually evolved in the direction of a fundamental emancipation of the military domain from parliament and the nation as a whole. ("Militarism" should not be equated with the numerical strength of military preparedness, but with the presence of a separate power within the state exempt from political-parliamentary control, the existence of a military estate as an autonomous group.) Several circumstances contributed to this evolution: one was the fierce insistence on septennial budgets on the basis of "technical military" requirements (the change to a quinquennial budget and the concomitant adjustment to the length of the Reichstag's legislature was only an apparent concession and a superficial alteration, which had no impact on the increasingly well-defined dualism, but only attenuated the Reichstag's concern with

4]

the problem by this apparent concession to its wishes);[g] another contributing circumstance was the exploitation and polemical exaggeration of foreign policy problems, especially at the time of the *Kartell* elections.[h] However, the general trend was not so much toward an emasculation of parliamentary authority over the military, which would then serve as a personal weapon of the Crown against the nation—as seemed likely in the sixties—as it was in the direction of a transformation of the military into an independent power alongside the political authorities, bound conceptually to the monarch by the special ties of feudal loyalty and obedience to the Commander-in-Chief. This was a relationship from which the ordinary citizen of the state was excluded. But in the last analysis the military faced the monarch as a power in their own right, opposing even him—a power which by a logical extension would evolve into a *de jure* or at least a *de facto* military dictatorship once the monarch had been removed from the picture.

The politico-military dualism found its constitutional expression in the Cabinet orders of 1883, 1889, and 1899—if such a term is appropriate for a political process which by its very nature was taking place beyond the confines of the "constitution" and of which not a single textbook of German constitutional law has taken cognizance, although it had a determining influence on the legal system of the state, its makeup, and its progressive elaboration. The Cabinet orders granted the Chief of the General Staff direct access to the Emperor, and removed the Military Cabinet from the jurisdiction of the War Ministry, a state of affairs that was concealed from the Reichstag by continuing to list it hierarchically as under the personnel division of the War Ministry.[1] In addition, the Cabinet orders split the Admiralty into the Reich Naval Office *(Reichsmarineamt)*, the Naval High Command *(Oberkommando der Marine)*, and the Naval Cabinet *(Marinekabinett)*, although in 1899, ten years after its establishment, the Naval High Command was once more eliminated, leaving the Reich Naval Office as the highest authority over the fleet.

These last mentioned developments are the first to have a bearing on the navy's involvement in this dualism.[4]

After authority over the fleet had been divided between the High

4. For further factual information on this question, see E. Kehr, *Schlachtflottenbau und Parteipolitik* (Berlin, 1930).

Command and the War Ministry in the sixties, the Admiralty was established in 1871, and its head combined the military prerogatives of a commander of the fleet with the political one of Minister of the Navy. In this instance, a unique way had been found to bridge the dualism. The significance of William II's dissolution of the Admiralty is not to be found only in the emperor's determination to take matters in his own hands, though this was precisely his aim. He was also carrying further the emancipation of the armed forces by removing the Naval Cabinet from the State Secretary's control. More significantly, however, the fragmentation of the Admiralty put an end to the hybrid position of its chief as both military and political head of the Navy and placed these two functions in the hands of independent authorities. By being able to issue whatever orders he pleased to his Commanding Admiral, the emperor gained greater influence over the navy—and he fully exploited this increased power—although his influence was limited to its internal and technical military arrangement. But at the same time the Reichstag won a greater influence over the Secretary than it had had over the Chief of the Admiralty, since the former never had the military support and, with it, the absolute cover of the emperor's authority as supreme military commander. This institutional innovation extended to the navy the same dualism that characterized the army, where General Staff, War Ministry, and Military Cabinets were, respectively, its technical-military, political, and personnel ministries. It created an arrangement that was bound to lead to a struggle for power between the state and the nation; that is, between emperor and Commanding Admiral on the one hand (represented by the Chief of the Cabinet through their alliance with the autocracy of the military personnel and who thus must be equated with the military pole of the dualism) and State Secretary and Reichstag on the other. The situation was further confused by the fact that the State Secretary belonged to the political bureaucracy, which in this conflict between nation and state, or between the nation and the military, vacillated in its allegiance between the opposing forces, sometimes allying itself with the military against the parliament, sometimes going along with the parliament against the military.

The struggles relating to the build-up of the fleet, which on casual inspection seem to be a series of minor squabbles, coincided with the period in which the naval administration was divided into a political and a military authority, and these struggles came to an end with the elimination of this dualism in 1899 when the Naval High Command was abolished and the Secretary of State was put in charge, gradually becoming the parliament's spokesman in the Reich government.

There is an intimate connection between the navy's involvement in this dualism as a result of the 1889 Cabinet order and the development of the fleet into a combat-ready military weapon. The army was already in existence when the dualism first appeared and was under no compulsion to prove itself as an autonomous power alongside the political one; it was effective because it existed. In contrast, the navy had to expand to a certain size before it could assume its place in the dualism and exert significant weight in it; or rather it had first to justify its right to this expansion, to outgrow its status as an institution serving its own end and to acquire a function in modern social life, under the difficult circumstance that the German empire was becoming more obsessed with capitalistic methods of cost accounting, in the light of which armaments were viewed as economically unjustifiable expenses. Yet this capitalistic spirit also served as a condition for the navy's subsequent popularity. For while the army developed as a factor in the dualism by means of conflict, in which it opposed its irrational power to the wishes of parliament and nation, the German fleet expanded to the impressive size it reached in 1914 not solely as a result of a sharp conflict with the nation, but by means of the closest collaboration with the nation's most modern forces, with parliament and the capitalist economy. The fleet was integrated into the economic system and the economic expansion of the Reich; and the big industrialists and shipbuilders knew what they were doing when they besieged the Reichstag and the Reich Naval Office with letters and petitions for implementing and further extending naval legislation. Although, from a constitutional point of view, the army and navy occupied the same position, the navy was part and parcel of a world policy oriented toward capitalist interests, while the army remained a pillar of the continent-oriented policy, which was conceived in the same vein as the agrarian-oriented constitution. The expansion of the fleet was

[7

justified on the ground that it contributed to industrial-commercial expansion, which implied a subordination of military power to capitalist profit objectives. The army was motivated by the slogan "enemies on all sides," but remained aloof from the international economic conflicts of interest. The fleet was a component of the capitalist profit economy, while the army could at best be viewed as a support for a subsistence economy. Only from the point of view of Marxist ideology could the fleet in the "service of maritime interests" be branded a "military tool of finance capital."

Although this economic justification played a crucial role in making public opinion accept the expansion of the fleet, and hence, unwittingly, its incorporation into the dualism, this should not blind us to motives of a different nature, which carried considerable weight with persons in high places in favor of naval expansion. It is difficult to say what determined the emperor's predilection for the fleet, but economic motives could hardly have influenced his attitude. Even Sea Captain Alfred Tirpitz, the Naval High Command's Chief of Staff,[1] whose technical naval arguments for expanding the fleet seem self-evident enough, leaves one puzzled when one reads the introductory remarks of the lengthy Memorandum IX *(Dienstschrift* IX) of June 15, 1894, in which he summarizes the "over-all experience of the maneuvers of the fall training fleet" in these words: "The uncertainty regarding the nature and purpose of the fleet has played a major role in hindering its development. Even if, in keeping with your Majesty's wishes, a change should occur in this respect, it is in the nature of things that it will take many years' effort before this change will be publicly recognized." Aside from this personal intervention on the part of the emperor, who was eager to eliminate the "filthy mess" *(Schweinerei)* in the navy, there were undoubtedly more serious military considerations, as well as the urge to lay the groundwork for a fleet that could serve in a two-front war and hold its own simultaneously against the French and Russian fleets, as can be seen in Captain Tirpitz's tendency to reduce the multiplicity of ship designs and evolve a doctrine of naval tactics that would be effective in a war. The concept of a two-front war on the sea led the emperor to stipulate as late as the spring of 1897 that the normal strength of the German fleet should be half the strength of the combined Franco-Russian fleets. This too was the underlying concept of the great fleet maneuver of 1896, in which a French fleet was supposed to penetrate the Elbe, and in which the simulation of wartime conditions was carried to such lengths that the actual names of French battleships and cruisers was given to the attacking vessels and their actual firing capability was taken into account. Tirpitz's vision of a battle fleet was not yet based on anti-British sentiment or shaped by the ideology of *Weltpolitik*. Despite the characteristic role that the battle fleet was to play later in the age of imperialism, it was first planned and trained in maneuvers in Germany's preimperialist period, when the Reich still pursued a continental policy, and France was the enemy that had to be defeated in a naval engagement off Cherbourg. The standardization Tirpitz envisaged for the German fleet in 1894 corresponded to this objective, a naval battle with the French armored fleet, although this completely ignored France's preference for the *guerre de cours*. The battle fleet that Tirpitz planned was to consist of seventeen battleships, six Class I and twelve Class III cruisers, in addition to six torpedo-boat flotillas and the requisite auxiliary fleet and a small reserve of armored ships and cruisers.

When Tirpitz took over the Reich Naval Office and was asked what requests he would make of the Reichstag, he haughtily replied: "Exactly what is stated in Memorandum IX." But this reply reveals a self-deception on his part. For instead of requesting about twenty-one cruisers and nineteen battleships, as he had planned in 1894, Tirpitz was already requesting forty-eight cruisers in the first naval bill, and thirteen of these were intended for overseas service, a figure that increased to twenty-six cruisers for overseas service by 1900. The doubling of the number of cruisers did not yet imply a shift in emphasis from a battleship fleet, but the Wiesbaden plans of May 1897 with fifty-four cruisers—up to twenty-one of which were meant for overseas—already put greater emphasis on the cruiser fleet. But Tirpitz's original concept of a battleship fleet with a tiny appendage of cruisers was long since obsolete even in his own eyes. His battle fleet never approximated his original 1894 concept: world politics had opened up new vistas and posed new demands, which were reflected in the construction of an overseas fleet alongside the domestic fighter squadrons and reconnaissance groups.

The 1894 fleet plans were therefore much more strongly motivated along military lines than the later plans, in which the emphasis on cruisers clearly demonstrated that this increase in armaments was motivated primarily by imperialist and economic arguments.

But even then Tirpitz had already discovered the key formulas, which were to serve him later for propaganda purposes, though the slogan that the fleet was merely a function of maritime interests was coined only at the end of 1895 and expressed most vividly by Ernst von Halle:[k]

A state with maritime or global interests (which in this respect comes to the same thing) must be in a position to back up these interests and make its power felt beyond its territorial waters. It would be unthinkable to engage on a national basis in world trade or world industry or even, up to a point, in deep-sea fishing, international transportation, and colonization, without the backing of an offensive fleet. Unless the state has maritime strength, that is, power beyond its own shores, with which to support these interests, conflicts among nations and the lack of confidence these would engender among the owners of capital and in the business world would either snuff out these vital national activities or even prevent them from getting started. Therein lies the fleet's prime justification.

He had no compunction about reinterpreting the course of history to achieve his goal of fitting military power into the context of a capitalist economy and thereby extricating military power from the paralyzing dualism:

Germany lost out as a maritime and world state when the Hansa's sea power collapsed. Holland's world trade declined from first to seventh place after the decisive defeat of De Ruyter's fleet. Conversely we see today that trade-oriented America is building up an offensive combat fleet in order to acquire maritime trade and protect her maritime interest. The European nations, with their highly developed cultures, which can no longer survive on what their own soil can produce, are all the more destined to follow this course.

The basic lines of argument are already apparent, but they were not yet fully worked out. Little remained to be done about the economic infrastructure, except to strengthen and improve details, but the question of tactics, artillery, use of armor-plating remained unsettled. The squadron tactics were already elaborated in theory, but on maneuvers, ancient frigate cruisers were often needed to fill up the empty spaces. Other vessels had to use flags to indicate that they were actually twice, three times, or even five times as numerous. But the linear tactical theory was still imperfect: the issue of the relative superiority of the line-ahead or line-abreast approach remained unresolved. The compromise of a T-formation was nothing more than a complicated way of circumventing the dilemma. These tactical problems determined Tirpitz's ideas about the placement of artillery: middle-range artillery was concentrated on the bow and stern for preliminary skirmishes of the fleets moving line abreast, while heavy artillery was placed midships and intended for broadside gunnery during skirmishes in which lines of ships moved past each other. He estimated the strength of armor-plating on the basis of the penetrating power of middle-range artillery, which implies that he had not yet worked out his principle of heavily armored battleships. But even at that time he paid little attention to speed and regretted the fact that new ships were invulnerable to explosions caused by torpedoes.

This residual uncertainty in his views reasserted itself on a higher plane in his opinions about the fleet as an offensive weapon. He felt that sea power required the possession of aggressive weapons; a fleet designed to defend the coastline "would be only marginally justifiable." His first argument for an offensive fleet was based on military considerations: "Only control of the seas offers the real means to force the enemy to come to terms," by troop landings, construction of military bases, blockades, inflicting damage on the enemy's maritime interests, and—in this respect he was a disciple of the *jeune école* [1]—destruction of the enemy's coastal cities. Elevating tactical and strategic considerations above their strictly military context, he showed the connection between an offensive fleet and the demands of international economic policy. But he remained a military man, limited to his own jurisdiction, his side of the dualism. While stressing the difference between the defensive character of the modern conscripted armies and the aggressive bent of the developing fleet, he failed to visualize the place of this fleet in the political system of the great powers and obviously never gave deep thought to the concrete political consequences of his plans for the fleet. He probably did not anticipate the revolutionary effect of his fleet construction on foreign policy and recognized even less its revolutionary impact on domestic policy, its influence on the social structure of the nation. He may have had his first glimpse of the relations between politics and armament expansion in 1895, when he was drawn into the political conflict in connection with his plans for the fleet. As an argument in favor of building up the fleet, he mentioned the intractability of social problems: "This great new national undertaking and the economic gains connected with it will serve as potent palliatives against educated and uneducated Social Democrats." Here a fleeting vista opens up before our eyes of the connections between the politico-military dualism and the dualism of the class struggle. Just as the real *principium movens* behind the origins of the politico-military dualism in pre-March Prussia was the conservative-feudal state's resistance against the revolutionary bourgeoisie, the underlying reason for its persistence in imperial Germany was the fear of a proletarian upheaval, which reunited the military with the now feudalized bourgeoisie.

Captain Tirpitz's unwillingness to step beyond his own jurisdictional area gives special weight to some of his brilliant predictions as a strategist. Might not the enemy, he wondered, refrain from attacking the German coast, remaining at a cautious distance in mid-ocean, and thus leave "our own fleet only two alternatives: inactivity, that is, moral self-destruction, and a decisive battle on the open sea?" This most difficult eventuality was precisely what the fleet must be equipped to handle: it must be ready to seek out the enemy and initiate combat. How prophetic are his subsequent musings for the navy's strategic position in the fall of 1914:

"We must be especially careful to avoid overestimating the strength of the enemy. This is a tendency deeply rooted in human nature, and it is further reinforced by the tension of all spiritual and mental forces in time of war, by the element of danger, by the feeling of responsibility. An additional factor is that we have exact information about our own weaknesses and inadequacies as far as personnel and equipment are concerned, and that we are well informed about the elimination of ships, etc. at the time of mobilization or later because of sea damage to machines and boilers, etc., while we lack information on this score about our enemy. For the above-mentioned reasons and on the basis of past military experience, it therefore seems less urgent to warn against the converse danger of underestimating the strength of the enemy. In attempting to avoid both mistakes, one is more likely in most cases to approximate the truth if one endeavors to underestimate the strength of the enemy, in opposition to one's emotionally biased conviction.

He concluded on the basis of past experiences with the English blockade fleet "that the moral superiority of the aggressor is greatest at the very outset. A prolonged period of inactivity in enemy territory, during which there is an inevitable attrition of personnel and equipment, may mean the loss of this moral superiority and even its transformation into its opposite."

Precise thinking about the politico-economic, tactical, and strategic tasks of the fleet, the introduction of order into the chaotic multiplicity of types of vessels, these were the goals Tirpitz had set for himself. He was consciously seeking to herald a new era in the development of the fleet. The obverse of his goals emerges from his negative comments about the Italian fleet, of which he observed that "because of national characteristics and internal political circumstances, effort and money have been obviously misallocated through a misguided emphasis on numerical strength and large amounts of equipment rather than on the organization of the fleet and its military capability. The same could of course be said until recently of almost all European navies."

But this seemingly military-technical quest for new solutions can only be understood against the backdrop of a hidden rationalism. What we have here is perhaps a quest not for the "ideal state" but for the "ideal fleet." By means of maneuvers "we can provide ourselves with a wealth of evaluations about questions that are insoluble in peace time, but which can facilitate wise action in war time." And just as rationalism turned the ideal state it had just determined into an absolute, so did Tirpitz make an absolute out of his ideal fleet, the battleship fleet. "The experiences from our maneuvers confirm that the contemporary battleship represents the nucleus of naval power, just as it did in the days of the sailing ship. There is some justification in comparing the strength of the different national fleets roughly on the basis of the number of available ships of battleship caliber." Just as the salvation of mankind or of individual man could be assured only in the ideal state, so could control over the seas be gained only through the "ideal fleet," which meant not

[13

only that it was the most battle-worthy possible in the technical sense, but that in the specifically rational meaning of the word, it was meant to be an absolute guarantee of victory. Tirpitz's pessimism about the emperor's fleet plans of January 1896[m] can only be explained in the light of this "ideal fleet" ideology; in his eyes the demand for cruisers would lead to the collapse of the whole plan, as he observed to Senden[n] at that time. His theory about the "risk fleet" (Risikoflotte)[o] makes sense only on this basis; the battle fleet as the ideal fleet would inevitably guarantee victory.

Leaving aside the irrational fact of mere existence, which applied equally to both poles of the dualism, rationalism prevailed among the military just as it did in its parliamentary-political counterpart. Moltke had erected a rational strategic structure through a rigorous elaboration and development of Napoleonic military concepts; Tirpitz was creating his own rational system, for which he derived much less guidance from his predecessors. The political system was built on rational foundations, but so was Moltke's army with its rational and systematic strategy and so was Tirpitz's fleet, whose rational features were even more conspicuous than the army's: not only was it endowed with rational tactics and strategy, which it had lacked until the early 1890's, but as a fleet of armored vessels it was also based on advanced technology and mathematical calculations, and above all it was publicly justified by the theory that it was a factor in the calculable capitalist process of production.

In the first years of the last decade before the turn of the century, even before the increase in the fleet's strength came to public attention, its inner strength grew and its future commander discovered the path along which he wished to lead it and laid down the arguments with which to justify its expansion, as well as the tactics and strategy for future naval battles. But what was the relation between this fleet and the Reichstag? How were tension and easing of tension shaped between the two poles of the dualism?

Without explicit comment, but with an obvious reference to German conditions, Tirpitz observed in 1893, in his second memorandum (Dienstschrift II), which dealt with the most recent maneuvers of the Italian fleet, that it had now actually been recognized in Italy "that the fleet was decisive for Italy's role as a Mediterranean power ... The concomitant reliance on a growing Italian fleet and the determination to bring about the necessary strength is shared by most people of consequence in Italy." The position of the German navy in the military-political dualism was strongly affected, however, by the fact that at the time of its initial build-up it lacked adequate external representation.

While Stosch[p] had succeeded in creating what was a respectable fleet for his days, in closest collaboration with the Reichstag majority, Caprivi[q] had put a halt to further expansion of the fleet in view of the total confusion about the type of vessel needed, limiting himself to the encouragement of torpedo boats. Even when some clarity concerning tactics and types of vessels gradually emerged between 1892 and 1894, the navy's political representation—Admiral Hollman had been named State Secretary after the brief interludes of Count Monts and Rear Admiral Heusner, who succeeded Caprivi in 1888 and 1889—still groped around in the dark; its requests to the Reichstag were based not on any grand design but simply on whatever had some prospect of being acceptable to parliament: coastal armored ships one day, armored ships the next, and cruisers the day after that. Whenever the outlook for approval of these erratic requests became too bleak, since even the tolerant Reichstag got tired of such scandalous goings-on, the Reichstag was presented with an infinitely verbose jeremiad about the decline of German sea power and a request for a ship with a pompous title like "admiral ship for the high seas" or was brazenly told some lies about the purposes of the requested vessel: "Supplying intelligence for high-ranking command groups." Hollman had the most confused notions about the respective merits of a battleship fleet as against those of a cruiser fleet and gave relatively greater weight to armored ships or to cruisers depending on the changing pressures emanating from the Kaiser, the Supreme Command, and the Reichstag. The term "marasmus" which a highly placed official of the Hollmann era applied to the over-all condition of the Reich Naval Office was quite justified.

By the nature of things, the Reichstag was itself confused about the question of ship designs, so that the opinions expressed about armored ships and cruisers were always highly muddled. But the Reichstag had no desire to act as arbiter in this question. All it expected was that the specialists in the Reich Naval Office should state

[15

clearly what they had in mind. The Reichstag was almost pleading for an acceptable military plan for the expansion of the fleet and was ready to submit to any leadership that knew what it wanted. However, Hollman kept telling it, with disarming candor and a complete misapprehension of his position with respect to the Reichstag, that the Navy had no plan, that it had to live from hand to mouth, nay, that such a plan would be harmful, because it would be binding only on the Reichstag but not on the technical administration. Hollmann never understood that this apparently recalcitrant parliament was raising so many difficulties only because of his incapacity to provide leadership. What the Reichstag resented was not the abuse of authority but its absence.

The Reichstag demanded an unambiguous plan. It was difficult, however, to determine what form this should take. If it was imprecise and without commitments, as was true of the 1873, 1884, 1887, and 1889 plans, then the government had to worry about the refusal of the now anarchic Reichstag to carry it out.[r] If the plan was proposed to the Reichstag in legislative form, then that amounted to a limitation of that body's budgetary prerogative and an encouragement of imperial absolutism. And such was precisely the Kaiser's motivation when on May 19, 1897 'he ordered a legislative draft to be prepared by winter incorporating the plans which Hollmann had presented in March before the Reichstag and which the latter had turned down. The composition of the circle where the decision about this legislative proposal was reached is characteristic of the dualism. The only political organs of the Reich represented in it were the Kaiser and the Deputy State Secretary from the Reich Naval Office, Rear Admiral Büchsel, and these two actually belonged to the military rather than the political pole of the dualism. The other participants were clearly representatives either of the military pole or of personal autocracy: Commanding Admiral von Knorr, Chief of the Naval Cabinet von Senden-Bibran, the head of the Civilian Cabinet von Lucanus[s] and the head of Imperial Headquarters von Plessen.[t] People whose orientation was primarily political and governmental were missing from this important conference. Military-technical arguments easily prevailed over political considerations, while the political case for the expansion of the fleet in the light of the current diplomatic situation was not made as strongly as it would have been by politicians. Even Tirpitz was no exception. As a military man, he felt that his efforts to expand the fleet were being checked by a superfluous institution, the Reichstag, and he had no appreciation for the fact that the limitations imposed by the parliamentary budgetary prerogative had more than technical significance. As early as January 1896, when the first grand plans for the fleet were being presented, Tirpitz, who was later to complain so bitterly about cabinet politicking, had tried to implement his ideas with the help of the head of the Naval Cabinet and had tried to organize an agitation for that purpose. At that time he definitely worked hand in glove with the personal autocracy in opposition to parliament and the political leadership.

When the first law was presented also, he was still dominated by the idea that, in the interest of a favorable evolution of military forces, the hands of the recalcitrant parliament should be tied as tightly as possible. The septennial budget appropriation should exclude parliament from decisions about the expansion of the fleet and leave these up to the competent military authorities. It is true that to all appearances he was not intrinsically opposed to parliament; he did object to its intervention in the technical question of how the fleet should be built up and knew of no other way to circumvent this interference than the septennial budget. He thought of himself in every way as an officer, not even as an officer with political responsibilities, but as a military technician viewing political problems primarily from the perspective of their military-technical repercussions. When he resigned from the cruiser squadron in 1897, he pointed out in his farewell address on board the "Irene" that he was a fighting man and was basically unsuited for the office of State Secretary.

Tirpitz had introduced the septennial budget request accompanying the proposed law as a technical military matter, not a political one. But he was soon compelled to broaden his point of view and to learn new ways, absorbing more political modes of thinking and feeling in his determination to carry through the military technical expansion of the fleet. For parliament rebelled against its exclusion from decisions about national defense and, unable to shake off the yoke of the septennial budget, in turn limited the government's freedom of action by setting an upper limit of 407 million marks for expenditures during the new septennial period, which meant that Tirpitz, as a result of unwise procurement policy, could not build the anticipated number of vessels. In this way, the Reichstag was able to assert indirectly its budgetary prerogative against the semiabsolutist government without registering formal dissent. The passage of this limiting paragraph was one of Ernst Lieber's finest pieces of technical-parliamentary manipulation.[u]

This parliamentary victory stands out above the ordinary level of parliamentary conflict, since it served as a point of departure for conciliating the dualism between political and military elements. Under the pressure of this parliamentary countermaneuver, which did not rely on brutal obstruction of the state's demands but instead agreed to these demands with reservations that sorely penalized the state for its lack of confidence in parliament, Tirpitz presented his second proposed law. He set aside the military-technical approach he had previously used and on his own initiative brought the Reichstag into closer contact with the state and the military. He abandoned the attempt to protect the state and its defense forces by suppressing the Jacobin tendencies in parliament; he voluntarily gave up the fetters of the septennial budget and instituted an open relationship between the Reichstag and the government. Thereupon the Reichstag felt less shackled, and out of this freedom that Tirpitz had granted it and which the army did not dare to emulate, grew the Reichstag's great sympathy for the fleet and its inclination to approve naval demands more readily than those of the army. From the point of view of the state and the military, the Prussian method of keeping the military at arm's length from the Reichstag, the nation, and the civilian sector, allowing as little parliamentary influence over the armed forces as possible, proved to be less effective than Tirpitz's approach. He enhanced it further in the course of inspection visits by Reichstag deputies by creating the impression that the Reichstag was a control organ for the accomplishments of the navy, an impression that was, characteristically, sufficient to evoke angry protests on the part of the Prussian State Ministry. In reality relations between the Reich Naval Office and the Reichstag might be characterized, on a smaller scale, in the same way as those between Pericles and the Athenian *demos:* "It was called democracy, but in reality it was rule by the top man."

Tirpitz's methods as State Secretary of the Reich Naval Office find their closest modern parallel in the governmental methods elaborated in England and France during the final stages of the World War, the methods that gave these powers the strength to withstand the last German onslaught in the spring of 1918; in Max Weber's terminology: leadership by great demagogues and government by parliamentary dictatorship. There was one basic difference, however, between Tirpitz's leadership and that of Lloyd George and Clemenceau, a difference that hinges on the most deep-seated aspect of the German dualism. Tirpitz had achieved his position of leadership only within the narrow circle of his naval administration, not within the government of the state and its policies as a whole. He did succeed in strengthening his Reich Naval Office militarily and in gaining primacy for it within the Navy after the break-up of the Naval High Command, but he failed in his efforts to expand the Reich Naval Office into a great Reich Commerce Office, about which he had written Stosch (and the conquest of the Chinese base of Kiaochow was only a poor consolation for the miscarriage of this project); he was even less successful in attaining the post of Reich Chancellor and bringing to this office the relations he had established with the political parties. The reason for these large failures was that Tirpitz could think as a politician, yet he always remained a military man. The dualism in the Reich made it unthinkable for an officer to exercise a parliamentary dictatorship, which left only two mutually exclusive possibilities: a parliamentary dictatorship subjugating the military and a purely antiparliamentarian military dictatorship.

Without breaking away from the principles of Bismarck's constitution, which rested more firmly on this dualism than has been generally supposed, there was no hope of finding a satisfactory solution to the politico-military dualism either on the parliamentary or on the military side. Tirpitz was drawn into this tragic dilemma; even so, in attempting to resolve the problem, he stood alone among the German statesmen of the prewar era. The army remained internally a hybrid creature, which exhausted its energy in the interminable struggle between the old and new tendencies inside it. The navy was completely modern and unified. It consciously drew its support from the economy and the parliament. When Tirpitz struggled with Bethmann about the Haldane proposals,[v] he represented the military side of the dualism differently from the way it was represented in 1913 by the General Staff in the question of expanding the army.[w] Why Tirpitz was on an equal footing with Bethmann politically and why he exerted political influence could be explained, one might say, on the technical grounds of the Admiral's and the Reich Chancellor's personal qualifications. But the historian must get to the bottom of things: if the dualism between the army and parliament could be equated with the military expression of the conflict between state and nation, which in terms of party politics was reflected in the conflict between conservatism and liberalism, the navy belonged to the military side of the dualism only so far as it, like the army, served as a fighting instrument for the German state. Never lacking in economic justifications and built up in closest collaboration with industrial and commercial forces (as exemplified by the subsidizing of the Navy League *[Flottenverein]* and the lobbying of heavy industry in favor of the new naval legislation between May 1899 and December 1901), the navy showed none of the misgivings, so typical of the Prussian military, about the Jacobinism implied in policies supported by popular enthusiasms. Consider the Jacobin heedlessness with which the naval agitation was conducted and the skill with which it fanned national emotion and popular lust for booty! The navy was the most complete incarnation of the modern, national-democratic, and capitalist-imperialist notion of power, through which the 20th century carried over the French Revolution's ideas of human rights into the realm of foreign affairs; by contrast, the Reich's political leadership before the war had hardly progressed beyond the feeble and helpless conservative foreign policy of pre-1848 days.

It would be a mistake to explain the elimination of the State Secretary and the failure to create a unified Supreme Command for Naval Warfare in August 1914 as the result of personal intrigues and personal inadequacies. In reality, they were the consequence of the type of organization produced by the political-military dualism. When parliament was barred from political intervention and when military responsibility was transfered to the Admiralty Staff—the remnant of the former Naval High Command—which Tirpitz had opposed in the interest of his parliamentary power and of alleviating the dualism, Tirpitz too was deprived of his power. He suddenly found himself in a vacuum. One can only hint at the magnitude of the problem without getting to the root of it if one insists on tracing the organized anarchy of the conduct of naval warfare back to the breaking up of the Naval High Command and the transfer of power to the Reich Naval Office. Even at the time he took office, Tirpitz was already limited in his freedom of action because the institutional organization of the Navy until 1899 was untenable on purely technical grounds and therefore had to be changed, and because he had become involved in the dualism. The situation in 1914 was the inevitable consequence of the 1899 reorganization, and this reorganization of the navy was itself an attempt to cope with the pressure of the preexisting politico-military dualism, both by eliminating it within the navy and by placing the relationship between the armed forces and parliament on a new foundation. The problem of the conduct of ground warfare and of political action in general, as well as the problem of naval combat in 1914 and the conduct of naval warfare throughout the war in particular, boils down to the question of the position of the German army and navy within the politico-military dualism of the Empire and hence to a crucial feature of the political organization of the Bismarckian Reich, which is nowhere spelled out in the articles of its constitution.

CHAPTER II

Anglophobia and *Weltpolitik*

*A Study of the Internal Political and Social Foundations of
German Foreign Policy at the Turn of the Century*

1

The fact that the Bismarckian Reich was founded by the state and
against the wishes of society had a determinative effect on the
political theory and the political writing of the empire, so that they
became indifferent to the problems of social movements and concentrated on the history of political organization.[1] In the history of
the state, moreover, foreign policy above all was regarded as the
most specifically characteristic expression of the state's power, and
the key to the understanding of all other aspects of its political,
economic, and social life. Indeed, belief in the primacy of foreign
policy found universal acceptance in the historiography and political writings of the Reich, in sharp contrast to prevailing views in
other countries, unless those views happened to have been shaped
by German influence, as was true for Seeley,[a] and could thus be regarded in Germany as a foreign confirmation of its interpretation.

The real question, however, is whether this German thesis, which
attempts to establish foreign policy as a realm of autonomous and
objective political norms, in which social and internal political conflicts have no place, is not actually an intimate reflection of the internal political and social organization of the Bismarckian Reich; and
whether the period during which this thesis won such wide acclaim
in German scholarship was not, on the level of real political life,

1. In his *Der Historismus und seine Probleme* (Tubingen, 1922) p. 216, Troeltsch
underestimates the influence of Bismarck's policies on historiography.

characterized by the strong influence on foreign policy, if not the primacy, of domestic politics and social stratification.

The major turning point in the foreign policy of the imperialist era is the outcome of negotiations for an Anglo-German alliance around the turn of the century.[2] In the Foreign Office's documentary publications, the internal political motivation behind this foreign-policy decision can be glimpsed only between the lines, but there is, nevertheless, enough there to show the way in which German leadership responded to public opinion. Miquel's *Sammlungspolitik*[b] provided the basic reasons for the foreign policy that set the course for war. The fundamental issue is not whether domestic political considerations sometimes cause foreign policy to deviate from its predetermined course in minor details; it goes further than that. It is the extent to which prewar foreign policy was determined all along the line by the social structure of the Reich. An assessment of German foreign policy is inadequate not only when it fails to take account of English policy.[3] A foreign policy has—this may sound trivial but it is often overlooked—not only an antagonist in front of it but a homeland behind it. A foreign policy is contending with the adversary and also fighting for its own country; it is guided by the opponent's moves but also—and to an even larger extent—by the will and needs of the homeland, whose concerns are primarily domestic. The question whether a broader war guilt existed should not be decided exclusively by determining how far the general situation in 1914 was a result of England's diplomatic alliances, but should also take into account the influence of Germany's social structure on its foreign policy. This is not tantamount to accepting the absurd French thesis[4] that places all blame for the war on the mythical monster, "le generalstab prussien"; it does mean facing up to the fact that the social conflicts of the nineties set foreign policy on a course that encouraged the expansion of the fleet and the rejection of the English alliance. Let us go one step further even than Brentano with his courageous hypothesis that the German tariff

2. Hermann Bächthold, "Der entscheidende weltpolitische Wendepunkt der Vorkriegszeit," *Weltwirtschaftliches Archiv* 20, 1924; Fr. Meinecke, *Die Geschichte des deutsch-englischen Bündnisproblems* (München, 1927).

3. H. Rothfels, "Zur Beurteilung der englischen Vorkriegspolitik," *Archiv für Politik und Geschichte*, 1926/II, p. 602.

4. An interpretation that is even offered by Seignobos.

policy contributed to the outbreak of the war[5] and investigate the social factors underlying this aggressive tariff system.

It goes without saying that foreign policy may determine the attitude of parties and classes. Proof of this is afforded, not only by the Irish, Egyptian, Indian, and Chinese independence movements (which have not, however, been free of social motivation), but also by the history of European nation states, where parliaments have not infrequently toppled governments because of their foreign policies, and where loss of parliamentary confidence has often enough culminated in mass revolution. Between the fall of the Cuno Cabinet[c] and the overthrow of the Hohenzollern dynasty there is a difference of degree but not of essence. But for the classes and parties the influence of foreign policy is always secondary. Much more intensive in their case is the exploitation of the external situation for internal political, social, and economic ends.

In making their decisions, the parties proceed from the objectives of their domestic and economic policies. Foreign policy is in their eyes only a means to their domestic ends. For the conservatives, this tactic is the basic principle of their national agitation, despite the contrived reversal of means and ends in their propaganda. For the nineteenth-century liberal-bourgeois parties, however, one must distinguish between two opposite eras in the way foreign policy intervened in the implementation of domestic policies.

Since its genesis in the pre-1848 period, conservatism has tended to use state power as a means of self-preservation, that is, the preservation of a more backward social and economic system than that represented by the bourgeoisie. Whenever conservatism has been in a position of political power, it has applied this power ruthlessly to protect the interests of the agrarian patriarchal system, or later of agrarian capitalism, against industrial and commercial capitalism. It has conducted foreign policy entirely in accordance with agrarian interests, disregarding city-based manufacturers and workers.

Bourgeois liberalism on the other hand has not used foreign policy for domestic purposes with the absolute singlemindedness with which conservatives turned it into a defensive weapon against more advanced economic institutions. Bourgeois nationalism has

5. Lujo Brentano, *Ist das "System Brentano" zusammengebrochen?* (Berlin, 1918), p. 67.

never been lacking in internal political motives and has always been responsive to social conditions, both in the narrow, self-explanatory sense of its being based on the support of some domestic political and social groups, and in the broader sense that it has been used by these groups to attain political and social power or to increase this power, making foreign policy and even the concept of foreign policy serve as weapons in the internal political and economic struggle. Everyone knows about the opposition of the Prussian liberals in 1859 to a government that in its opinion was failing to represent the national interest in an adequate manner.[d]

The bourgeoisie originally used nationalism, from a social point of view, as an offensive internal political weapon, but nationalism— and this was symptomatic of the revolutionary bourgeoisie's having become conservative—gradually acquired a socially defensive coloration. Where a nationalist foreign policy had at one time served as a weapon against dynastic feudalism, as a weapon, that is, for social development, nationalism came to be advanced as a weapon against the proletariat, that is, as a weapon against social development or *for* social reaction. We must look for the sociologically most deeply rooted, even if psychologically often unconscious reason, for the overwhelming victory of Ranke's thesis of the primacy of foreign policy in the German empire's unofficial and official philosophy of power and in its political theory, which were always closely linked with historiography. The demand for a policy of national strength (*Machtpolitik*) was gradually converted from a weapon of the progressive bourgeoisie against the feudal-absolutist state into a weapon against the politically threatening proletariat.

When we have done this, the significance of the backwardness of the ruling class for the empire's foreign policy comes clearly into focus, but it remains important to discriminate between the different motives compelling agrarian conservatives and the originally revolutionary but later more rightist bourgeoisie to put primary emphasis on internal political considerations.

2

At the turn of the century, the principal problem of foreign policy for conservatism was the relation between agrarian and industrial states on the one hand—Germany and England—and between competing agrarian states—Germany and Russia—on the other. This view of foreign policy originated in the internal political and social sphere, in Germany's industrialization and the concomitant development of large cities.

German conservatism carried its detestation of cities and industry over into foreign policy. England was the country with the most advanced industry and commerce, and it was a far more dangerous example and model than the far-off United States, which in 1900 still contained, or seemed to contain, large uncultivated stretches of open land. Inasmuch as the English represented a socially advanced type, everything about them was criticized, and their policies were accused of reflecting their "shop-keeper" mentality. They were maligned for their "business as usual" outlook, in contrast to the Germans' responsiveness to the deepest ethical values. People boasted about Germany's not having been conquered as yet by the cursed motto "time is money," though they knew that the old tradition of German loyalty and honesty had succumbed to the onslaught of modern corruption. As Adolf Wagner[e] once expressed it with delightful naivete, "A noble spirit and refined being could not avoid shaking his head in comparing the present with the days of old, with the time of a hundred years ago, with the time of Goethe and Schiller, of Schleiermacher and Wilhelm von Humboldt, and, refusing to condone the praise of the present and retreating into isolation with a feeling of rejection, could only take comfort in the sad and proud conviction *odi profanum vulgus et arceo.*"[6] The Boers were the object of praise and acclaim because they had been successful in preserving a country with immense mineral resources from the ravages of industrialization.[f] But the high esteem in which patriarchal principles were held as far as the economy and politics were concerned coincided with the defense of unpatriarchal elements. These agrarian conservatives were the most determined spokesmen of the modern power State *(Machtstaat),* which was based on rationality and on an urban bourgeois society. They had never asked themselves the question how a predominantly agrarian state could ever afford to pay its army. They had never understood that in order to exist at all as a power state, the modern national state had to be an industrial—capitalist or socialist—power state.

6. *Vom Territorialstaat zur Weltmacht.* (The Kaiser's birthday address for 1900.)

This total failure to think things through, which characterized the German conservatives' attitude toward foreign policy, is sufficient proof that the Anglo-German antagonism was not the product of a conflict in intellectual values, a conflict between traders and heroes, but that it reflected the attempt to preserve at all costs their own position in the face of capitalist-industrial growth. The English victory over the Boers had the same internal political and social implications for the conservatives that Königgrätz had had for Napoleon III. The crushing defeat of Metternich's principle of intervention in South America[g] was echoed by the English victory over the Boers at Kimberley and the Modder River. By their victory, the English also dealt a crushing defeat to the Boers' social allies, the Prussian conservatives. Much as the conservatives used to despise the fleet "in the service of maritime interests" and refer to it as the "horrible fleet," the fleet was still the military weapon to be brandished against victorious England by the agrarian state under the Prussian conservatives' control. The Boers' agrarian state had been vanquished by capitalist England; the German agrarian state had to be protected against that very England, whose victory had just demonstrated that God was not on the side of the backward economic system but on the side of the stronger batallions and even on the side of the horrible fleet. The anti-British sentiment of the conservatives was not an outgrowth of a nationalism that expressed the natural foreign-policy outlook of a bourgeois-controlled national state; it was in fact the product of the prenational and antinational fear of agrarian leaders that the victory of the English industrial state over the Boers might be a dangerous blow to their own well-established dominance, and that the outcome in South Africa might create a precedent for East Elbia that would be fatal from the conservative point of view. Had it not been for the British victory in South Africa, the conservatives could never have become reconciled to the fleet, which in their eyes would always have remained a weapon of industry. In the nineties, conservative circles looked askance at *Weltpolitik;* the reversal dated from the turn of the century, and the unconditional acceptance of *Weltpolitik* came only as a response to the final English victory. It took the English victory in the Transvaal to compel the agrarians to rely on such a dubious instrument as the fleet for protection against industrial-

[27

commercial England. It was only from that time on that they clung to the German industrial state with that last ounce of strength derived from the feeling of defeat. They hated that state, which threatened to break their own class rule, and yet they were dependent on it to keep hostile England at bay with its fleet and its superior financial power. Only the English victory in the Transvaal made the fleet and *Weltpolitik* acceptable in the eyes of the conservatives and assured the success of the *Sammlungspolitik* by preventing the agrarians from imposing strongly restrictive measures against German capitalism. Foreign policy, the expansion of the fleet, a successful *Weltpolitik* were viewed by the conservatives not in terms of the state or the—theoretically unified but effectively nonexistent—nation, but rather as a means of preserving their own class rule. Even though conservatism had made its peace with the modern rational power state, it did not hesitate to attack this state ruthlessly whenever it felt its own influence threatened and had no qualms about weakening military preparedness, which it was constantly advocating verbally, rather than sacrifice conservative, bureaucratic interests. The Prussian government loudly protested against Tirpitz' habit of showing Reichstag deputies a few warships on occasion in the hope of creating a favorable mood in the Reichstag by such harmless gestures. It justified this protest by stating that "this might easily lead to a transgression of the bounds constitutionally imposed on the legislative bodies and to a weakening of the government's executive power."[7] The decisive motive why the Prussian Minister of War von Heeringen turned down the General Staff's request for the famous three army corps[h] was the desire to maintain a conservative officer corps, because a large expansion of the army would inevitably necessitate the inclusion of "quite unsuitable social groups" in the officers' reserve corps, thereby exposing the officer corps, "aside from other threats, to the danger of democratization."[8] The available historical material is adequate to establish the class character of conservative nationalism; and the primacy of internal political considerations

---

7. Communication of the Minister of War to the General Staff, January 20, 1913 in Herzfeld, *Die Deutsche Rüstungspolitik vor dem Weltkrieg,* (Bonn, 1923) p. 63.
8. Hans Rothfels, *Bismarcks englische Bündnispolitik* (Stuttgart, 1924), p. 126.

and agrarian class interest in the conservatives' attitude toward England around the turn of the century is also clearly recognizable.

This primacy comes even more sharply into focus if one examines the attitude of the agrarians toward the Baghdad railroad construction program[1] in terms of its internal political foundations and its foreign-policy consequences. The agrarians despised industrial England and therefore reconciled themselves even to German industry's institution of the fleet. This anti-British outlook was the exact counterpart to the struggle against the Baghdad railroad. The prospect that the competition from Russian grain products, which they were so desperately resisting, would reassert itself in Mesopotamia as part of an expanded Germany led them to a relentless struggle against the pro-Turkish policy of the German government and the German Bank. If the limitations imposed on German policies by the enmity with England should impose restrictions on such experiments in national grain production, then they had every reason to give their approval to the horrible fleet in order to intensify British hostility and thereby maintain their East Elbian grain monopoly.

German foreign policy of the prewar period was in no position to choose between a pro-British and a pro-Russian stance. As long as the conservatives maintained their political influence in Germany, and as long as the whole economic policy was geared primarily to government subsidies for agrarian-capitalist grain production in the form of customs barriers, no foreign-policy decision either in favor of England or in favor of Russia could have had any solid foundation. The social structure of the Bismarckian Reich, combined with the crisis of the debt-ridden but politically powerful landholders east of the Elbe, permitted only one harmonious solution: a foreign policy directed against both England and Russia.

3

There is no point in talking about the Anglophobia that gripped the whole nationalist half of the German people at the turn of the century and substantially influenced the government that represented it in its anti-English policy, without taking into account the social background of those who shared this sentiment. We are not doing full justice to the complexity of Anglo-German relations if we maintain that the inherent contradictions of the problem rendered it incapable of decisive resolution, a position that relieves the diplomats of any responsibility for the failure of an alliance to materialize.[9] This foreign-policy antinomy was merely part of the greater antinomy that was the consequence of the social structure of the Bismarckian Reich. It was present before 1890 and played a role even in Bismarck's foreign policy; but it was particularly pronounced in the decade 1890–1900, because of the change in the social and domestic political situation, and after that time became determinative.

The foreign views of the conservatives, agrarians, public servants, and academicians were decisively influenced by Germany's social backwardness compared to England, the awareness of which, consciously or unconsciously, alienated them from the economically superior and more highly developed enemy. The other motive for this Anglophobia was that the nationalist circles that were antagonistic to England in their foreign views constituted the ruling strata within the Reich. They ruled over a class that had not yet thrown off its yoke but that constantly threatened social and intellectual rebellion, and against it they could think of no intellectually, socially, and politically effective means of repression. The class division of the German people into bourgeoisie and proletariat had a direct causal relationship with the implementation of an anti-English world policy and the development of the German battle fleet.

If one accepted the thesis of the primacy of foreign policy, one would have to uncover motives for this Anglophobia in foreign policy. Or, to put it another way, one would have to find a common foundation shared more or less by the whole nation determining its attitude in foreign policy. For if it should turn out that the nation's foreign-policy demands were divided, then the burning question would arise what caused this divergence and how it was related to the internal political and social situation.

Two sets of public opinion, bourgeois-nationalist and proletarian-socialist, coexisted in Germany, and from them two opposite foreign policy lines emerged. The Social Democrats were as outspoken in demanding an alliance with England as the bourgeois half

9. Prussian State Ministry, signed Studt, to the Reich Chancellor, July 27, 1906. Files of the Reichswehrministerium.

was passionate in advocating an undying enmity against England. The foreign policy demanded by the ruling strata was opposite to the one demanded by the group subjected to its rule. It is a rare occurrence that public opinion displays such uniformity of views about foreign policy, which is usually too remote from the average person and becomes relevant to domestic politics only under special circumstances. In this instance, however, the division of the nation into two classes coincided with the demands for taking hostile action against England and demands for an alliance with England. It is technically impossible to isolate foreign policy from all other aspects of life and consider it purely a matter of governmental concern, although such a view has been encouraged by the documentary publications of the Foreign Office. Such a view may be valid for the detailed course of a single negotiation and the methods used during it, which are revealed in the documents, but it fails to do justice to the fundamental factors in the foreign policy of a whole era. The great scholars of absolutism presented as the central problem of that period the close and unbreakable interconnection of foreign policy and military organization, of internal political developments and mercantilism, and regarded the process of forming states in the age of absolutism as a living totality in which each organ was adjusted to the other and depended on the other for its own existence. This recognition of the interplay of all forces is precisely what is missing for the age of imperialism. It will be an important task of the historiography of the immediate future to reverse the tendency to view post-1871 foreign policy in isolation, a failing for which the historical research of the postwar period, sinking to dismayingly low levels from the heights that had been reached before the war in the exploration of absolutism, must bear the blame. Only thus can we hope to write the history of foreign policy instead of merely analyzing diplomatic techniques.

Before we turn to the problem of the interaction among the bourgeoisie, the threat of socialism, and foreign policy, we will have to turn back to the agrarian question, not so much in terms of international relations but as an internal political and social matter. The decisive question hinges on the underlying motives for the tariff legislation of 1902. From all we know up to now about the German government's views on foreign policy around the turn of the century,[10] it is unlikely that the Sino-Japanese, Spanish-American, and Transvaal wars "were viewed as portents of an age of international political conflicts, which clearly indicated the need to prepare economically for the possibility of war."[11] In reality, they merely offered a fine pretext for economically motivated agitation to hide special interests behind a smokescreen of nationalism and to invert the primacy of internal political and class interests by propaganda and ideology. It is especially difficult to find motives in foreign policy for the expansion of the fleet and the tariff policy in the light of the German government's serene and optimistic outlook on the international situation, which was based on the marked relaxation of continental relations in the wake of the Anglo-Russian confrontation in the Far East.[j] Considerations of foreign policy had played no part in the attitudes of the political parties even at the time of the military budget proposals of 1893, so around the turn of the century foreign policy was given a new look to make it capable of serving as a weapon in internal political battles and the class struggle. The agrarians had the habit in the nineties of raising the specter of a hunger blockade against Germany, but long before the East was allowed to resume its exports of rye (1909), this possibility ceased to preoccupy them: that is, from the moment that the Reichstag approved grain tariffs. The primacy of foreign policy and the wish to take into account foreign-policy requirements of the German state by developing the fleet and instituting grain tariffs were not determining factors in the attitude of the German agrarian class. What really moved them was the realization that the world economy had primacy over the national economy. But this had a contradictory effect on them. Precisely because they saw that their position was becoming untenable in the world economy, while their will to survive remained strong, the agrarians fought bitterly to defend an autarchic national economy based on tariffs against world trade. In their eyes, both protective tariffs and the expansion of the fleet were intended not as instruments for assuring the success of the German

10. *Cf.* for instance in very compressed form Bülow's intention "of patiently and serenely awaiting the further irresistible turn of events under the protection of a good fleet and with continued friendly relations with Russia and England," November 24, 1899, in *Grosse Politik* XV, 420.

11. Fritz Hartung, *Deutsche Geschichte 1870 bis 1912,* 2nd ed. (Leipzig, 1922), p. 203.

national economy within the world economy but as means of shutting off the national economy from the world economy. Even the existence of the national state was a matter of secondary importance to them, a mere tool for improving their economic condition. Five years earlier, when the national state was apparently paying more attention to industry than to agriculture, they had shown the same support for a pan-European, or at least a Central European, customs union[12] as they showed for the national state at the turn of the century, when the *Sammlungspolitik* promised an increase in the tariff on grain. As far as industry was concerned, foreign policy and national motivations were equally secondary: it had agreed to the increase in the grain tariff just at a time when it was basking in its rapid growth, when no foreign-policy concerns darkened its horizon and long before it was jarred out of its boundless optimism by the severe crisis[k] of 1900.[13]

The period around 1900 is especially well suited from a methodological point of view for dealing a critical blow to the thesis of the primacy of foreign policy. It also serves to cast doubt on the method of reading foreign-policy motives into situations where internal political factors are not only present but determinative. For the tariff policies and navy laws were passed by the Reichstag not out of concern for the security of the national state but as weapons in the class conflict, which became entangled in foreign-policy issues and was to be fought out with foreign-policy weapons, because it could not be resolved domestically.

The influence of public opinion, so far as it can be interpreted, notwithstanding all its finer nuances, as a homogeneous expression of the national will and as an unstable factor that is relatively independent of government tendencies and has a driving force of its own, must not be overestimated in the question of the decision to conclude or to reject the British alliance. The German government had sufficient backbone at the turn of the century to bear with fortitude the indignation of the masses with respect to the tariff policy,

12. J. Pentmann, *Die Zollunionsidee* (Jena, 1917), pp. 87 f.
13. Vossberg-Rekow, "Bericht," *Schriften der Zentralstelle für Vorbereitung von Handelsverträgen,* Heft 11; Ernst Loeb, "Die Berliner Grossbanken in den Jahren 1895 bis 1902 und die Krise der Jahre 1900 und 1901," *Schriften des Vereins für Sozialpolitik,* Vol. 110 (Leipzig, 1903), passim; F. Pinner, *Emil Rathenau und das elektrische Zeitalter* (Leipzig, 1918), pp. 223 ff.

[33

which markedly affected their standard of living, and to implement the tariff policy that it deemed appropriate despite the opposition. It was not, therefore, out of weakness that it yielded to the anti-British sentiment.[14] Only if we assume that the rationale for the government's attitude was the interest of the united national state does there appear to be a contradiction between its stubborn persistence in carrying through its tariff policy despite its social and political consequences and in the face of a sizable increase of the Social Democratic vote as a result of this legislation, and its subsequent susceptibility to the anti-English tendencies. In reality, these apparent inconsistencies in the attitude toward the demands of the imperialistic and socialist parts of the nation reveal a class-determined policy that favored the imperialist half of the social dualism and worked to the detriment of the socialist half. There is an inseparable connection between the outcome of the social crisis in the nineties, which was resolved by the *Sammlungspolitik* for the benefit of the industrialists and agrarians and at the expense of the proletariat, and the foreign-policy decision to abandon any plans for an alliance with England. The positive or negative stand with respect to foreign policy was contingent on a simultaneous stand with respect to domestic politics and the resolution of the social crisis. It is as unthinkable to separate these decisions from each other as it is to separate the political life of the ancient *polis* from the creation of its statuary. However strongly a deeply rooted, or, to be more exact, a deeply implanted feeling may impel us to separate the two in order to escape the painful consequences of historicism, which does not respect venerable prejudices, historical consciousness must resist letting these consequences seduce us into accepting untruths.

4

What were the broad lines of development that led to the *Sammlungspolitik?*

The *Sammlungspolitik* brought to an end a phase of the class struggle. In Germany the nineties were the crucial years of the social struggle. The great change of direction that was effected in 1879[1] brought a reasonable reconciliation between industry and agriculture, which as late as 1873 had still wished to ruin industry by lifting

14. Meinecke, *op. cit.,* pp. 258–259.

the tariff on steel[15] and had supported the social legislation of the 1870's for the same reason. In face of this new bloc, the proletariat was powerless. It was still numerically weak. Moreover, the bloc possessed an inherent strength. Internal disharmonies had not yet manifested themselves, because industry was experiencing an enormous upsurge as a result of the opening up of the United States (*not* as a consequence of the fictitious "protection of national labor," for indeed the industrialization of Central and Western Europe everywhere "reflects the opening up of large territories"[16]), while simultaneously a great upward movement of the grain tariffs took place, raising them from 1 to 3.50 and then to 5 marks. Both industry and agriculture benefited, and neither therefore complained about the policy of the state. Herein lies the deeper meaning of Minister of Agriculture Lucius's remark, *"Juvat vivere."* In addition, Bismarck's policy, characterized by precapitalist, diplomatic techniques, saw to it that class conflicts did not erupt with excessive violence. The years 1890–1892 mark a decisive change. Bismarck's fall eliminated the dictator whose politically oriented and government-centered will to power had led him to believe he could direct the social struggle from an uneconomic perspective, and had tried to do so, but who had never understood the importance of the establishment of the British Empire as a problem of German policy and who had kept mixing up the problems of the proletariat in the factories with those of the farm workers. And with the relaxation of governmental pressure, the class struggle for power, which had not been smothered by Bismarck but only superficially covered over, reasserted itself openly. It was then that the ruthless struggle to gain control of the legislative machinery began between the highly capitalist industrial sector and the increasingly capitalist agricultural sector. Industry had just recovered from the crisis of 1888, but agriculture, which for decades had forced up the prices of its products according to a carefully planned policy,[17] experienced a catastrophic collapse in grain prices after 1892. Both industry and

15. Elisabeth von Richthofen, *Über die historischen Wandlungen in der Stellung der autoritären Parteien zur Arbeiterschützgesetzgebung und die Motive dieser Wandlungen,* Diss. (Heidelberg, 1901), p. 37.

16. Sering, *Agrarkrisen und Agrarzölle* (Berlin, 1925), p. 17.

17. Theodor v.d. Goltz, *Geschichte der deutschen Landwirtschaft* (Stuttgart, 1903), II, 354, 405 ff.

[35

agriculture found themselves in a struggle for survival, which was at stake for each of them if the legislative influence of the other were to increase even slightly. It was not so much the introduction of ruthless intrigues and petty conflicts that characterized the chaotic nature of this new course, as it was the persistence of the power struggle waged by these two social estates. The policy of the New Course was merely an expression of this struggle. Nothing illustrates more strikingly the overwhelming influence of social and economic developments on politics and the political parties than the answer to the question: when political and economic factors are on a collision course, which of the two has the prevailing influence on political decisions and political parties? According to their ideological and constitutional views, conservatives should have sided with the Russian tsarist regime against French democracy. In reality, their policy was to wage a relentless battle against Russia as their main agricultural competitor and to attempt to introduce into Germany French commercial policy, which under Méline[m] happened to favor small farmers at the expense of industrial expansion. They were faced with a sharp conflict between ideology and practical considerations, between political philosophy and economic policy; with the exception of a few outsiders, the conservatives unanimously opted against the Russian governmental model and for the French trade-policy model, against political ideology and in favor of practical economic advantages.[18]

The same conflict between ideology and economic practice affected the liberals (and we can lump all shades of opinion from Richter to Bennigsen[n] together without doing too much violence to the nuances). Liberalism was ideologically on the side of England, the country in which liberty was presumed to flourish, and in opposition to Russia, the country in which liberty was presumably suppressed. But conversely, from an economic point of view, England was the competitor and Russia the country whose grain exports would not only theoretically obviate the necessity of supporting estate owners east of the Elbe, who were its social and internal political adversaries, but would practically dislodge them

18. Even in Meinecke's *Bündnisproblem* this fact is not sufficiently emphasized. The conservatives were quite ambivalent about Russia and not altogether in favor of a political alliance with Russia.

from power. Caprivi's trade treaties were accepted by the Left against the Right.° Their official justification was to assure foreign markets for German industrial exports, but their actual purpose was to strengthen Germany's position in its international economic competition with England. In the economic sphere, their impact was comparable to that of the navy law in the military sphere. An ideological agrarian like Johannes Haller—who, as is true of anticapitalist orthodox conservatives generally, often has a clear view of things—is right in maintaining that Germany's "misfortune" did not begin with its anti-British *Weltpolitik* and naval policy, but with Caprivi's commercial policy.[19] As a counterpart to the struggle of capitalist liberalism against its industrial and commercial English competitor, a change took place in liberalism's attitude toward Russia. Henceforth, the empire of the tsars, formerly conceived as a stronghold of reaction and barbarism, became the land of grain exports. Although liberals were incapable of feeling any sympathy for Russia on ideological grounds, the situation was different in the economic sphere. Now that Russia, as a result of its state-financed railroad construction, had begun to export grain, it became the best ally of German liberalism in its struggle against the predominance of the East Elbians.

German foreign policy had a double thrust, against England and against Russia, against the industrial and commercial state and against the agrarian state, against the liberal state and against the despotic one. The decision for or against Russia and for or against England was made all along the line on the basis of the adversary's economic and not his political posture. Germany's anti-Russian policy was socially motivated, not by liberalism's freedom-loving opposition against despotism, but by the competitive struggle of the East Elbian agrarians against agrarian Russia. Similarly, Germany's anti-British policy was socially motivated not by the authoritarian conservatives' struggle against parliamentarian England but by the opposition of West German industry and the Hanseatic shipbuilding industry to the capitalist competitor and by German agriculture, which wanted to protect itself against the industrial nation. It was not political but economic antagonism that determined this double-pronged policy of hostility on the part of the Reich. The fun-

19. *Die Ära Bülow* (Stuttgart, 1922).

damental lines of foreign policy were set much more by anonymous social pressure from within than by ephemeral diplomatic maneuvers.

5

Industry and agriculture were pursuing opposite objectives in terms of foreign and domestic policies. As the ruling strata, they determined the over-all political direction. But as long as agrarian and industrial interests could not be reduced to a common denominator, there was no way of producing a unified policy.

It was Miquel's achievement to bring together the mutually antagonistic industrial and agricultural sectors. This political strategy of "gathering together" (Sammlung) was characterized by its disregard for party lines in that it did not use the state's authority as arbiter above the parliamentary parties to repress the parties' combative tendencies. In fact, it was a pure expression of class politics: industry and agriculture agreed that neither would seek a monopoly of power in the state and that neither would try to eliminate its defeated rival from the levers of legislative machinery; instead, they would establish an agrarian-industrial condominium against the proletariat.

The decisive motive for this joining of forces and the mutual renunciation of absolute primacy in favor of a condominium with reciprocal favors was the miscarriage of all measures intended to stem the growing tide of the proletariat and to win its loyalty to the state. Both the social-insurance policy and the Subversion and Penitentiary Bills,[p] both the carrot and the stick, had proved equally ineffective, and these repeated failures evoked a feeling of impotence and helplessness. But one weapon against the proletariat had not as yet been exploited until the Sammlungspolitik: namely, that of redressing the intolerable social and internal political situation by a successful foreign policy, which would be credited to the prevailing political and social order, whose survival was now so gravely threatened by the proletariat. The Sammlungspolitik proposed to carry to unprecedented lengths Bismarck's method of exploiting foreign-policy situations, and, if necessary, artificially creating them, to solve domestic problems or at least achieve a temporary or apparent solution for them. The Sammlungspolitik was not satisfied with temporary successes having a short-lived internal impact, but hoped to free foreign policy from the continental limitations of the Bismarck era and introduce a grandiose *Weltpolitik* based on the expanded fleet. Tirpitz himself was to write Stosch that Germany would have to convert to a world policy "not least because this great new national task and the economic gains derived therefrom will serve as a strong palliative against both educated and uneducated Social Democrats."[20] *Weltpolitik* and its accompanying successes were to be a means of securing and reinforcing the socially threatened position of the ruling strata.[21]

It remains an open question whether this objective could possibly have been accomplished. Our point here is only that a definite kind of foreign policy was proposed in the hope of redressing the internal situation. As it happened, the government soon lost control of the genii it had let out of the bottle, and it was the genii that later determined foreign policy. In any case, this change of course in the overall foreign policy line, which had been induced by internal political and social factors, became the decisive element in the rejection of the proffered alliance with England.

If we put aside the legal arguments about the dictated war-guilt clause of the Versailles treaty and try to approach the question of responsibility for the war from a more general perspective, it is not enough to ask whether England, in accordance with the highest demands of *raison d'état,* involved the continent in the fatal tensions that eventually led to the world war in order to be left to rule its empire in peace. England's anti-German policy was not something positive but merely a reaction to the German attitude. Before appraising England's guilt, therefore, one must go into the question of what compelled the German government, under the pressure of public opinion, to act in such a way as to make England give up the idea of solving the problems of its world empire with the help of a German alliance and forced it to adopt an anti-German solution. And this formulation of the question makes us confront head on the entire set of problems associated with the social and economic conflicts in Germany in the nineties. The anti-British and anti-Rus-

20. December 21, 1895 in Tirpitz, *Erinnerungen,* p. 52.

21. Cf. also Max Weber's formulation in *Wirtschaft und Gesellschaft: Grundriss der Sozialökonomik* III, 2, 2nd ed. (Tübingen, 1924), p. 626.

sian policy around the turn of the century were the outgrowth in the realm of foreign policy of the *Sammlungspolitik* and its establishment of an agrarian-industrial condominium against social democracy.

The concrete expression of the industrial-agrarian coaltion's two-front campaign against the neighboring states was to be found in the second navy law, 1900, and the proposed tariff legislation of 1902, which at the same time reflected their internal political collaboration against the proletariat. The agrarians gave their consent to the horrible fleet, and industry compensated the agrarians for this concession by agreeing to tariffs that would raise prices. The agrarians gave their support to industry' competitive capitalist struggle against England, and industry in exchange supported the struggle of the agrarians against the Russian production of rye. It is true that, even while this decision was being reached, there were men who drew attention to the close connection between the protective tariff and the second navy law: Walter Lotz in his *Handelspolitik des Deutschen Reiches unter Graf Caprivi und Fürst Hohenlohe* (1901) and somewhat later, in 1913, Gerloff in his *Finanz- und Zollpolitik des Deutschen Reiches.* Nevertheless, this connection between power politics and trade policies, which is much more meaningful than the commonly accepted notion of the need for warships to protect overseas trade, failed to penetrate public consciousness; and no one has yet recognized the connection between the tariff proposal and the navy law as a means of reconciling agrarian and industrial interests struggling for state control[22] or reinterpreted them as measures in support of a nation-wide *Machtpolitik*. Never was national security invoked as clearly as a propaganda tool in the struggle between the ruling and the ruled classes as it was when the agrarian conservatives approved the second navy law. It can be pinpointed with chronological accuracy in the stenographic record of the Reichstag Budget Commission[23]— between April 27 and May 1, 1900—that the conservatives voted for the German battle fleet because, after cautious tactical maneuvering, they were assured of an increase in grain tariffs as a compensation for this considerable sacrifice.

22. *Cf.,* however, Fr. Meinecke, *Bündnisproblem* p. 260.
23. In the archives of the Reichstag but also reproduced in detail in the contemporary press. *Cf.* the above-mentioned articles by W. Lotz and W. Gerloff.

Industry needed the fleet and the power it would provide to prevail over its English competitor, even if war should break out. Only thus could Germany be transformed into an industrial state. Agriculture needed protective tariffs in order to reinstate the old policy of obtaining higher prices for the products of the estates, a policy that had broken down in the nineties. Only thus could Germany be preserved as an agrarian state. The basis for the *Sammlungspolitik's* compromise solution, which had been reached under the pressure of the proletariat, was that the agrarians denied industry an internal political and social victory but in exchange gave up their anti-industrial and agrarian-patriarchal ideology, as well as their attacks on capitalism and particularly on the stock exchange,[24] while at the same time clearing industry's path for foreign expansion by approving the build-up of the fleet and, because of their dismay about the Transvaal victory, actively participating in anti-British policy. Prussian domestic economic policy, which since the eighteenth century had had as its foreign policy basis the exploitation of the industrially underdeveloped East, beginning with the Prussian-Polish trade agreement of 1775, rather than colonial rule and protection of overseas interests, reversed its general direction in the wake of the agrarian crisis that broke out in 1875. Bismarck's tariff policy of 1879 had the result of making Russia reduce German imports by nearly half during the eighties;[25] and in the nineties, it energetically pursued its currency reform and expanded its own industry, to become independent of German trade policies, repeating the experience of the 1820's by surrounding itself with high tariff walls, so that segments of German industry were forced to move across the border and to leave German national territory in response to the Russian reprisals against German exports.[26] There

24. In January 1900, to be exact, the stock exchange law of 1896 had to be practically abandoned. *Cf.* W. Pinner, *Der Getreideterminhandel in Deutschland vor und seit der Reichsbörsengesetzgebung* (Berlin, 1914), p. 62.
25. Whereas Russian exports to Germany fluctuated around 160 million rubles between 1876 and 1895, imports from Germany fell from 230 million rubles in 1871–1875 and 1876–1880 to 176 million in 1881–1885, 115 million in 1886–1890, and 124 million in 1891–1895. As a percentage of total imports, Germany's share fell from 44% in 1876–1880 to 20% in 1886–1890. *Cf.* Mertens, "1882–1911: Dreissig Jahre russische Eisenbahnpolitik und deren wirtschaftliche Rückwirkung," *Archiv für Eisenbahnwesen*, 41 (1918), p. 448.
26. W. Lotz, *Handelspolitik*, p. 65. Schmoller's basically devasting verdict is

is a complete contradiction between Bismarck's political friendship with Russia and his economic hostility toward that same country. Here we can see more clearly than is generally admitted how the elaborate edifice of his foreign-policy system was an anachronistic and artificial construct produced by his old-fashioned diplomacy *(Kabinettpolitik)*, alongside of which economic policy was isolated and autonomous, a situation whose contradictory consequences were not taken into account. Bismarck was all too conscious of this weakness in his system, but sought to persuade others that the inconsistency between economic and foreign policy was natural and harmless, and he used this thesis to keep a line of retreat open for himself.

Concern for the economic interests of the agrarian conservatives, whose political views were actually pro-Russian, resulted first in an economic and finally in a political opposition between Russia and Germany. Bismarck changed the basic direction of the Prussian economy, which had consisted of opening up the industrially undeveloped East to its own industry, and forced industry to concentrate on overseas expansion. The responsibility for German imperialism must be attributed not to capitalism but to the power positions of the agrarians, who forced industry to expand in new directions. And German industry, whose leading figures subordinated themselves to the wishes of the state—in the often described feudalization of the German bourgeoisie—submitted to the will of the agrarians, whom the state supported. In England the aristocracy had to yield to the wishes of the bourgeoisie even at the sacrifice of its own most immediate economic agrarian interests, although the bourgeoisie was not in direct control of political power there either. In Germany around the turn of the century, on the contrary, industry and finance capital sacrificed their interests, which lay in a capitalist penetration of the Russian agrarian economy, to agrarian aristocratic-conservative interests, which required a throttling of Russo-German trade relations. The decision reached in 1900 was motivated less by the opposition of German capitalism to England than by the fact that agriculture had thwarted capitalist expansion in Russia and had thereby induced maritime expansion, which in

couched in very cautious terms in "Staatenbildung und Finanzentwicklung," *Schmollers Jahrbuch,* 33, 1909, p. 55.

turn led to the military confrontation with England. In the nineties, German capital investment in Russia fell behind Belgian and French investments and even dropped below the German level of the eighties. Characteristically, the German stock exchange reacted much more sharply to the Russian monetary crisis of autumn 1899 than the Paris and the Brussels stock exchanges in manifesting increased caution. In the wake of this Russian crisis, German capital expansion moved exclusively in a direction that brought it into competition with England. In 1906 only 4 out of 26 billion marks of German holdings abroad were invested in neighboring Russia.[27] The primacy of the agrarians compelled German capital to choose the dangerous confrontation with England instead of pouring, unhindered, into capital-starved Russia. The tariff policy inaugurated immediately after the collapse of the English alliance negotiations, as a result of which Germany's coastline became vulnerable to British attack, had the result of exacerbating the opposition provoked by Bismarck's tariff measures to the point of irrevocable enmity. For the protective tariff of 1902 eliminated the competition between German and Russian rye production, made it altogether impossible for Russia to find a foreign market for its rye, and left no alternative after 1905 but to supply Germany with increased barley exports to expand its cattle production.[28] It was not simply a matter of improving the international agricultural division of labor in Europe, as was suggested in a grotesque distortion of the real situation;[29] it was a brutal intervention into Russia's economy. If another country had attempted doing anything of the sort toward Germany, German agrarian conservatives would have described this behavior as economic rape. At the same time, England, which around the turn of the century wished to encircle Europe for the sake of its colonial policy and not out of envy for the growth of German trade, as Hans Rothfels expressed it with pan-European acuity,[30] was forced to give up the idea of a rapprochement with Germany as a result of German foreign policy and left no choice but

27. Ischchanian, *Die ausländischen Elemente in der russischen Volkswirtschaft* (Leipzig, 1913), p. 252.

28. *Cf.* the statistics in Leo Inrowsky, "Der russische Getreideexport," *Münchener Volkswirtschaftliche Studien,* 105 (Stuttgart, 1910), p. 175.

29. Fritz Beckmann, *Die agrarische internationale Arbeitsteilung* (Jena, 1926).

30. *Op. cit.*

to move toward an alliance with France and Russia. And it was England's joining the French-Russian entente that finally determined the outcome of the war. The social underpinnings for this course of events lay in the fact that capitalists and agrarians in Germany were united in their hostility toward England. Agrarians like Diedrich Hahn might carry on intrigues [31] against the "horrible fleet" or assert, like Gustav Roesicke, that the fleet was a knife that would be used to "slaughter" German agriculture,[32] but agrarians were just as ready to give financial backing to the anti-British agitation as industry was willing to finance the propaganda for the fleet. The interests of agriculture and industry could be reconciled in the struggle against England. Despite their internal political, economic, and social hostility, in terms of foreign policy they were allies in their opposition to England. The hostility toward England provided the safety valve which permitted the clashing forces of industry and agriculture to find a common denominator in a foreign policy that allowed them both a "nationalist" attitude. This hostility was anything but a hysterical ideological nationalism on the part of persons ignorant of the foreign political situation, and the idolizing of the Boers was anything but an expression of the ideologically oriented but "unpolitical" German temperament and of the urge to defend the liberty of oppressed peoples. Had this been the case, it would have been a more or less academic matter. Its angry intensity and, especially, its persistence were derived from its significance in the struggle for state power on the part of industry and agriculture in their opposition to the proletariat. It was not muddy-minded popular attitudes that triumphed over the clarity of *raison d'état,* but the clear-sighted class interests of agrarians, industrialists, and shipbuilders, whose enmity of England, rooted as it was in domestic, economic, and social considerations, won out over the equally obvious interests of the German people, because the German government, in its pursuit of the *Sammlungspolitik,* identified itself with the interests of these classes against the interest of the German people.

31. *Reichstagsverhandlungen,* February 10, 1900, X, 1, Vol. 3, pp. 4025, 4028, 4043–4045.
32. *Ibid.,* December 14, 1899, X, 1, Vol. 5, p. 3386. *Cf.* his conversation with Tirpitz, August 13, 1915, in Tirpitz, *op. cit.,* p. 492.

In terms of internal politics, the buildup of the fleet and *Weltpolitik* meant a reinforcement of capitalist, liberal, bourgeois elements; the government itself justified the navy laws with the need to protect capitalist expansion. In terms of foreign policy, however, this domestic liberalism did not portend a rapprochement with the Western powers, whose social structure resembled its own, but hostility toward them. Just as in the sixties Germany's national unification (that is, its attainment of a political framework comparable with that of France) had taken place in conflict with the latter and under the protection of tsarist Russia, German industrialization (that is, its attainment of an economic framework like England's) brought it into conflict with the latter. As in the sixties, it was imperative for Germany to maintain its friendship with Russia and to conclude an alliance with it, but that would have been feasible only if both countries, in view of the severe European agricultural crisis, had been willing to adjust to each other's economic needs. That kind of alliance could not be implemented in 1900. As a background to the nonrenewal of the Reinsurance Treaty between Russia and Germany, to which little research has been devoted so far, one must take into account developments that go as far back as 1890: Vyshnegradsky's fiscal protective tariff policy, the forced export of grain combined with a sharp reduction of German imports in response to Bismarck's tariff policy, and the introduction of the capitalist profit motive in the management of the Russian railroads.[q] It is not possible to estimate what the prospects would have been for a Russo-German alliance, if it was meant to be more than a mere exercise in diplomatic virtuosity, unless we take into account the effects of Witte's complicated financial policy[r] and the competitive anti-Russian stance of German agriculture, that is, of the smaller, debt-ridden large-scale landholdings East of the Elbe. This Russo-German alliance was the precondition for any anti-British policy, but it was impossible for Germany to conclude this alliance as long as the German government allowed the East Elbian estate owners to dictate its agricultural policy. As a result, both the naval policy and *Weltpolitik* lacked a solid foundation, because the agrarians dictated an anti-Russian foreign policy, whereas the capitalist anti-British forces in the Reich were hampered by the *Sammlungspolitik* in their efforts to promote a political friendship with the Russians, through which they might then control the latter financially and industrially. The Russians made no secret in Berlin of their deep satisfaction about the buildup of the German fleet,[33] but the German tariff legislation of 1902 probably evoked similar pleasure in England. Instead of exacting a *quid pro quo* from England for the anti-Russian policy that England had urged on Germany between 1898 and 1901,[s] Germany voluntarily took part in England's encirclement of Russia after the collapse of the Anglo-German alliance. The German protective tariff against Russian agriculture was enacted simultaneously with the Anglo-Japanese alliance against Russia in the Far East.[t] Although after the collapse of the alliance negotiations England and Germany assumed a determinedly antagonistic stance that led to the outbreak of war in 1914, Germany made inestimable contributions to England's anti-Russian policy under the pressure of its own East Elbian anti-Russian agrarians.

From the standpoint of internal political developments, the expansion of the fleet and the competitive anti-British industrial and commercial policies raised the question how a state socially and politically dominated by agrarians could conduct an obviously capitalist foreign policy, and how a state whose grain policy drove its factory workers to violent protests against high food prices and lowered their real wages[34] could rely entirely on the country's industrial growth when it came to its foreign policy. From the standpoint of foreign policy, the question arose whether the Russian alliance, which was the necessary counterpart to the anti-British policy, could be maintained in the face of Germany's agrarian competition with Russia, whose intensity was as great as its capitalist competition with England. It has been customary to blame Germany's unfavorable geographic situation for what should be blamed on its economic policy, which, in contrast to geography, is not intrinsically static but open to dynamic change. It has been stated that the industrial competition between Germany and England need not have entailed a political antagonism between the two countries. But the agricultural competition between Russia and Germany had to

33. Report of the Hamburg representative to the Bundesrat, Senator Dr. Burchard to Senator Dr. Lappenberg, November 21, 1899, in Staatsarchiv Hamburg, *Cf.* Tirpitz, *op. cit.*, p. 105 and Meinecke, *op. cit.*, pp. 122, 142.
34. Sering, *op. cit.*, pp. 80–81.

lead to political antagonism, because the closing of the German market to Russian rye, which, given the insignificance of the international market, could now find an outlet only in Scandinavia, threw the Witte financial policy into disarray, reduced to an even lower level the already dismally low standard of living of the Russian peasantry, and by the destruction of this internal market, placed an additional obstacle in the path of Russian industrialization. Germany in the nineties assumed the same stance in its economic policy toward Russia that America is now (1928) assuming toward vanquished Germany with its Dawes Plan.ᵘ Under such economic conditions a political alliance would have been nothing but a tactical diplomatic move, from Russia's point of view; the earlier Reinsurance Treaty of 1887 and the Russian attempts to renew it in 1890 were mere expedients on the part of Russian diplomacy of that small circle around the powerless Foreign Minister von Giersᵛ who was faced with an imminent "internal Cabinet crisis" unless he could present some foreign policy successes to the man actually dictating Russian policy as a whole, namely the minister of finance. Giers attempted to keep Germany in line through political-technical methods, at the time that Vyshnegradsky was collecting the necessary capital from Germany's enemies in Paris. But if Germany had wished in 1900 to seek a Russian alliance in response to an ultimative English treaty offer,⁽³⁵⁾ it would have had first to eliminate the international agrarian crisis (which was terminated for reasons that had nothing to do with the German protective tariff measures),⁽³⁶⁾ and in addition to split up into small family farms the East Elbian landholdings; these were most heavily affected by the agrarian crisis, and their owners, despite their political and social sympathies for tsarist despotism, were among the most vocal advocates of an anti-Russian policy. Otherwise, how could a political alliance have had any solidity, if German economic policy was geared to harming its ally?⁽³⁷⁾ And the most important point:

35. Rothfels, "Zur Beurteilung der englischen Vorkriegspolitik," *Archiv für Politik und Geschichte,* 1926/II, p. 613.
36. Magnificently summarized in Sering's work.
37. This does not do justice to the obstacle presented by Austro-Hungary, particularly Czechoslovakia, a point that Meinecke has treated in detail in his *Bündnisproblem.* Here we are dealing primarily with the social impediments in the way of the foreign-policy decision.

Germany would have had to replace Franco-Belgian capital in Russia with its own. Bismarck had taken a negative stand toward such a means of shackling the Russian ally with capitalist chains not only in his well-known monetary policy of 1887[w] but also in his entire protective tariff policy, which had been adversely affecting the Russian economy since 1879. The precondition for binding Russia politically was always the guarantee of credit. The Franco-Russian alliance[x] and the Anglo-Russian Entente of 1907 represent to a large extent retroactive political confirmations of financial ties that may well have been of recent origin. But was Germany, with the constitution it had at that time, ever in a position to make an alliance with Russia? A conservative state could no longer conclude such an alliance. In truth, obsolete dynastic friendship and feudal opposition against revolution weighed less heavily in the scales than the need of the Russian agrarian state to complement its own resources with money from a capitalist state; a conservative-agrarian protective-tariff-oriented Germany would always give priority to agrarian as against capitalist interests in its relations with Russia. When the tsar rose to his feet at the playing of the Marseillaise,[y] this symbolized the alliance of the Russian agrarian state with French money, not only against Germany as a political power, but even more: the effective rejection of all monarchical solidarity on the part of the Eastern powers under the pressure of Russia's overriding need to complement its economic resources, a need that Germany was incapable of satisfying.

Yet, even on the assumption that Germany had tried to put its policy toward Russia on a sound financial footing, the Petersburg stock market crash of September 23, 1899, which terminated Witte's *Gründerzeit,*[z] presented an insurmountable obstacle to any policy leading to the injection of German capital into Russia. This situation of the Russian money market was only one of the factors that condemned any Russo-German alliance to a mere diplomatic-technical episode; the other factor was the social distribution of power within the German Reich. The agrarian conservatives were the opponents of a grain-exporting Russia, and internal and economic policy from 1897 on made every effort to take their wishes into account. How could an exception now be made in foreign policy? How could a Reich Chancellor think of courting the agrarians domesti-

cally and slapping them in the face in foreign affairs? The conclusion of an alliance with England as well as with Russia would
have confronted the man in charge of German foreign policy with
the task of squaring the circle: he would have had to force the East
Elbian agrarians, without whose participation the *Sammlungspolitik* was unworkable, to agree to a foreign policy that was altogether
odious to them.

The fact that the Reich Chancellor was responsible for the conduct of foreign policy as well as internal and economic policy makes
it inevitable that German foreign policy (and the foreign policy of
all other states) can never be understood merely as a diplomatic
technique to be analyzed with the help of the Foreign Office files and
the memoirs of diplomats. The question of the alliance with England cannot be viewed as an isolated diplomatic action, not only
because it is a link in a lengthy chain of foreign policy developments,
but also because it is inextricably tied to questions relating to the
severe social and economic upheavals of the nineties, for which
the *Sammlungspolitik* offered an unsatisfactory over-all solution.
Around the turn of the century, internal and foreign policy—the
latter in both its economic and its diplomatic guise—were notwithstanding their apparent incoherence pursuing a common objective,
namely to make this over-all solution effective. The protective-tariff proposal was the economic facet, the Penitentiary Bill the social facet, the second navy law the power-political facet, and the
combination of an anti-British and an anti-Russian policy the
foreign policy facet of one and the same tendency: that of the
Sammlungspolitik.

CHAPTER III

Class Struggle and Armament Policy in Imperial Germany

1

The crucial precondition for the bourgeois nation-state's acceptance by its inhabitants is a generally shared confidence that the state's actions are not guided by class interests: the "state" as an institution transcending individual classes—and, in Prussian Germany, under the aegis of a special class, the bureaucracy—follows the dictates of its inner necessity and acts as a state among states. For the ideology of the German national state in the nineteenth century, the primacy of foreign policy was an iron law, and it would have been as serious a crime to challenge this law as to claim in the sixteenth century that the earth rotated around the sun.

As a state within a system of states, the national state is surrounded by a hostile world. Its own actions are defensive measures against the unjustified lust for power of its enemies. The actions of other states are aggressive[1] and indicate plans for eliminating their competitors by force, possibly even by surprise attack in the midst of peace.[2] The army, whose purpose it is to safeguard the state from its competitors, thus represents to a high degree the state's foreign-

1. Typical of this view is the important armament memorandum of the General Staff of 21 December 1913. Printed in *Der Weltkrieg 1914 bis 1918, bearbeitet im Reichsarchiv: Kriegsrüstung und Kriegswirtschaft.* Vol. 1: *Die militärische, wirtschaftliche und finanzielle Rüstung Deutschlands von der Reichsgründung bis zum Ausbruch des Weltkrieges* (Berlin, 1930), p. 173 and Appendix I, pp. 158 ff.
2. Examples can be found in Franz Freiherr v. Edelsheim, *Operationen über See* (Berlin, 1901). For comments, see Eckart Kehr, *Schlachtflottenbau und Parteipolitik*

policy interests and is ideologically removed from internal political and social disputes within the national state.

Yet, can it be truthfully claimed that the army of the national state, and the army of the German empire in particular, kept aloof from class struggles? Is it not true that the social opposition, which rejected the ideology of a unified national state, recognized the class character of the army and was actually joined in this view by the ruling class, which also viewed the development of the army in terms of the social division of power rather than in terms of foreign-policy considerations?

The direct approach to this question, that is, the marshaling of evidence for the dependence of military ideology on the social and economic structure, is valid *per se*. However, it may be more effective from a methodological point of view to deal with the problem of armament policy and class bias from an apparently purely military standpoint by raising the question to what extent the execution of military operations and modern strategy, with its focus on the grand offensive, were determined by the requirements of advanced capitalism. Or, to put it more concretely, we may ask what were the economic presuppositions for the *ancien régime's* widely held theory that the next war would of necessity be a short war and what were the economic and social conditions for Schlieffen's mobilization plan?

2

Frederick the Great's determination to keep his wars *"bref et vif,"* short and fast, was certainly not based on any compulsion to adjust his military strategy to the state's capitalist economy. Capitalism was still so immature that it had nothing to contribute to military strategy. To prevent the financial collapse of the state, the entire productive apparatus had to be kept working at full capacity, without demanding military service of those engaged in it even in wartime, so that the flow of taxes would not be interrupted. The principle that the citizen should not be aware of the wars the king

---

(Berlin, 1930), p. 355. See also the General Staff's communication to the Ministry of War of 25 November 1912, which had been drafted by Col. Ludendorff (quoted in Appendix I, p. 147 of the work just cited above).

was waging was less an intrinsic feature of political despotism than the consequence of the low productivity of eighteenth-century cottage industry. The incipient capitalist economy was perfectly capable of withstanding a protracted war—industry had developed out of the delivery of war supplies, and loan capital had first appeared in Prussia in the wake of the coin and subsidy transactions of the Seven Years' War and had expanded so rapidly as a result of the high-interest loans extended to the estates and the government between 1806 and 1813 that it began in a true sense to deserve that designation—but its earnings were still insufficient for financing a war. What inspired Frederick to depart from the usual rules of eighteenth-century strategy and to fight resolutely, to attack, and to risk battles, rather than merely to engage in maneuvers, was the prince's desperate situation as the ruler of an agrarian state fighting against a coalition of states with a much more advanced form of capitalism. And the monarch's unique qualities, his personal courage, and the fact that he combined in one person the attributes of military commander and king, thus avoiding the usual inhibitions restraining generals acting under orders,[3] were strokes of fortune that allowed him to exploit the given situation to the utmost.

There is no connection between the strategy of Frederick the Great and that of the late nineteenth century. The theory of the inevitability of short wars in the era of advanced capitalism begins with Clausewitz,[a] and then only indirectly. For in his writings, neither the question of the economic burden of war nor the impact of weapons plays a prominent role. His concept of "the culminating point of attack"[4] is predicated on what he knows about the size of armies and does not take into account the economic or social basis for differences in their internal strength. Clausewitz takes for granted that "most wars will continue" to be ones in which "the crushing of the opponent cannot be the military objective," and he simultaneously assumes the economic vulnerability of the states supporting the opposing armies. Although in his theory about the "absoluteness" of warfare this vulnerability of the states is perceived

---

3. This inhibition had a much greater impact under absolutism than in the nineteenth century in view of the costliness of the Army and the ease with which military setbacks had repercussions on court intrigues.

4. *Vom Kriege,* Appendix to Book 7.

as a limiting factor, he shows no desire to explore its causes, because in his eyes "absolute war in all its destructive energy" is merely an exaggerated mental construct.[5]

Clausewitz's theory about the culminating point of the attack, his observation that the attacker may well, "in the dynamics of the operation," be carried beyond "the culminating point without realizing it," and that most field commanders out of lack of self-confidence "prefer to keep at a safe distance from the goal [the culminating point] rather than come too close to it," was bound to lead to the conclusion that attack at the outset of the war must seek to bring about the speediest possible annihilation of the enemy. This conclusion was particularly convincing when Clausewitz's theoretical framework was examined in the light of concrete economic and technical reality. It was then that General Moltke recognized that, in the wake of the revolution in weapons technology that had begun in the mid-nineteenth century, the army had become so closely tied to the economy and technology that the culminating point had moved frightfully close to the outbreak of the war. While Clausewitz, on the basis of the experiences of the great wars of coalition, had integrated war with politics—presenting war as a continuation of politics by other methods and transferring responsibility for military plans from the general to the politician—but had left the question of human resources and weapons effectiveness out of account in the analysis of tactics, Moltke for his part isolated war ideologically from the requirements of politics.[6] He made strategy completely subservient to the demands of the capitalist economy and allowed weapons technology to determine tactics. "Modern warfare is characterized by the urge to achieve a decisive and rapid conclusion," we find in the 1869 instructions for upper-echelon commanders.[7] "The strength of the armies, the problems of keeping them provisioned, the expense of keeping them under arms, the interruption of trade and transportation, combined with the speed

---

5. Eberhard Kessel, "Doppelpolige Strategie," *Wissen und Wehr*, 1931, p. 631.

6. In his essay "Über Strategie," one of the most important sources for the shaping of military ideology in the German empire (*Militärische Werke*, II:2, p. 287).

7. *Militärische Werke*, II:2, p. 173. See also an almost identical passage in *Militärische Korrespondenz*, 1870, p. 115. It would be interesting to investigate the question whether the Prussian military leadership accepted and applied this superstructure-infrastructure theory.

of troop organization and the ease with which they can be mobilized, all these factors make a rapid conclusion of the war imperative." "In view of the huge size of the assembled troops, both sides will try to engage in a decisive battle in the first eight days" and "whoever is familiar with the way the Prussian army and *Landwehr* [militia] are organized, must know that we cannot stand by idly once these resources have been mobilized; thus, mobilization will inevitably lead to an attack."[8]

Just as the conditions of a highly developed capitalist state imposed a strategy that was designed to bring a decision as quickly as possible, so did weapons technology determine the nature of this decision. It was the breach loader and the rifled gun that transformed the Napoleonic bayonet attack and frontal penetration by massed columns into the tactics of encirclement. "In facing the enemy's infantry, if it is still well-organized, that is, if it is still firm and has not yet suffered very heavy losses, bayonet attack is not likely to lead to 'success,' and whenever such masses of firearms are assembled, as was the case in the Austrian position at Königgrätz,[b] the high command will have to consider whether the frontal attack should not give way to a flank attack."[9] This encirclement of the enemy, made invulnerable to frontal attack because of strong fire power based on modern weapons technology, increasingly became in the next decades the central operational problem of the German army, both on a small and on a large scale, tactically and strategically, beginning with the encirclement of a single company and expanding to the most gigantic encirclement operation in world history, Schlieffen's invasion of Belgium,[c] adopted in preference to a frontal assault on the impregnable French fortified line of Belfort-Verdun.

Helmut von Moltke was both the theorist and the practitioner, not of the long, but of the short war that was necessitated by the wartime vulnerability of the capitalist economy as well as by the incipient escalation in weapons development in the second third of the nineteenth century. Moltke's strategy was one of securing a rapid decision through the initial attack. We must attribute to the discouragement of old age Moltke's address to the Reichstag in 1890

8. To General Hartmann, 17 May 1867 and to his brother Adolf, July 1859.
9. *Militärische Werke*, II:2, p. 101. Memorandum of 1868.

with its reference to the possibility of a seven-year or a thirty-year war. This was his reaction to the difficult challenge which the fortification of Paris and the vastly overrated French system of defensive strong points posed for a German army that put a higher valuation on open battle and the heroism of an onrushing and self-sacrificing infantry than on siege warfare and its attendant technical problems.

In the early years of the twentieth century, Tirpitz and Schlieffen carried Moltke's theory of warfare as a function of capitalism one step further. Tirpitz based his navy propaganda on the thesis that the fleet was "in the service of maritime interests," and Schlieffen based his strategy of a colossal advance through Belgium that would decide the war in the West at the first blow on the impossibility of a protracted war at a time "when the very existence of a nation depends on the uninterrupted flow of trade and industry, and when the immobilized wheels of the economy must be reactivated by a rapid decision."[10]

Moltke, Schlieffen, and Tirpitz founded their strategy on the assumption that the next war must be short because the advanced capitalist state could no longer tolerate a protracted one. This belief had two consequences:

1. the renunciation of economic mobilization and of a transition to a war of attrition;

2. a vacillation between increasing and limiting the size of the army.

3

Before 1914, preparations for war had to remain on an intermediate level. Unless the economy was coordinated with the direction of the war, it would be impossible to conduct war; yet an economic preparation for war, which organized the General Staff and the War Ministry as military bureaus in a comprehensive economic-political war directorate, and abstained from the mechanical piling up of giant stocks of weapons and equipment in order to concentrate upon "the determination of types of weapons and the preparation

10. *Der Krieg in der Gegenwart: Gesammelte Schriften* (Berlin, 1913), I, 17. See also the valuable comments by Walter Elze, *Tannenberg: Das deutsche Heer von 1914* (Breslau, 1928), p. 366.

for their mass production in time of need"[11]—this was impossible as long as it was assumed that the war would be so short that it would be over before the war directorate had defined its area of activity and before the mass production of material could be initiated.

It was precisely because Moltke and Schlieffen consciously subordinated their strategy to their realization that the state had a vital interest in the uninterrupted functioning of an unregulated economy even in time of war—because they were receptive to the idea of an intimate relationship between strategy and the operation of the economic process—that they were unable to understand that the next war must be an economic one. They felt that justice had been done to all requirements of the economy when they had taken all possible measures to cut short military operations, thereby sparing capitalism the convulsions of wartime. In reality, the only result achieved by Moltke and Schlieffen in this adaptation of their strategy to an extremely short war was that the military administration was saved all real concern regarding the economic difficulties of a protracted war and thus never gave them any thought. "All plans and measures were dominated by the question of replacing material used in the field, but there was no effort to spur to the utmost industrial production as a whole in order to supply ever larger quantities of equipment for the struggle."[12] And the problem then arose quite logically what should be done with a million unemployed that were to be anticipated as a result of the interruption of peacetime production and a serious consumption crisis; the question how the few fully able-bodied persons that had not been mobilized could maintain both agricultural and military production was not even raised. It was impossible to implement economic mobilization before 1914 and to place industry under a unified policy geared to a war economy, not because of the backwardness of the military, but because of a view that was in tune with the times and led it to try to circumvent the wartime economic difficulties of capitalist states by seeking a speedy termination of the war through a mighty initial offensive rather than attempting to face inherently insuperable difficulties. As a New York banker recently expressed it: "People who

11. Colonel-General von Seeckt, *Gedanken eines Soldaten* (Berlin, 1929), p. 99.
12. *Kriegsrüstung,* I, 395. [For complete reference, see note 1.]

stated in August 1914 that for financial reasons war could last no more than four months and who became laughingstocks in 1918, were right after all."[13]

At the same time, the prewar policy of meeting the requirements of the anticipated war by stocking equipment was given further impetus by the fact that the wartime strength of the armies was increasing faster than the population. The second- and third-line formations that had been newly set up, especially in the 1890's, and for which no weapons were yet available, took over the old equipment discarded by the front-line troops and thus permitted the standing army, notwithstanding its size, to be consistently supplied with new weapons. In view of the stagnating population and the rapidly developing technology, it would have imposed an intolerable financial burden to scrap weapons as soon as they become obsolete.

4

The problem of provisioning the population with food in wartime was handled as ambivalently as was the weapons problem.

Neither foreign policy nor the demands of the military had started the debate over the question of starvation in the event of war; it resulted from the agricultural crisis and the agitation of the great landowners who were economically threatened by it. Caprivi, who lowered the tariffs on grain, and, by the pressure exerted by this on agriculture, significantly increased both grain and cattle production, spoke before the Reichstag in 1893[14] of the possibility that, in the next war, a force of enemy cruisers might cut off food imports to Germany by blockading the English Channel and the waters as far north as Scotland. As the first politician courageous enough to designate Germany as a predominantly industrial country, he was not intending by this statement to give agriculture a nationally privileged position; against the possibility of a hunger blockade he proposed the building of a blockade-breaking fleet, and he showed that Germany's agriculture was relatively superfluous in wartime,

13. Paul Scheffer, "Kreditpsychose und ihre Gründe," *Berliner Tageblatt*, 23 October 1931, no. 501.
14. 8 March 1893—a remark that, strangely enough, has generally been overlooked by scholars.

as long as the Reich maintained tolerable political relations with England.[d]

The representatives of large-scale agriculture, thrust into a secondary role, became the sociological group who made the argument that Germany's food supplies in wartime would be inadequate and who opposed any fleet whose purpose it would be to keep the path clear for imports in the event of war. Anti-agrarian proponents of a *Weltpolitik,* like Delbrück and Dietzel,[e] and the Reich Naval Office in their footsteps, therefore insisted on the adequacy of the German food supply. What finally laid this controversy to rest was not that one of the opponents became convinced by scientific evidence but that the protective tariffs of 1902 satisfied agricultural demands and prevented agrarians from further stressing their incapacity to satisfy wartime needs. A reversal in the official stand toward the hunger blockade now manifested itself. The Ministry of War, with its close ties to the aristocratic agrarian ruling group, felt that there was no reason to worry about problems of food supply even in the face of English hostility; the Ministry of the Interior felt that it was superfluous to investigate the relations between consumption and production, because the protective tariff was bound to lead to a sufficient increase in agricultural production. For a searching investigation of the question of food supply would have amounted to a repudiation of the official rationale for the tariff legislation of 1902, which was that it had been a national necessity. It was therefore natural that when the rhetoric of the tariff debate receded into the past and the War Ministry began to have renewed doubts, the Ministry of the Interior, which was responsible for tariff policy, sought to distract its attention from the question of securing food supply without revealing the reasons for this transparent delaying maneuver.[15] When consultations finally got under way in 1912 (taking a very Platonic course), the discussions, characteristically enough, focused on supplying the population with grains from the large estates. Grains were thus quietly given first priority among items of wartime nutrition, while meat and fat, which were the products of small-farm cultivation, were "forgotten" as they had been in the tariff legislation. There was a simple way in which the

15. *Kriegsrüstung.* I, 302, 306–307, 313, 320, 322, 334.

question of meat supply could be disposed of for propaganda purposes: the argument that 95 percent of the meat consumed was produced within the borders of the Reich. The fact that this production required large imports of fodder was never considered.

The question of import permits was handled in the same way. These were supposed to make it possible for the great landowners of East Elbia to export rye, which would be compensated for by duty-free imports from the West. As a result of this certificate system and of the additional circumstance that postponement of payment of duties on grain imports was allowed only at the cost of interest charges (which made it cheaper to store grain for import abroad than at home), there was a marked scarcity in the German grain market from May to July, in which the threat of war typically loomed large: in southwest Germany grain reserves did not exceed two weeks' supply. The Ministry of War finally raised an uproar about this constant denuding of Germany's grain reserves solely in the interest of the great landholders. But these methods had been provided for in the tariff laws of 1902, with full exploitation of nationalist phraseology. The fact that it would have been necessary to admit that national protection of agricultural production was a stab in the back of the army in the interest of the ruling clique of aristocratic estate owners made it impossible before 1914, despite all attempts by the military, to do away with the system of import certificates and tariff postponement.

It was the Reich Naval Office that assumed the most unambiguous ideological stand among the agencies concerned with the food problem, even if it failed to implement it practically. This was the agency that justified its policies along Marxist lines and was in agreement with the Social Democrats that armament policy for the German Reich was in the service of capitalist interests, though it evaluated this fact positively. Starting from these assumptions, the Reich Naval Office was also the first German central authority unwilling to view the question of wartime food supplies from a purely fiscal point of view; it perceived agriculture, transportation, and industry as a large, interconnected economic apparatus, whose proper functioning in wartime was a precondition of victory.[16] And, in line

16. *Ibid.*, pp. 310–311.

with its sceptical evaluation of the concrete prospects of the German fleet in a confrontation with England,[17] it became a proponent of the hunger theory from 1905 on. It did not succeed, however, in making its opinion prevail, and scholarly discussion of the food question, which was resumed in 1907, had equally little impact, because basically the agricultural group, which could not admit the inadequacy of the tariff policy, was in the saddle. The problem never got beyond a discussion for the files, and no action was taken that might have jeopardized the big landowners' position. In this trench warfare between military and agricultural interests, the agrarians, with the official support of the Reich Ministry of the Interior, were successful in repelling all attacks on the part of the military, whether they came from the navy or from the army.

When the agrarians were hard-pressed in the nineties, they had urged preparation for the assuring of adequate food in time of war. Now that they were sheltered by a tariff wall, they saw to it that nothing was done to promote it, except by talk. The resultant lack of action was due, not to a negligent bureaucracy but to the compulsion exercised by a power constellation against which individual ministers, and even an uninvolved agency like the Reich Naval Office, were helpless. The direct pressure of agrarian interests was too strong and, even in the absence of this pressure, the state felt that it was not competent, in an era of unorganized but highly developed capitalism, to assume tasks like the feeding of the civilian population in wartime. Even in the eighties, in the early stage of neomercantilism, the Ministry of Agriculture turned down "an excellent storage system" in spite of the inadequacy of agricultural production, for fear of involving the state in the grain business "in an undesirable manner."[18] The highly developed capitalist state, functioning as a war-making institution, was no longer in a position to relegate such problems *ad acta,* but power relationships in the economic sector that was supposed to be brought under regulation, as well as the lack of adequate economic training on the part of the

17. Weniger, "Die Entwicklung des Operationsplans für die deutsche Schlachtenflotte," *Marinerundschau,* 1930.
18. *Kriegsrüstung.* I, 297.

bureaucracy and its still (compared with its present condition) underdeveloped drive for power, all combined to make the solution of this problem practically impossible.

5

The distribution of social power in the empire had an impact on the basic problem of German armament policy in the narrower sense, that is, the expansion of the size of the army, comparable to its weight in the question of regulating the food supply: it prevented an unequivocal answer to the question of quantity versus quality. Caprivi expressed the strategic dilemma in these terms: "In the beginning of a campaign, the quality of the troops carries great weight, but in the long run, larger numbers come into their own."[19] But from the German point of view, this dilemma of military strategy, which, like many other matters, Caprivi had brilliantly grasped, concealed the dilemma of the Reich's social structure, which turned upon the question of size versus quality.

The army reform that began in 1859 had abolished the dual system, which comprised a front-line army *(Linienarmee)* and a militia *(Landwehr)*, the former viewed as aristocratic territory, the latter as reserved for the bourgeoisie. This was replaced by a somewhat expanded, unified line army, which, however, because of the elimination of the antiabsolutist characteristics of the Landwehr,[20] closer control of the officers, the purging of bourgeois elements among the cadets, and the limitation of military duty to the twelve youngest contingents, became a much more praetorian instrument of power in the hands of the Crown than the earlier army. As long as the distribution of power, which had been stabilized in the conflict between the Crown and parliament,[f] remained intact—not only politically but socially—and as long as capitalist interests had no direct influence on the political decisions of the highest state authorities,[21] this character of the Prussian army remained unaltered. The

19. *Ibid.,* p. 36.
20. Described most incisively in Roon's classical memorandum: "Bemerkungen und Entwürfe zur vaterländischen Heeresverfassung" (Kolberg, 21 July 1858). *Militärische Schriften Kaiser Wilhelms des Grossen* (1897), particularly II, 347–352.
21. Much could be said about their indirect influence, but that would lead us too far afield here.

speeding vehicle of power politics that Bismarck had let loose, he personally held to the middle of the road,[22] nor was he sympathetic to the plan of competitive armaments which, from the seventies onward, called for matching every battalion of the enemy with a new one of one's own. But the key to his "politics of peace" cannot be explained in psychological terms. The successful balancing act among the large powers can only be understood by recognizing that between 1873 and the nineties all states were affected by the declining prices of goods and stocks. No big power is inclined to go to war when its economy is in the grips of a latent crisis: in such a situation even the armament industry is under no illusion that prosperity can be restored by large armament orders and new naval laws. Armament interests are faced with this opportunity only during short, sudden spells of depression.[23] The recklessness of Bismarck's successors was much less a function of their inferior intellectual capacities than of the rise in prices—which, beginning with the mid-nineties, always exceeded the peak reached by the previous boom, despite the intervening deep troughs of depression—and of the attraction of the stock market, in which, after the nationalization of the railroads and the leveling off of bank dividend payments, a shift occurred in typical shareholding from the railroads and banks to mining and armament shares. The economic depression was a force for peace; the economic boom aroused the joyful hope that a political-military boom would follow on the heels of the economic boom. For it is no accident, though political historiography refuses to acknowledge it and is in fact incapable of seeing it with the psychological methods at its disposal, that the last and most massive increases in the size of the army before the world war coincided with a new business upturn, which improved the Reich's finances, so

22. Hans Rothfels in his introduction to *Bismarck und der Staat* (München, 1925), pp. XXXII f. But this interpretation neglects the fact that Bismarck could afford the luxury of inconsistency as long as he was in office and in charge of things, but that after his abdication the logic of his actions was more important than his personal preferences. The psychological approach, by disregarding this distinction, distorts the truth.

23. For the German crisis of 1901, see also Prince Salm's letter to Tirpitz of 3 December 1901 (cited in Kehr, *Schlachtflottenbau*, p. 457); for the English crisis of 1908, Fritz Uplegger, *Die englische Flottenpolitik vor dem Weltkrieg 1904–1909* (Stuttgart, 1903) is informative.

that the excess revenue could easily be diverted to the financing of armaments.

But the basis of the first large armament wave at the end of the eighties and in the early nineties was not economic but social in nature. The bourgeoisie of the eighties finally gave up its opposition to the military monarchy under the pressure of the Socialist menace and entered into a coalition with the dynasty and the aristocracy for a mutual protection of property rights. This feudalized bourgeoisie could, from the internal political point of view, be counted upon to supply the Crown with an absolutely reliable reserve officer corps, thereby permitting the conscription law of 1888 to extend military service through the forty-fifth year and subsequently to expand the peacetime army by 27 percent, that is by 125,000 soldiers, without any imminent danger of a democratic dilution of the army.

As a result of this change and, even more, the shift to a two-year military service,[24] with its concomitant 30 percent increase in the quota of recruits, new formations could now be established for mobilization, and an ambitious reserve system could be set up for the first time. An operational army consisting of active and numerous reserve corps could thus be formed. Beginning with the addition of a fourth reserve battalion to all active regiments, and continuing with a transitional stage of *Kriegskorps,* composed of active and partly supernumerary troops, which in turn were replaced by reservists, an arrangement still reflecting the strong scepticism toward reserve formations, a point was finally reached where separate reserve divisions and reserve corps were created, to which a special *Landwehrkorps* was added in 1914. It is true that these reserve formations were equipped with only half as much artillery as the active formations: the human resources expanded more rapidly than did the possibility of supplying them with adequate weapons. But the military strength of the German army in terms of human resources

---

24. The maintenance of the three-year military service under William I in the period of constitutional conflict could be attributed only to the class struggle against the bourgeoisie, because it had no military-technical justification. Bismarck's marginal comment on Moltke's 1879 communication is revealing. In response to Moltke's doubts about whether the Russian army reform was motivated by foreign or domestic considerations, he noted: "Not domestic ones, since it entails a reduction of the period of military service." *Kriegsrüstung,* Appendix I, 25.

kept increasing. The number of men increased from 750,000 to 1,200,000 between 1875 and 1888, then rose rapidly to two million by 1902. The ratio of the field army to the total population increased from 1.7 percent in 1875 to 2.5 percent in 1888 and 3.4 percent in 1902.

This unusual increase in the size of the fighting army up to the turn of the century, which far exceeded the increase in population, inevitably contained within it the seed of the dissolution of the army's praetorian character; and, as a result, the question arose once more how far the old state, from an internal political point of view, could still rely on an army that conscripted all those fit for military service, including almost the whole Socialist laboring class. Recruitment methods were consciously manipulated in such a way that the ratio between those fit for service and those called to military duty differed in the city and in the country: almost all those fit for service in the country were called to duty, while in the city a considerably larger percentage of those fit for service were immediately pronounced supernumerary and transferred to the *Landsturm* or the auxiliary reserves.[25] This meant that a larger percentage of the reliable rural population and a smaller percentage of the unreliable workers were serving in the army. An increase in the size of the army had the unavoidable consequence that the number of workers increased disproportionately fast, since almost all the rural population was already serving in the army, so that the degree of reliability of the army declined faster than was visible from its external expansion. Ten years after the extension of military duty up to the forty-fifth year, the Ministry of War had reached the point where it seriously considered once more lowering the period of service to the thirty-second year and reducing the size of the field army from 900 to 750 battalions.

At least as threatening as the disproportionate increase in unreliability of the recruits compared with the increase in the army's

---

25. Lujo Brentano and Robert Kuczynski, *Die heutigen Grundlagen der deutschen Wehrkraft* (München, 1898), p. 132. And this happened even after the increased call-up of all able-bodied men from the time of the army expansion of 1893. Until that time each corps district had to find its own recruits, and since the corps borders had only been altered once—in frontier areas—since 1867, the uneven population increase had resulted in placing a much smaller burden on the industrial areas, whose development came at a later date.

size was the uncertainty about the reliability of the officers. The Prussian army had always limited the size of its officer corps, in contrast to France, which drew on the pool of noncommissioned officers and thereby prevented the officer corps from turning into a separate caste closed off at the bottom toward the lower classes. Was it conceivable that in Germany a small but segregated officer corps with its own *esprit de corps* could find its place in a thoroughly capitalistic state, whose interests and ideology could never be those of the—relatively speaking—backward military element? But the apparatus was already in existence, and nothing short of a revolution could have eliminated this inconsistency. In peacetime, the only critical problem was that of officer replacement. Only 91 percent of the billets for infantry officers could be filled in 1889. The social strata that had been the mainstay of old Prussia could no longer supply enough officers for the growing army, and although the increasing feudalization of the bourgeoisie made the shortage of officers less acute in the nineties, the question had to be faced whether the new and expanded generation of officers would remain homogeneous. If the army were to grow beyond bounds, there would be no way to avoid "taking on more democratic and other elements that were not fit for this career"[26] and inevitably "reaching down into circles unsuitable for the expansion of the officer corps, which aside from other threats, would expose it to the danger of democratization."[27]

The General Staff, which played an opposing role to the Ministry of War, had the advantage of being an institution not responsible to parliament, since it was constitutionally an agency directly under the Kaiser's control rather than a branch of the Ministry of War.[28] Nevertheless, it could not regard the increase in army size from a purely military and operational point of view, because, despite the conflicts between the General Staff and the Ministry of War, the social homogeneity of the officers in both these agencies acted as a bond strong enough to counterbalance the conflict in respon-

26. Minister of War von Einem to Chief of the General Staff Count Schlieffen, 19 April 1904, in *Kriegsrüstung, Appendix I*, p. 91.

27. Minister of War von Heeringen to Chief of the General Staff von Moltke, 20 January 1913, *ibid*, p. 180.

28. Günther Wohlers, *Die staatsrechtliche Stellung des Generalstabs in Preussen* (Bonn, 1920).

sibilities for the operational superiority of the army and its social reliability. Still, once an apparatus has been established it follows its own laws, and the social reliability of the army was therefore only a secondary consideration for the General Staff; Schlieffen himself in later years gave up his thesis about the uselessness of the reserve formations in the front lines, which he had been reiterating around the turn of the century, in his desire to give the requisite momentum to the initial offensive push that was to lead to a rapid victory. In supporting Ludendorff's efforts to expand the size of the army by three army corps in 1912/13, the General Staff closed its eyes to the social problems that were of sufficient concern to the Ministry of War to make them take the opposite stand.

But even from an operational point of view, the situation of the General Staff remained ambiguous. For the field army, which had been so drastically enlarged, contained quite a few formations with soldiers over the age of thirty, who, being encapsulated in active corps, significantly reduced the capacity of those units for action. On the other hand, the General Staff needed a large army to avoid great operational inferiority to the Russians and the French: "It is our hope," wrote Schlieffen,[29] "that our army is superior to those of France and Russia. It remains to be demonstrated that it is socially superior in the way, let us say, Europeans are when compared with Indians and Negroes, and that is what would be needed in view of the numerical ratio. Up till now we have owed our victories at least in part to our larger numbers: 1813–1814, 1864, 1866, 1870."

The General Staff vacillated between these two extremes. There was no way out of the dilemma that strategically the army must be large and composed of young soldiers, while from the internal political perspective, it must be small and reliable. Therefore the protracted debate was terminated in 1900 by a truce between the Ministry of War and the General Staff on the following basis: things were to remain as they were, the extended period of military service would stay in force, the active army would not be expanded any further, and the gaps in the organizational scheme would not be filled. In keeping with this compromise, the new formations to be called in time of war, which had risen from 457 to 575 battalions between 1888 and 1902, were not to be reduced, as the Ministry of

29. Schlieffen to his sister, 13 November 1892, in *Kriegsrüstung* I, 43.

War would have preferred, but at least they were increased only by 21 battalions between 1902 and 1910. In ten years, wartime strength increased only from 2 to 2.3 million, and the ratio of the field army to the total population only from 3.4 to 3.6 percent. Whereas every increase of population by five million had raised wartime strength by 330,000 between 1875 and 1888, and by 500,000 between 1888 and 1902, it increased it by only 175,000 between 1902 and 1910.

6

This truce, unwritten but definitely concluded, was the basis of the standstill in the growth of the German army up to 1911, foreign policy crises notwithstanding, and no other considerations entered in, certainly not the expansion of the fleet, which began concurrently.[30] Armament policy was determined not from the outside but from within. While the outside world was being told in wild outbursts of rhetoric that for "national" reasons armaments could not be limited, with complete disregard for the bad impression Germany thereby created at the first Hague Conference,[g] German military preparations were in fact stabilized at that time. And as though to rub the noses of even the most obtuse into the neglected inconsistency between armament growth and foreign policy, the same gruesome spectacle recurred at the Second Hague Conference. The Ministry of War and the General Staff had agreed that the army had now reached its ultimate size.[31] There was neither an objective nor a genuinely national reason preventing Germany from urging a halt at least in the expansion of land armaments, since it was neither desirous nor capable of expanding its own armaments. Yet for reasons of internal politics and social prestige, it could not sacrifice the glamour of armaments and a pseudoautonomy, particularly in military matters, which must appear to be impervious to prescriptions from either the traditional enemy, France, or the contemptible shopkeeper England, and so the gap was allowed to widen between foreign political saber-rattling and the actual desire to keep ar-

30. It is psychologically understandable that the Reichsarchiv, which was administered by army (rather than navy) officers, was inclined to blame the navy as an obstacle to the expansion of the army. But repetition of an inaccurate assertion does not make it more accurate.
31. *Kriegsrüstung,* I, 91; Appendix I, p. 106.

maments in a dormant state.[32] The German tactics at both Hague conferences were dictated by internal political considerations, but not by a fanatically pro-armament "militarism," rather by a deplorable degree of consideration for a politically incapable, feudalized and militarized bourgeoisie. This bourgeoisie would have interpreted an international treaty committing Germany to do what its own military authorities were forced to do anyway under the pressure of internal social difficulties as a brutal encroachment by aggressive enemies on German honor and the German nation's right to self-determination. This bourgeoisie, further, had to have the glamor of military autonomy and the right to boundless expansion of armaments paraded before it daily, even though those at the head of the parade fully realized that, in the interests of this bourgeoisie, this autonomy could not be exploited any further. German policy at the Hague conferences was an example of grotesqueness without a parallel: precisely because Germany had put a halt to its land armaments, this halt could not be allowed to penetrate the consciousness of the militaristic bourgeoisie and therefore had to be hidden by propaganda and by a refusal to accept any international limitation upon armaments. Germany refused disarmament because it was unwilling to continue arming for fear of proletarianizing its army, but simultaneously it dared not admit this situation to its own bourgeoisie.

Although this fundamental reversal in armament policies can be clearly perceived, the question remains unsettled whether any conflict over this armament limitation arose between the armament industry on the one hand and the Ministry of War and the General Staff on the other. It is known that the director-general of the Berlin-Karlsruher Industriewerke, von Gontard, attempted to incite the Budget Commission to demand increased armaments from the Ministry of War by spreading false information,[33] and the King of

32. A comparable scissor effect manifested itself in the expansion of the German fleet. It was equally impossible to combine the buildup of the fleet, which was a conspicuous method of increasing armaments and one likely to impress the patriotic bourgeois chauvinist, with the intention of avoiding war in the hope that England would be oblivious of Germany's surpassing it in armaments and thereby let Germany gain world rule without bloodshed. Kehr, *Schlachtflottenbau,* especially p. 317.

33. Hans Wehrberg, *Die internationale Beschränkung der Rüstungen* (Stuttgart, 1919).

Italy believed that Germany could not agree to armament limitations at the Second Hague Conference for the very reason that the Kaiser would not want to reduce Krupp's profits.[34] It may be assumed, however, that the armament industry agreed to let the military keep the army at its existing size and that it tolerated the concomitant loss of new orders that would have followed an expansion of the army, because the numerical stabilization of the army coincided with the buildup of the navy with its unusually large steel requirements and with the rearming of the field artillery and the infantry, which were being equipped with the recoil-barrel gun 96nA (which represented a compromise solution) and the 98 rifle respectively. It remains an open question whether the armament industry, after this reequipment had been completed in 1908, then insisted on new orders or whether it found sufficient compensation in the building program of the navy, now accelerated to four keels a year.

7

It was not the navy with its extensive financial requirements that interfered with the development of the army—the navy budget increased by only 240 million compared with 188 million for the army budget [35]—but probably it was thanks only to the diversion of the armament interests to the navy that the army found it possible to carry through its stabilization of the troop buildup, to which it had been compelled by the pressure of social tensions, without becoming embroiled in an embittered conflict with the armament industry. And aside from providing the army with this inadvertent but certainly welcome relief, the navy was responsible in 1911 for setting off a second round in the armament race, which led directly to the world war.

Like the period of armament limitation, this new spurt in the armament race was not externally induced by the competitive arming of foreign powers. Russia was still poorly armed; France, under the pressure of its own troublesome manpower shortage, was still shying away from further arming. Austria, on the other hand, was beginning to improve its neglected army, which was hardly fit for wartime use. The proportional strength of the different armies had

34. A. Nevins, *Henry White* (New York, 1930), p. 252.
35. In interpreting these figures, price rises must be taken into account.

not shifted in recent years. Foreign political tensions were not so marked that the "respectable increase and expansion of the organization" and the increased fighting potential of its military formations[36] needed to be upgraded by the army after the conscription law *(Präsenzgesetz)* of 1911. The Ministry of War therefore had every intention of maintaining for the whole decade up to 1921 its policy of expanding the army slowly, limiting reinforcement only to technical troops.

The navy shattered this intention. Tirpitz never admitted that foreign-policy considerations should guide the development of the fleet. But he did allow the fleet to grow in accordance with the plan laid down in 1900, and he exploited every international incident as an argument for its further expansion.

The diplomatic defeat in Morocco,[h] which had no connection with the strength of armaments, became the pretext for the new supplementary navy law, which was to prevent the reduction of the building program from four to two keels a year. "The greater our disgrace, the more vigorous the indignation. The prospects of a supplementary law are improved thereby." Tirpitz wished to turn an "impression into a fact, making it seem as though Germany had been forced to yield to France because of a lack of warships."[37] The supplementary law, which had been formulated with brilliant psychological insight, had every chance of success on its side; and, in order to prevent its passage, the circle of opponents to the fleet expansion around Bethmann and Wermuth[i] saw no other remedy than to ask simultaneously for a large expansion of the army, thereby making armament demands so exorbitant that the naval proposal would be out of the question. It was a spectacle to delight the gods to see Wermuth, and Bethmann after him, working on the Minister of War, who bitterly resisted the expansion of the army that was being forced on him.[38] It was only after his own subordinates had switched over to the pro-expansion party and after the thesis "quality rather than quantity" was for the first time in two decades

---

36. *Kriegsrüstung* I, 152.

37. Tirpitz to Vice Admiral Capelle, 3 August 1911, in A. von Tirpitz, *Der Aufbau der deutschen Weltmacht* (Stuttgart, 1924), p. 200; see also pp. 208, 209, 222.

38. September to November 1911. The material is organized (but without drawing the above conclusions) in *Kriegsrüstung,* I, 119 and Appendix I, p. 152.

replaced once more by the persuasive slogan "full utilization of all those fit for military duty," and only after Tirpitz had actually convinced the emperor to insert the supplementary naval law in the 1912 budget, that Heeringen, a few days later, abruptly jettisoned the old system of stable army strength and demanded an expansion of the army on grounds that showed only too clearly the real reason for his request: namely, that the new German naval proposal would "certainly" provoke a war, because England would not stand by idly while its armaments were being surpassed and that, in this war, "the fate of the Hohenzollern crown" and Germany's destiny would rest not on the sea but "on the victory or failure of the German army."

This allusion to the endangering of his crown by the supplementary naval law cleverly maneuvered the emperor into the right position and from that point on, the Reich Secretary of the Treasury succeeded in reducing navy demands. He did not succeed in forcing their withdrawal, because the Minister of War, who requested an expansion of the army that he really did not want because he could not maintain himself against Bethmann and Wermuth without doing so, had a pressing interest in seeing that "a navy proposal was presented alongside it,"[39] so that this increase in naval costs would "force" a reduction of his own request.[40]

The 1912 army expansion was a wild intrigue, which was set in motion by Tirpitz's uninhibited exploitation of all opportunities for expanding the fleet. The foreign-policy consequences of this petty struggle were disastrous. France viewed this expansion of the army by 29,000 men as an obvious preparation for an imminent German attack, because there was no external provocation and because it was outside the regular quinquennial plan, and Russia significantly accelerated the reorganization of its armed forces.[41] But even before these two countermeasures had gone into effect, before there had been any international repercussions to this internal German jurisdictional conflict, Germany at the end of 1912 introduced yet another proposal for an expansion of the army, which again, like

39. Heeringen's note of 4 December 1911.
40. Instruction to the Allgemeines Kriegsdepartment of 29 November 1911: "I am asking you to think about the areas in which we now want to cut down our budget."
41. *Kriegsrüstung* I, 146.

that of the previous year, was not the result of external pressure but of conflicts between government agencies.

8

At a conference held on October 13, 1912, the Kaiser, the Minister of War, and the Chief of the General Staff[j] agreed that there were no foreign-policy considerations warranting an increase in armaments. The previous increase in army size was considered adequate.[42]

On the next day, the Minister of War received a communication from the Chief of the General Staff requesting a "truly decisive" expansion of the size of the army and "very substantial increases in military call-ups." The head of the Mobilization Section, Colonel Ludendorff, had drafted this memorandum and had simply gone over the head of his superior, who was of a different opinion. An energetic, ruthless section head, whose only concern was for his department, and a weak man at the head of the General Staff, who, twenty-four hours after having expressed one opinion, put his signature to a paper saying the opposite—this combination provided the impetus for a 20 percent increase in the size of the German army, amounting to 137,000 additional men. The Minister of War, totally dumbfounded, laid the memorandum *ad acta,* since he did not take it seriously. But at the end of November, when the war in the Balkans was developing into a European crisis,[k] Ludendorff again pressed his proposal and, through Moltke, requested that conscription be fully implemented on the ground that Germany must be capable of repelling French or Russian attacks on German soil with its peacetime army.[43] Moltke himself put no faith in his section chief, whose letter he himself had signed, and told the Minister of War to maintain the old army strength. Three weeks later, a new communication from the General Staff arrived with the request to increase army strength by 300,000 men. Once more the Minister of War was taken by surprise by the General Staff's view and once

42. The emperor first wished to increase the number of machine-gun companies. A few days later, he dropped this plan. This is how the Reichsarchiv describes the situation (p. 154): "All these circumstances do not show Germany's military-political position at this time to be unfavorable if the Balkan disputes were to expand into a general European conflict."

43. Moltke to Heeringen, 25 November 1912. Ludendorff's draft.

more the Chief of the General Staff did not approve of his own demands.

That is how the lines were drawn: on the one side, the section chief in the General Staff, who compared the number of battalions in the hostile armies with his own on a purely mechanical basis and whose only concern was for numerical and material equalization in any circumstances; on the other, the Minister of War, who was expected to come before the Reichstag for the third year in a row (1911 marked the usual quinquennial period; the bill that competed with the naval demands came early in 1912, and the new demands of the General Staff came at the end of 1912) and was now supposed to throw overboard all the organizational and social misgivings about a rapid and extensive expansion of the army that had prevailed in the Ministry of War for half a generation. If the General Staff were to have its way, a democratization of the officer corps could no longer be held at bay,[44] and the whole ruling system in Prussia would fall apart, because the ruling class could not maintain itself in the face of the large mass of new officers from other strata that would have to be absorbed, its assimilating capacity, already impaired, would fail altogether, and the revolution would come "within a few years."[45]

The Minister of War fought ruthlessly against the General Staff, whose mechanical-military approach threatened to blow the social fabric of the Reich sky high. He could not prevent everything, but the 300,000 men that had been requested were reduced to nearly a third, and Colonel Ludendorff, the leading advocate for the army expansion in the General Staff, was hastily transferred to the provinces. The new army law for the fiscal year 1913/14 included an increase in army expenditures of only about 550 million, about 50 percent of the previous army budget.

At the end of January 1913, the new increase in German armaments became public knowledge. On March 6, the French government published a proposed law for the resumption of three-year military service; in December 1913 Russia received a French

44. See note 27.
45. General Wandel, head of the Allgemeines Kriegsdepartment, to Ludendorff, in Hans Herzfeld, *Die deutsche Rüstungspolitik vor dem Weltkrieg* (Bonn, 1923), p. 77.

loan of 2.5 billion francs to expand its railroad network, and the practice of keeping the men who had just completed their service in the barracks over the winter—a practice that had been introduced during the turmoil of the Balkan war—was retained during a period that was supposed to be one of peace.

9

Ranke once observed in his *History of the Popes:*[46] "At first glance the course of world events, the progress of unfolding developments, has an air of inevitability. But one only needs to step closer to discover, in many cases, that the foundation on which everything rests is flimsy and delicate, almost personal in nature, sympathy or dislike, and not difficult to shatter."

If we look at the history of the army proposals of 1912 and 1913, in which personal factors played such a large part and objective necessity none at all, this resolution of the historical process into the restless interplay of personal interventions seems appropriate. Yet in fact these personal rivalries take place within the framework of large institutions; and the problem of history is not the wilfulness of the human beings who appear to be directing these institutions, but the fact that they are the captives of the laws that govern their institutions and their class and are subordinate to their interests without even being aware of their dependence. The strategy of Moltke and Schlieffen was determined by the vulnerability of the unorganized capitalist economy; the handling of food provisioning was determined by the dominant power position of the large-scale agrarians; and in evaluating the army proposals of 1911/13, two points must not be overlooked:

1. Had this been a period of financial stringency Tirpitz would not have succeeded in getting his supplemental law presented, and Ludendorff would not have even considered requesting 300,000 men.

2. In these jurisdictional disputes and personal conflicts, the proponents of military expansion were successful only because their counterstrokes of 1911 and their mechanical notions of armament equalization of 1912 found a perfect breeding ground in the militarist and feudalized German bourgeoisie. The Reichstag showed

46. *Sämtliche Werke,* XXXVIII, 345.

almost no opposition to the increase in armaments; it was willing to swallow everything that was left over from the jurisdictional power struggle as long as it was presented as a national necessity. The Reichstag would even have gone along with Ludendorff's request for the additional 300,000 soldiers.

The actors were under the impression that they were acting independently, and yet, in their intrigues, they merely executed what was predetermined by social power relations. Just as capitalism brought about its own downfall on the economic plane, so did the militarized bourgeoisie effect its destruction on the social plane. An international conflict even of the severity anticipated before 1914 would have shattered the social system of the national state in any case.[47] Yet the militarized bourgeoisie blithely demanded and approved an armament policy that was in no wise justified by the foreign situation and blindly waved aside the serious misgivings that the military had about the reliability of such mammoth armies.

47. See also Bethmann's remark to the Bavarian ambassador, Count Lerchenfeld, on 4 June 1914 that "a world war, with its totally unforseeable consequences, will vastly increase the power of social democracy, because it has pleaded for peace, and might well tumble a number of thrones." *Bayerische Dokumente zum Kriegsausbruch und zum Versailler Schuldspruch,* ed. by Pius Dirr, 3rd edition (München, 1925), p. 113.

CHAPTER IV

The Social and Financial Foundations of Tirpitz's Naval Propaganda

"For reasons readily understandable, the subject of party finances, though one of the most important aspects of the party system, is the least accessible to research."[1] It is true that the history of German political parties is only in its earliest stages, and what little research has been done concerns their ideological history, rather than their concrete activities, their tactics, and their dependence on social or financial powers from which they receive their backing; and yet it is for political reasons that research has restrained itself from going behind the facade and investigating the financial aspects of party history that are to be found there.

For a long time, to be sure, there will be no prospect of exploring the financial history of any major German party: the modern state has no way of evading the financial accountability that is demanded of it by political parties (at least it cannot do so in theory), but the parties themselves maintain an absolutist system of financial secrecy. The less they rely on continuing, regular "taxes" from their subjects, that is, on membership dues, and the more dependent they are on unpredictable receipts attributable to the skill of their financial managers and the propitious situation of their contributors, the more pronounced will be their aversion to opening up their records.

1. Max Weber, *Wirtschaft und Gesellschaft: Grundriss der Sozialökonomik,* 2nd ed. (Tübingen, 1924), III:1, 169. [The English text is quoted from the translation *Economy and Society: An Outline of Interpretive Sociology,* ed. by Guenther Roth and Claus Wittich (New York, 1968) I, 288.]

76]

Chances are somewhat better for casting a quick glance through a chink in the door and looking at the financial backing of specific political campaigns. Just recently documents bearing on the financing of Bismarck's press propaganda from the "Reptile Fund"[a] have turned up, but their publication remains in doubt. In any case, it was only in the nineties of the past century that vast and far-reaching political and social propaganda campaigns requiring extensive financing began to play a significant role in Germany.

The social propaganda campaigns launched by the Social Democrats after the restrictions of the anti-Socialist law *(Sozialistengesetz)* had been lifted, were almost entirely financed with membership dues. The Farmers' League *(Bund der Landwirte)* followed the same system at least to the extent that the special contributions of East Elbian estate owners were not set aside in a separate category but were incorporated with the remaining contributions as higher membership dues, so that the funds collected by the Farmers' League, which in 1897, for instance, came to 492,000 marks,[2] could be considered as levied from a homogeneous source. On the other hand, the financial aspect of Bismarck's press propaganda lost its significance in the nineties; in the campaign devoted exclusively to asserting his own individuality, the dismissed Reich Chancellor could rely on the support of the *Hamburger Neueste Nachrichten* without resorting to monetary contributions.[b]

By the early nineties, the Reich government itself was beginning to take an interest in press propaganda (the campaign of the eighties had been mainly a private undertaking on Bismarck's part). As Chief of the Admiralty, Caprivi had forbidden journalistic activity by naval officers; [3] now that he was Reich Chancellor, he was quick to realize the importance of the press and appointed Otto Hammann as the government's press spokesman. Aside from restoring an official atmosphere, this new activity by the Reich government had its greatest impact in the question of armament expansion, first in connection with the enlargment of the army proposed in the four major billls of 1887, 1888, 1890, and 1893, and later in the fleet expansion from 1896 to 1900.

2. Von Kiesenwetter, *Zum 18. Februar 1903: Zehn Jahre wirtschaftlichen Kampfes* (Berlin, 1903), p. 102.

3. Paul Koch, *General von Caprivi als Chef der Admiralität* (Berlin, 1927), p. 25.

Interestingly enough, German armament expansion, which made Germany's military budget, from the eighties onward, surpass that of any other major power in relative or absolute terms, came to be financed differently from that in other countries. Since it was no longer possible to shift the burden of the military budget to the federal states by increasing their quota contributions *(Matrikularbeiträge)* to the Reich treasury,[c] the state could not cover the higher military costs by raising its own regular tax revenues. Hence the costs, which could not be met by taxation, were shifted to the next generation: the much-applauded system of government bonds was initiated with the armament increase of 1887.[4] Until the intervention of Reich Treasurer Wermuth, warships were also included among the "interest-bearing investments," to be built from funds raised by loans. On the other hand, the agitation that preceded armament expansion and accompanied the related parliamentary struggles developed an increasingly healthy financial basis. Although it is not yet possible to obtain detailed information about the financial support for the armament agitation of 1893, which was directed by the then Major Keim,[d] it is easy to see from its scope that substantial funds were required for its implementation.[5] And even without access to secret documents, it is easier yet to establish the basic approach and specific features of Tirpitz' fleet agitation, as well as its financial foundations.

Propaganda for the navy was inaugurated at a much earlier date than has been assumed until now. The emperor was aware of the success of the army's campaign in 1893, and his first instructions date from January 1894.[6] But that propaganda was a feeble effort. The Naval High Command did succeed in making contacts with the National Liberal press and in having some articles published in the party's provincial newspapers with the help of an editor of Stumm's *Post,*[e] and a press service was launched. But the agitation never acquired life. Tirpitz, who was still Chief of Staff of the High Command at that time, made a futile attempt to convert the *Ma-*

4. Wilhelm Gerloff, *Die Finanz- und Zollpolitik des Deutschen Reiches* (Jena, 1913), p. 311.

5. A. Keim, *Erlebtes und Erstrebtes* (Hannover, 1925), pp. 50, 67f., 73. Waldersee, *Denkwürdigkeiten* (Stuttgart, 1922), II, 270, 355.

6. Files of the former Naval High Command, presently in the Reichswehr Ministry (henceforth RWM).

rinerundschau into a livelier publication, but it refused to abandon its original charter,[7] according to which it was instructed, characteristically, not to discuss the German Navy and to talk about foreign navies only "if it could be done so as to avoid arousing idle public comment about the German navy." Tirpitz's thesis about the profitability of armaments, set down in his Memorandum IX (*Dienstschrift* IX) of 16 June 1894, to the effect that "money invested in the fleet can bear indirect interest even in peacetime, whereas army expenditures on the whole are essentially an insurance premium for war"[8] remained generally ignored, although it was later to serve as the ideological basis for the fleet expansion.[9] And it is typical of the degree of alacrity with which the navy was propagandizing its own cause that it felt that it had done its duty as long as "everyone interested in naval affairs"[10] could satisfy his curiosity on any technical question in the *Marinerundschau*. Admiral Hollmann, State Secretary of the Reich Naval Office, beset as he was by day-to-day bureaucratic problems, made it a point to keep clear of propaganda matters, which he specifically assigned to the individual sections of his office.

The crucial factor in the failure of this agitation, from the standpoint of its technical implementation, was not altogether the lack of enthusiasm of the persons in charge of its execution; inadequate financial support was also a major factor. The reason for this was not so much that the most directly affected circles in heavy industry were unwilling to make propaganda for their interests. The maritime shipyards were already complaining in the press that the "lack of orders" was a national misfortune,[11] despite the large backlog of commissions that accompanied the shift of the shipping lines to large ocean-going vessels.[12] Krupp, in whose plant the new method of armor-plating had just been invented—and for which licenses

7. Dated 16 March 1890 (RWM).
8. Reproduced incompletely and with a definite bias in *Nauticus 1926*.
9. Lieutenant Captain Ingenohl to Dr. Groddeck, editor-in-chief of the *Post*, 17 August 1894 (RWM).
10. Corvette Captain Pohl to the wife of Corvette Captain Hirschberg, 24 March 1896 (RWM).
11. Annual report of the Hamburg Chamber of Commerce for 1895, p. 5. See also Kurt Wiedenfeld, *Die nordwesteuropäischen Welthäfen in ihrer Verkehrs- und Handelsbedeutung* (Berlin, 1903), pp. 31 ff.
12. *Hamburger Neueste Nachrichten*, 25 September 1894 and 17 February 1895.

were soon to be issued to all foreign war fleets[13]—and whose Germania shipyard in Kiel was shortly to be converted to the construction of the largest ships, manifested his displeasure, innocuously enough, by publishing a booklet whose cover bore the title "What has the Reichstag done for the Navy in 1893/4?" with nothing but blank pages inside.[14] The Hanseatic cities, however, were opposed to building up the fleet; the representatives of the Hansa cities in the Bundesrat saw no use for a fleet against free-trading England.[15] Adolf Woermann, who converted Hamburg to a procolonial attitude,[16] could produce nothing more than a few languid petitions for an expansion of the fleet,[17] in response to the urgings of Count Dürkheim,[18] notwithstanding his position as president of the Chamber of Commerce (Handelskammer) and chairman of the Hamburg Shipowners' Association.[f] The agitation could not be launched as long as the fleet expansion had no resonance: conceived as a purely technical undertaking like the postal service or road construction, the navy could not hope to play a role in the Reich's social development and gain "popularity" in the process. In the technique of construction there was no clear line, only helpless vacillation between cruisers and battleships; and even on the strategic level the fleet lacked a value of its own, being viewed at best as the maritime extension of armies victoriously advancing against France.[19] The nostalgic recollection of a few old Liberals about the fleet of 1848[g] carried little weight. From the start—and this was the secret of his success—Tirpitz was determined to extricate the navy from its isolation and tie it to "German economic development since 1871." The

13. *Friedrich Alfred Krupp und sein Werk* (Braunschweig, 1904), p. 20. It is not clear whether there was a lump payment or whether payment was proportional to the volume of production.

14. Eugen von Jagemann, *Fünfundsiebzig Jahre des Erlebens und Erfahrens, 1849 bis 1924* (Heidelberg, 1925), p. 131.

15. *Ibid.*

16. *Cf.*, for instance, Ernst Baasch, *Die Handelskammer zu Hamburg 1665 bis 1915* (Hamburg, 1915), II, 320.

17. Annual report of the Hamburg Chamber of Commerce for 1894, p. 4. Petition by the Association of Hamburg Shipowners (*Verein Hamburger Reeder*) dated 10 March 1897, in the Reichstag Archive.

18. Count Dürkheim to Admiral Hollmann, Neumühlen Castle near Ottensen, 14 August 1894 (RWM).

19. Vice Admiral Valois, *Seemacht, Seegeltung, Seeherrschaft* (Berlin, 1899), p. 52.

fact that he cavalierly identified the global development since 1871 with the boom that had begun in 1895 is another story, but industry was not willing to contribute money to any naval campaign until this identification had sunk into popular consciousness and until the question of the fleet had been successfully harmonized with the economic and social framework.

Subsequent propaganda efforts for the fleet were doomed to rapid failure for lack of social support. Karl Peters,[h] hoping to avoid legal prosecution for his African misdeeds by running for a seat in the Reichstag and making propaganda for the fleet with the emperor's blessing, initiated his campaign at the end of 1895.[20] His efforts were as unsuccessful as those of the former Polish Reichstag leader, von Kosciol-Koscielski, nicknamed Admiralski because of his remarkable infatuation with the navy, who provided the Reich Naval Office with subsidies for printing a propaganda pamphlet. Admiral von Senden, the head of the Navy Cabinet, who had been trying since January 1896 to "enlighten the Reichstag *plenum* and create the right attitude nationally"[21] in connection with grand plans for a fleet expansion, met with equally little success. In addition to the negative factor of lack of support from the Ruhr industrialists and the Hanseatic cities, the fleet also had to contend with the positive opposition of the agrarians: in February 1895, Werdeck-Schorbus coined the phrase: "No Kanitz—no canoes" *(Kein Kanitz—keine Kähne)* and von Levetzow justified the Conservatives' resistance to the Kaiser's fleet plans in January 1896 with the classic phrase: "The agrarians would scarcely have their daily bread."[22]i

Although Tirpitz had been preparing the tactical, strategic, technical, and propagandistic-ideological basis for the building of the fleet since 1892, the expansion of the fleet was transformed from an officer's wishful thinking into reality only as a result of two major alterations in Germany's political and social structure in the second half of the nineties. One factor was the switch of the Center party, under Lieber's leadership, from the opposition to the government camp, after the party's antifeudal and democratic stand in the 1893

20. Karl Peters, *Lebenserinnerungen* (Hamburg, 1918), pp. 103 ff.
21. Diary of Admiral Baron von Senden-Bibran, 14 January 1896 (placed at my disposal by its present owner).
22. *Ibid.*

elections.[j] The other factor was the reconciliation of agriculture and industry, which had been locked in bitter struggle. It was the result of the impact of the progressively expanding Social Democratic movement and the influence of the economic boom that had begun in 1895, which undermined the resistance of the agrarians. Miquel introduced his *Sammlungspolitik* in mid-1897, and new state secretaries of Foreign Affairs, the Interior, and the Navy were appointed. The "New Course," which had been dominated by the power struggle between agriculture and industry for control over the legislative machinery, was replaced by a joining of forces between them against the proletariat, a policy that transcended such ephemeral and ill-fated measures as the Penitentiary Bill and culminated in the protective tariff of 1902 and the navy laws. "Every successful imperialist policy of coercing the outside normally—or at least at first—also strengthens the domestic prestige and therewith the power and influence of those classes, status groups, and parties, under whose leadership the success has been attained."[23] The expansion of the fleet was intended to provide the power-political basis for a successful foreign policy, which in turn was meant to stabilize the internal political and social position of the ruling strata against the threat of social democracy.[24]

We must place the propaganda effect of the emperor's infatuation with the fleet in the context of this change in orientation. William II was unable to translate his predilection for the fleet into an expansion of the navy by simply intervening in its favor as a monarch and by "preaching daily for ten years about this need in front of these asinine Reichstag deputies."[25] What actually brought about the change was the sudden recognition by the bourgeois part of the nation, which before 1897 had viewed the emperor's enthusiasm for the navy partly with impotent resignation and partly with irritation, that his *Weltpolitik* and naval program offered a promising social weapon in the struggle against the proletariat. "There is too much

23. Max Weber, *op cit.* III, 626. [For text quoted, see English translation, *op. cit,* II, 920].
24. *Cf.* Tirpitz's letter to Stosch, 21 December 1895, in Tirpitz, *Erinnerungen,* p. 52.
25. Marginal comment to report by Bülow dated 1 April 1899 in *Grosse Politik,* XIV, 592.

talk about the emperor's 'impulsiveness' and his personality generally. The blame lies with the political structure."[26] The personal argument which claims that the emperor's influence on the implementation of naval expansion was decisive fails to explain why William II succeeded in having his way only after 1897 and not before;[27] his victory was the result of the social consolidation of the ruling strata by means of the *Sammlungspolitik*.

This new situation accounts for the sudden effectiveness of the fleet propaganda, which had been launched in grand style in mid-1897. The Pan-German League *(Alldeutscher Verband)*[28] and the German Colonial Society *(Deutsche Kolonialgesellschaft)*[29]— whose agitation in early 1896 failed to take hold despite an approach that was, in theory at least, quite reasonable—established vast propaganda agencies.[k] The Hanseatic cities began to view the fleet in a favorable light. At a banquet in the Hamburg city hall,[30] Tirpitz, Heeringen (the new propaganda chief of the Reich Naval Office),[l] and Adolf Woermann discussed further plans. Woermann attempted to win over the German Chamber of Commerce *(Handelstag)* the next day by a surprise attack,[31] but he came up against the resistance of the Berlin banks. These organizations, which had a decisive voice in the Berlin Merchants Corporation, because all head clerks in the large banks had voting rights, were politically affiliated with one or the other progressive parties and therefore looked with disfavor on the *Sammlungspolitik* and had no desire to

26. Max Weber, *Politische Schriften*, p. 456. *Cf.* also Carl Brinkman's reference (*Gesellschaft* 1926/II, 137) to this frequently overlooked connection between the Emperor's personal politics and social realignment.

27. Neither does it offer an explanation for the construction of battleships instead of the planned cruiser fleet. The emperor was confused on the relative merits of battleships and cruisers.

28. 10 June 1897.

29. Retired Ambassador von Kusserow, the Colonial Society's propaganda chief, had already been preparing this agitation since April: Kusserow to Hohenlohe, Bassenheim, 29 June 1897 (RWM). Official decision 12 June 1897, start of propaganda in September.

30. 26 September, Hamburg State Archive.

31. The minutes of the executive committee meeting of the German Handelstag, 27 September 1897 (Membership report, vol. 37, no. 8, Berlin, 14 October 1897) make no mention of this, since Woermann's intervention occurred only at the end of the session. *Cf.* Woermann's version (reproduced on 25 January 1898 in the daily press and also printed as a manuscript) and *Der Deutsche Handelstag 1861 bis 1911*, ed. by the Deutscher Industrie- und Handelstag (Berlin, 1911) II, 335.

be its handymen. But from the start this resistance was slight. The senior members of the Merchants Corporation did not dare to motivate their negative stand publicly beyond stating that "the matter was political in nature and taking a stand on it might easily split the Chamber of Commerce" and that "the board itself has taken no stand on this matter and has moreover advised one of its representatives on the Chamber's executive committee to take no position on this political question."[32] It was only in a written communication to the *Handelstag*[33] that Max Weigert expressed the view that "there may be differences of opinion whether the war fleet should, given the present state of the commercial treaties,[34] be considered as a particularly effective means of increasing German exports, and whether the existing strength of the war fleet should not be considered as adequate, both to protect German trade, as far as protection can be attained in this manner at all, and to further the prestige of our fatherland."

The opposition did not hold out for long. Although, as far as one can tell from the documents, only the Mendelssohn banking house took an active interest in the Navy League *(Flottenverein),* the other Berlin banks at least offered no further resistance to the Chamber of Commerce's demonstrations in favor of the fleet at the time of the second navy law in 1900.[35] In June 1897 the Hamburg section of the German Colonial Society was still protesting against its participation in the naval campaign,[36] but at the banquet on 26 September the Hanseatic representatives were converted virtually completely into friends of the navy. In the propaganda drive for the first navy law, the Hamburg Chamber of Commerce actually became the directorate for the agitation of the special interests. The professional propaganda chief in the Reich Naval Office, Dr. Ernst Levy von

32. Minutes of the meeting of the senior members of the Berlin Merchants Corporation *(Alteste der Kaufmannschaft von Berlin)* held 16 November, 13 December 1897 and 17 January 1898. Files of the Industrie- und Handelskammer Berlin.

33. *Ibid.,* 16 December session, in reply to the latter's inquiry of 6 October 1897.

34. He probably meant to say the stage in which preparations were being made for commercial agreements favoring agrarian interests but damaging to commercial interests.

35. Handelstag resolution of 6 April 1900.

36. *Tägliche Rundschau,* 16 June 1897.

Halle, remained in touch with this organization,[37] using Hamburg and Bremen as sources for the material he needed as evidence of "German maritime interests" in his official memoranda. To prevent the opposition from making accusations about collaboration with private sectors of the economy, official communications of the Reich Naval Office with the Hamburg and Bremen chambers of commerce were regularly addressed to the proper local government channels.[38] The chambers of commerce, to whom these letters were then transmitted, went ahead and determined the overseas interests of the firms in their district by circulars, which were then turned over to Senate commissions and finally returned by them to the Reich Naval Office. If the overseas interests established by these inquiries proved to be slight, they were augmented as needed. The Reich Naval Office's practice of "improving" the Hamburg figures caused as much irritation in Hamburg as its endeavors to discover increases in the armament budgets of other countries when there had actually been a decline or when the increase lagged behind the German increase in armaments;[39] but none of this dampened the propagandistic fervor. When the attempt to include the German Chamber of Commerce in the agitation came to nought, at least every "ehrbare Kaufmann" in Hamburg was mobilized.[40] And the German industrial leaders who could not be reached through the *Handelstag* were gathered together in a hastily formed committee to organize an independent demonstration on 13 January 1898 in the Kaiserhof. The resolution presented in this demonstration, which had been prepared in closest collaboration with the head of the Navy Cabinet,[41] succeeded in overcoming even the opposition of the *Frankfurter Zeitung.*

37. v. Halle to Woermann, confidential, 7 November 1897; to Chamber of Commerce Secretary Dr. Gütschow, 17 November 1897. Regarding subsequent collaboration: Dr. Gütschow to Woermann, Feb. 10, 1898 in Hamburg Chamber of Commerce Archive.
38. 17 August, 9 November 1897, 9 February 1898, Hamburg State Archive and Hamburg Chamber of Commerce Archive.
39. Dr. Gütschow's letter to Woermann, 10 February 1898, Hamburg Chamber of Commerce Archive.
40. The opposition was a mere seven votes.
41. Telegram of Chamber of Commerce President Carl Ferdinand Laeisz to the Hamburg Chamber of Commerce, Berlin, 7 January 1898, regarding a discussion between Krogmann and Senden. Hamburg Chamber of Commerce Archive.

In the following period, however, the importance of the Hanseatic cities in this agitation fell behind the influence of heavy industry. At the time of the campaign for the second navy law, the Hanseatic cities intervened only through a petition of the chambers of commerce of all coastal cities, a petition with an interesting background. The confiscation of several German steamships by an overzealous British cruiser commander near Delagoa Bay at the end of December, 1899, on the ground that these might be transporting contraband war materials for the Boers, aroused great resentment among the anti-British bourgeoisie against this effrontery of "perfidious Albion." The capitalist press[42] for its part contemptuously shrugged off this ideological indignation, considering the incident as insignificant from a practical political standpoint. The Hanseatic cities in turn cleverly exploited nationalist fervor to carry out a financial maneuver of a private nature. At the meeting of the Deutsch-Ost-Africa Line (DOAL) board of directors in early January 1900, where the raising of 10 million marks in investment capital for the construction of a new steamship was discussed, the five participating bankers declared that "it would be unthinkable to invest new money in this enterprise until the question of compensation for the damage recently suffered is resolved."[43] Although Adolf Woermann's participation in DOAL stock was only one million out of six,[44] he took it upon himself, with his primitive-brutal aggressiveness, to see to it that the obstacle would be eliminated, by building a German fleet strong enough to discourage British highhandedness in the future. He was convinced that a joint petition from the various chambers of commerce with an interest in maritime trade would exert the necessary pressure on the Reichstag, and he expected that the public mention of the difficulties encountered by the DOAL in raising capital as a result of the Delagoa Bay incident would have a particularly strong impact on the German people and the German Reichstag, a stupidity that was too much even for his friends. The petition, in fact, was characterized by its repudia-

42. *Deutsche Industriezeitung, Organ des Zentralverbands,* January 1900, no. 4, p. 41.

43. Woermann to Dr. Gütschow, 10 January 1900. Hamburg Chamber of Commerce Archive.

44. O. Mathies, *Hamburgs Reederei 1814 bis 1914* (Hamburg, 1924), pp. 121 f.

tion of the Reich Naval Office's thesis that the build-up of the fleet was in the service of capitalist expansion, taking the line that it was a purely governmental, power-political necessity.

Aside from this isolated intervention, propaganda in favor of the second navy law was conducted not by the Hanseatic cities but by heavy industry. Obviously the demonstration at the Kaiserhof had also been subject to an earlier agreement with the Central Association of German Industrialists (Zentralverband deutscher Industrieller),[45] but at the time, the Zentralverband was willing to leave leadership in the hands of Woermann and to let him bear the brunt of the opposition's attack. Krupp had advised the gentlemen of the Zentralverband to exercise cautious restraint[46] and had refrained from personally participating in the appeal for the demonstration, so that only an unpolitical hothead like Emil Kirdorf appeared among the signatories.[m] This restraint did not imply that the attempt to influence public opinion in favor of industrial interests had been abandoned. It was just that the right time had not yet come. When in March 1897[47] cod-liver oil manufacturer Stroschein set out to found a navy league representing honest petty-bourgeois nationalist sentiments and the Berlin bankers declined to give it financial support, Krupp intervened through the intermediary of Victor Schweinburg, publisher of the Berliner Politische Nachrichten. When Stroschein failed to accept unconditionally the industrialist objectives, a counter-committee was set up under the leadership of Schweinburg and Landtag deputy Bueck, secretary-general of the Zentralverband. In order to hide the heavy-industry content under an idealistic veneer, the Free-Conservative leader Octavio Baron von Zedlitz-Neukirch was added to the committee and Prince Wied was asked to preside over the propaganda office. The German Navy League (Deutscher Flottenverein) was officially inaugurated on 30 April 1898.

This coverup technique was at first only partly successful. Stroschein, to be sure, was persuaded to join the new organization, but when Schweinburg turned to the professors of Berlin University,

45. Bueck to Tirpitz, 21 December 1897 (RWM).
46. Two letters to Privy Councillor Jencke, communication of the Krupp company's board of directors.
47. Circular and pamphlet printed as manuscript, March 16.

he encountered icy suspicions of his "interest group of conservatives, big industrialists, and financiers."[48] Baron von Stumm's attempt to correct Adolf Wagner's economic views at revolver point[49] were all too fresh in the professors' minds.[n] Heavy industry's psychological tactics for influencing public opinion were still too crude to succeed. The primitive style of its interventions, which was still apparent in Stinnes's take-over of the *D.A.Z.*,[o] was finally laid to rest by Alfred Hugenberg[p] in his practice of granting semi-autonomy to the newspapers under his control and of keeping business and politics sufficiently distinct in political propaganda to escape the notice of peaceable citizens. Both Stumm's *Post* and the *Berliner Neueste Nachrichten,* which came under Krupp's control at that time as a result of its financial plight and was reorganized by Schweinburg, became, like the Navy League, one-sided instruments for specific, limited objectives of heavy industry. In the process, as they were soon to discover to their discomfiture, they neglected the ideological-patriotic sensitivities of wider circles.[50]

The new propaganda office of heavy industry met its crucial test a mere twelve months after its establishment. An unpleasant squabble had broken out between England and Germany in March 1899 with respect to the possession of Samoa. Tirpitz began to regret that he had contented himself with such a modest fleet expansion in 1897 and that, as late as December 1898, he had decisively disavowed further naval plans. He negotiated with Hohenlohe[q] about a new navy law[51] and carefully inspected private shipyards to determine their existing capacity and the possibility of enlarging them. This inspection had the immediate result of setting off a lively agitation, beginning in early May, on the part of the two industrialist papers and of the Pan-Germans, who took the Samoa incident as a starting point. They did not urge the Reich Naval Office to disregard the

48. The exchange of letters between Delbrück and Schweinburg is printed in the *Berliner Neueste Nachrichten,* 7 January 1900 and in the *Post,* 8 January, *Cf.* Delbrück's letter to Rippler, *Tägliche Rundschau,* 1 December 1899.

49. *Cf.* Wagner, *Mein Konflikt mit dem Freiherrn v. Stumm-Halberg,* 1895.

50. For a description of the manner in which these purchases of bankrupt newspaper by heavy industry were carried out and their poor results, see Ludwig Bernhard, *Der "Hugenberg-Konzern": Psychologie und Technik einer Grossorganisation der Presse* (Berlin, 1928), pp. 57–58 in particular.

51. Report of the Hanseatic delegate Klügmann on the Bundesrat session of 2 November 1899, Hamburg State Archive.

navy law—for such an attempt was considered hopeless—but they asked the Reichstag to demonstrate its national sentiment by voluntarily relinquishing the restrictions on the expansion of the fleet for a six-year period. The people in the Reich Naval Office, however, who had incited this agitation in the first place, became unhappy about it when it became too lively, particularly since they didn't have a proposal for the winter anyway.[52] They were put off further when they noticed that the campaign, which was financially supported by heavy industry and gave "higher priority to business interests than to practical considerations,"[53] was not as susceptible to their direction as the Hanseatic enthusiasm of 1897/98.

Industry's first move against the Reich Naval Office and the Reichstag was a complete fiasco; what resulted was tension between the Navy League and the navy's administration. Shortly after the Kaiser's speech of 18 October 1899, in which he assigned the future of Germany to the water and announced the second navy law, Schweinburg became the object of a scandal, in the course of which the Reich Naval Office remained silent and refused to intervene in favor of the Navy League. It allowed Heinrich Rippler to publish his virulent attacks in the *Tägliche Rundschau* against the League's special interest lobbying, thereby forcing the withdrawal of Bueck, Schweinburg, and von Zedlitz in November and December, notwithstanding Prince Wied's vigorous protests and the emperor's great irritation. The Berlin professors founded a counter-committee to attack the Navy League and to act as an ideologically and morally irreproachable advocate for the new navy proposal. Lack of funds hampered the effectiveness of this "Free Association for Navy Lectures" *(Freie Vereinigung für Flottenvorträge)* because the collection of admission fees—for which the names of the most famous speakers were insufficient compensation—led to poorly attended gatherings, while the Navy League's free meetings for the public were well attended despite their empty and rhetorical content. And when the Free Association's speakers, who appeared at nineteen of the demonstrations organized by the Social Democrats against *Weltpolitik,* had a catastrophic lack of success, Stumm's *Post* loudly gloated over the despised professors' failure to sway the workers. It

52. Hollweg notes, 3 June 1899; Heeringen notes, 8 June (RWM).
53. Note of 26 June 1899 (RWM).

could vent its feelings freely, for the proponents of the *Sammlungs-politik* had meanwhile discovered that the professors' propaganda for their fleet was no longer needed. Moreover, the "Chinese justice by proxy"[54] that had resulted in Schweinburg's removal had in no way diminished the influence of heavy industry, which kept in the background, and mining stocks had at least temporarily reversed their downward trend in response to the anticipated fleet expansion. Stock prices rose or fell as follows:

	From Aug. 31 to Oct. 17		From Oct. 17 to Nov. 7	
Baroper Rolling Mill Co.	from 107 to 111	= + 4 pts	to 136	= +25 pts
Bismarck Foundry	from 326 to 290	= −36 pts	to 311	= +21 pts
Bochumer Cast Steel Co.	from 265 to 245	= −20 pts	to 257	= +12 pts
Charlotte Foundry	from 208 to 164	= −44 pts	to 194[55]	= +30 pts
Eschweiler Mining Co.	from 238 to 222	= −16 pts	to 245	= +23 pts
Hasper Iron-Works	from 385 to 335	= −50 pts	to 368	= +33 pts
Howaldt Shipyard	from 142 to 125[56]	= −17 pts	to 142	= +17 pts

The great success of the agitation carried on in favor of the second navy law, which surprised even the Reich Naval Office, was not based on any profound belief among the broad masses of the bourgeoisie in the "need for a strong sea power"; rather, it was induced by the general feeling that there was an urgent need for a suitable diversion after the defeat of the anti-Socialist coalition in the failure of the Penitentiary Bill[57] and the rebuff inflicted on the Prussian government by the agrarians in their defeat of the Canal Bill.[r] The other reason for the success was the systematic effort undertaken by a soundly financed center of propaganda outside the Reich Naval Office, heavy industry's Navy League, which remained under Krupp's control even after the withdrawal of its discredited founder. Here again the contrast between the inadequate methods for financing the increase in armaments and the brilliant private financing of armament propaganda is obvious. Thielmann, the incompetent Reich treasurer,[s] was no less unscrupulous in his presentation of the second navy law than he had been in the case of the

54. *Vorwärts,* 3 December 1899, p. 283.
55. 6 November quotation.
56. 18 October quotation.
57. Tirpitz, *op. cit.* p. 105. See also the report of the Hanseatic delegate of 2 November 1899.

first, resorting to the same reliable old stand-by for appeasing social crises and staving off the threat of revolution. The Reich's finances, which were again heading for a period of deficits, were presented in the most brilliant magic light, creating the impression that there was more money on hand than one knew how to spend,[58] and the Reichstag's intention of putting the program of naval construction on a firm financial foundation foundered on the passive resistance of the government.[59] The healthy financial basis of the agitation, on the other hand, is clearly apparent, if one avoids the mistake made by American scholars[60] of trying to tie the financial-organizational infrastructure of imperialist propaganda to the Pan-German League, for their information about its financial status is definitely unreliable. The Pan-German League, moreover, was a political-ideological consortium, which supplied "ideological" weapons to the other propaganda organizations—the Colonial Society, the Navy League, and later the Armament League (*Wehrverein*), and the like. The modest financial basis of the Pan-German umbrella organization is no yardstick for the true financial strength of imperialist propaganda.[61] The German Navy League had been founded specifically as the central agency for the naval campaign, and the financial policy behind the propaganda at the turn of the century can only be reconstructed on the basis of the finances of the real campaign organization. The Navy League's balance sheets for the years 1900 to 1903, published in its annual reports,[62] disclose the following rounded-off figures (in marks):

	Membership contributions	Special contributions
1900	348,000	412,000
1901	225,000	170,000
1902	247,000	410
1903	262,000	23,000

58. Minutes of the Budget Commission, 1 May 1900. Reichstag Archive.
59. Wilhelm Gerloff, *op. cit,* pp. 350, 359.
60. Mildred S. Wertheimer, *The Pan-German League 1890–1914* (New York, 1924).
61. In the course of a lengthy conversation, Miss Wertheimer agreed that my objections against her treating the Pan-German League in isolation were well founded.
62. The Navy League's financial files no longer exist.

The League never published the names of its special contributors. The Mendelssohn bank, whose head was the League's treasurer, was in control of its finances. There is a clue to the source of the funds in a little incident that occured during the executive committee meeting of 21 January 1901. Dietrich Schäfer sought to block the further acceptance of money from interest groups as unworthy of the national-minded Navy League. But the meeting rejected this naive proposal with a Homeric peal of laughter and the cry: *Non olet,*[t] for to accept it would have meant the end of the Navy League.[63]

The absence of balance sheets for the founding year 1898 and the year 1899, in which the first great campaign took place, makes it impossible to estimate the relationship between membership contributions—donated for the most part from ideological motives—and the "special contributions" of interest groups in this early period. For 1900, in which the second navy law was being negotiated, special contributions of 412,000 marks exceed membership contributions of 348,000 marks, although both figures remain highly suspect: it is conceivable that as much as 100,000 marks in special contributions were listed as membership contributions, and even that may not fully account for the real scope of the special contributions, since the reported expenses for propaganda meetings are unaccountably low.[64] For 1903, the balance sheet shows 23,000 marks in special contributions against 262,000 marks in membership contributions, which is a normal distribution of revenues. Both the year 1901, with special contributions amounting to 170,000 marks, despite the recent approval of the doubling of the fleet, and the year 1902, in which special contributions fell abruptly to 410 marks, seem to call for some explanation.

These figures are charmingly illuminated by a previously undisclosed episode dating from December 1901, which allows us a

63. *Die Flotte,* February 1901, p. 22–23. Tirpitz, *op. cit,* p. 97, stresses the fact that "the entire campaign was financed with voluntary contributions." A list in the files of the information division shows donations of about 100,000 marks based on ideological sympathy, 60,000 of them from a German-American. These funds were later used for the construction of a gun boat. It therefore appears that the agitation was not paid for by "patriotic contributions," but by special interests.

64. 27,000 marks for 3,000 lectures or 9 marks per lecture (*Die Flotte,* February 1901, pp. 18–19). A regional committee needed 150 to 200 marks per lecture (*Die Flotte* 1900, no. 7–8, p. 10) and the expenses for lectures reported by the German Colonial Society were also higher (its annual report for 1899, p. 61).

meager but highly instructive glimpse into the interrelations between business conditions and armament expansion.

During the weeks in which the fate of the second navy law hung in the balance, a collapse ended the protracted business boom that had served as a backdrop for the turn of the century's ambivalent mood, in which gloomy fear of a proletarian revolution and a transparently unproblematical enjoyment of the continuing high profits had both played a part. The critical situation that faced the German economy as a result of this crisis is well known. There appeared to be two ways out of the difficulty. The first, as defined by Emil Rathenau,[u] was to "reduce to a minimum costs of experimentation, manufacture, and sales by purposeful organization and rational division of labor in the more efficient enterprises" and to conclude favorable commercial treaties that could "keep the markets of friendly nations open to our goods."[65] But the people in the Ruhr area remembered the stock-market profits that came in the wake of the announcement of the second navy law at a time when market values were already crumbling, and they decided to duplicate that course of events artificially by pressure on the Reich Naval Office. Maximilian Harden[v] had already observed in January 1900[66] that the main impetus for industry's energetic naval propaganda came from the impending crisis, but he was mistaken at that time: as far as one can tell, industry was taken completely by surprise by the onset of the crisis in April. A connection between the economic crisis and the expansion of the fleet cannot be proved until 1901. Between mid-October and mid-November,[67] Krupp's *Berliner Neueste Nachrichten* published a series of articles requesting the Reich Naval Office to revise the timing of the ship-building program, by which construction was to proceed at a fairly even rate until 1917, so that a large number of ships could be laid down immediately. Two weeks later, the president of the German Navy League—Prince Salm-Horstmar had by this time taken over Prince Wied's position—addressed the following letter to the State Secretary of the Reich Naval Office:

65. In the AEG's business report for 1900/01, reproduced in Felix Pinner, *Emil Rathenau und das elektrische Zeitalter* (Leipzig, 1918).
66. *Zukunft*, 13 January 1900, XXXI, 93.
67. 20 and 22 October, 6, 7, 19 November 1901.

Varlar Castle, 3 December 1901

Your Excellency:

I am pleased to report the following good news:

I was asked by gentlemen with different party affiliations to activate a movement to induce the Reichstag to ask the government to accelerate the building of warships, in view of the depressed business conditions, the unfavorable state of commerce and industry, and the related unemployment of thousands of workers.

The acceleration of the ship-building program that was approved in the last navy bill up to the maximum capacity of the German shipyards would result in new orders for many branches of industry, which would not only keep these industries alive but would also enable them to keep the workers they have busy and rehire those that have been dismissed. One of the most important factors at stake would be that this order for new warships and the concomitant revival of commerce and industry would *raise the prices of the relevant stocks on the stock market, saving many stock issues and permitting a consolidation of the market.*[68]

A single party cannot go to the government with such a request for fear of being accused of selfish or partisan motives.

It is therefore felt that such a suggestion should originate in neutral territory and that the German Navy League, in which all parties are represented, is the most suitable terrain for bringing the parties together in this question, to instigate the Reichstag's petition to the government. Although I am firmly convinced that such a decision on the part of the Reichstag would be eagerly welcomed by the government, I do not want to neglect informing Your Excellency on this subject and to beg you to notify the Reich Chancellor of this communication, so that I may get some idea of what the position of the Reich government would be if I were to proceed as suggested. In case of an affirmative response, I would try to get the matter rolling after Christmas and to set the propaganda organs of the DFV [the Navy League] in motion.

If the Reich Chancellor desires, I will be glad to take part in a preliminary discussion, and I sign this letter with the expression of my sincerest respect,

Your Excellency's most obedient
Otto Prince von Salm

In reply to this demand that the weightiest armament decisions be reached simply on the basis of whether "they would raise the prices

68. My italics.

of the relevant stocks," Tirpitz wrote the president of the German Navy League in these terms:

Berlin, 14 December 1901

Your Highness,

I am very much obliged for your letter of December 3, which, in accordance with your desire, I have brought to the attention of the Reich Chancellor.

If it were possible to persuade a majority of the Reichstag to approve a resolution asking the Reich government to accelerate ship building, this would be of the greatest significance for reinforcing our country's military strength.

Your Highness should keep in mind, however, that an acceleration of the ship-building program by itself would not take care of the matter. It would have to coincide with an accelerated expansion of the maritime shipyards and harbor facilities, as well as a speeding up of the training of personnel and an increase in the disposable manpower.

If only one additional battleship were launched each year compared with the present building program of the navy law, this would imply additional expenditures of 30–35 million marks annually to defray the above-mentioned complementary costs. But if the goal is to give maximum employment to German shipyards, what would be needed would be not one but two or three additional large ships per year and corresponding complementary expenditures of 65 or 100 million marks respectively.

Unfortunately, it seems quite impossible in the present constellation of political parties and in the light of the exceedingly difficult financial situation to obtain a majority for such a resolution in the Reichstag. Under these circumstances, the government must regretfully decline to give either direct or indirect support to an agitation in favor of accelerating the current building rate. The time is not yet ripe for such an acceleration. I have the honor to remain very faithfully

Your Highness's obedient
Tirpitz

Only two minor newspaper items gave any public indication of what had gone on backstage, providing, incidentally, a neat methodological example of the possibility of reconstructing reality, at least in its general outlines, from stray comments in the press. On 28 December 1901 it was reported in the Munich *Allgemeine Zeitung* that authoritative quarters had taken a negative stand on the suggestion made in one sector of the press that the fleet be enlarged "to eliminate the state of economic distress." On 11 January 1902, the *Rheinisch-Westfälische Zeitung* regretfully acknowledged the government's lack of boldness "in the interests of industry, labor, and the German war fleet."

The special contributions received by the German Navy League dropped from 170,000 marks in 1901 to 410 marks in 1902.

CHAPTER V

The Genesis of the
Royal Prussian Reserve Officer

1

The absolutist Prussian state had its political center of gravity in the open plain. The recruitment of the East Elbian lower nobility into administrative and military ranks from the eighteenth century on had the effect of scattering the ruling class over the entire territory. This served a twofold purpose: it helped to unify individual segments of the "Royal Prussian State" and, by having the estate owners (*Rittergutbesitzer*) congregate in the nearest larger and smaller administrative towns, it made it possible to keep a check on the provincial bureaucracy's "reliability" in terms of the landed nobility's interests, thereby compensating for the remoteness of central authorities and the infiltration of bourgeois elements into the local administration.

Like the ruling stratum, which had its roots in the countryside, the army too was recruited in rural areas whenever mercenaries proved to be inadequate. The estate owners were officers *par excellence,* and their cottagers, the farm laborers indentured to their estates (*Inste*), were the ideal common soldiers of the Prussian monarchy. The scattering of the ruling class over the open plain was not altogether a function of Prussia's agricultural situation —Russia's political center of gravity had always been in the cities —but the purely agrarian structure of the army could not fail to suffer from the political and social crises of the nineteenth century. The army of the absolutist state was a socially self-contained body;

the attempt was made in the nineteenth century to break through this isolation and in fact, in the course of three generations, it was overcome both in Prussia-Germany and in France. The dynamics of this process, however, diverged: in France the army was fused with the bourgeoisie, which had sided with the nation; in Germany, the bourgeoisie was forced, in the wake of its defeats in the revolution of 1848 and in the conflict with the military, to accept the army's position of power and its ideology.

What we see in pre-1914 France is a bourgeois, civilian-minded officer corps and rank and file incapable of being driven to an assault that made no sense even by the most emphatic command and unwilling to sacrifice themselves unless their officers could give rational explanations of their orders which they themselves expressly accepted.[1] Military discipline paralleled relations between parliament and the government that issued from it; it proved its superiority during the world war by withstanding a crisis that strained it to the utmost, at a time when all armies gradually turned into citizens' armies, and Prussian drill seemed to have lost its effectiveness. In Germany, subordination to the military was carried over into civilian life in a process that we shall examine more closely; a major technical instrument of this transformation was the unique development of the reserve-officer system, above all under William II. France offers the ultimate example of the nationalization of an army that reached its culminating point in the last conscription law, in which differences between the army and the nation were erased; Germany, on the contrary, is a prime example of the militarization of a nation that produced excellent results in the time of the empire, but in the long run caused serious evil.

"Militarism" can never be automatically identified with the numerical strength of the army. With an army of 750,000 men, France is not, sociologically speaking, "militaristic," just as Germany, with 100,000 men, is not "unmilitaristic."[a]

Militarism exists

1. where we find a class of officers who do not look upon themselves as military technicians, as public servants executing the will of political superiors, and do not regard their military calling as a form

1. Retired Captain Hans Ritter, *Die französische Armee von heute* (Leipzig, 1924), pp. 18 ff.

of service after which they will belong to the citizenry of the nation in the same way as other citizens in public or private employment; but where these officers regard their profession as that of a "warrior caste" with its own code of honor, its own form of law, and its own set of beliefs, and when this view of the military profession as a way of life superior to and more estimable than bourgeois standards is generally accepted; and

2. where this evaluation of the military is voluntarily affirmed by a substantial fraction of the bourgeoisie, which willingly submits to this military caste, a process that was closely tied in Prussia to the realignment of capitalist society after the emergence of the industrial proletariat.

2

On two occasions the Kingdom of Prussia showed remarkable skill in keeping the upper hand against powerful social strata. The political subjugation of these adversaries did not lead to their economic and social defeat; on the contrary, it was the precondition for their integration into the state and for the concession of economic and social privileges, which were conferred upon them in ample measure.

In the seventeenth and eighteenth centuries, the Hohenzollerns politically defeated the degenerate lower nobility in their realm, which was in no way superior to the Polish aristocracy, the Szlachta,[2] using as their most potent weapon the judicial proceedings of the administrative courts, which claimed the estates *(Rittergüter)* as part of the royal domain. When Frederick the Great called a halt to these proceedings, thereby officially recognizing the aristocracy's claims to their lands and granting it exclusive ownership rights to the estates, he set out simultaneously to replace the ill-assorted, predominantly mercenary and nonaristocratic officer corps with an exclusively aristocratic corps, thereby putting the finishing touch on the political subjugation of the aristocracy under princely absolutism. It is to this peace treaty that we must attribute the aristocracy's "feudal loyalty" *(Vasallentreue)* which Oswald Speng-

2. Gustav von Schmoller, *Umrisse und Untersuchungen zur Verfassungs-, Verwaltungs- und Wirtschaftsgeschichte, besonders des preussischen Staats im 18. und 19. Jahrhundert* (Leipzig, 1898), p. 283.

ler, in his admiration for "organic" reaction, would be only too happy to legitimize by tracing it back to the Teutonic orders.[b]

After the French Revolution, the Kingdom of Prussia was forced to come to terms with the bourgeoisie as an ideological threat and, after the thirties and forties of the nineteenth century, as a social threat as well. It is to the Hohenzollerns' credit that they found a positive solution to this conflict, even if this solution, in the end, led to grief.

The first confrontation took shape in the Prussian reform movement, whose leaders wished to unify nation and state. The bourgeoisie inside Prussia was still too weakly developed, however, and revolutionary pressure by the third estate against the absolutist states lost its external impetus with Napoleon's fall. The *Landwehr*[c] remained a well-intentioned utopian idea and general conscription an excellent means of acquiring a good-sized army without the high costs a large mercenary force would have entailed. The democratic merging of state and nation, which in a state like Prussia, where power rested in the hands of public servants and the military, could only have come about by a joining of forces between the bureaucracy and officer corps and the third estate, became a possibility only with the emergence of a broad bourgeois stratum and a concomitant accumulation of capital. The problem was resolved from the sixties on, both financially and in terms of personnel recruitment.

The fiscal solution was found in the Prussian state's special method of raising a major part of its budget through the increasing revenues of state-owned enterprises and, in the empire, in the fact that, after the fiscal reform of 1879, its financial resources stemmed from the expansion of tariffs and indirect taxes, which could be exacted without the consent of parliament,[3] at that time under the control of a progressive-minded bourgeoisie. The paradoxical result of this situation was that the politically reactionary state developed a specifically capitalist state economy in its fight against the bourgeoisie. On the other hand, beginning with the last years of the Bismarckian era, this same bourgeoisie, which was relatively unaffected by government expenditures because of the policy of collecting

3. The earlier American fiscal policy of using the sale of land and tariffs as the cornerstone of the budget was presumably attributable to an aversion against a strong state, the opposite of the German situation.

revenues from state enterprises, tariffs, and indirect taxes, came to have an ever-increasing financial stake in the existing political order as a result of the large loans floated originally to cover military requirements and later to cover the Reich's chronic budgetary deficit.

From the point of view of recruitment, the subjugation of the bourgeoisie by the military monarchy dates from the eighties, the period of Puttkamer's ministry (1881–1888),[d] in which the road to administrative promotion was blocked for any assistant judge who did not espouse conservative views. Liberal officials disappeared in Prussia with surprising speed. The price that had to be paid by the bourgeoisie for keeping its share of government offices was simply to abandon political liberalism, and it paid this price. The political realignment of the Prussian officials from liberalism to conservatism is a brilliant example of the way in which an existing social situation can be exploited by the state vigorously and successfully through a systematic policy of personnel recruitment and replacement. The huge loss of seats in the Reichstag by the National Liberals and the Progressives between 1878 and 1893 is a revealing reflection of this feudalization of capitalist society in Germany. And indeed this process of selecting and cultivating men with reliable convictions assumed its most complete form in the academic world, the breeding ground for future government officials.

3

Royal Prussia's victory with respect to the army proceeded in two stages. The first, negative, stage consisted in the destruction of the *Landwehr* by the army "reform" of 1860; the second, positive, stage consisted in a building up of the reserve officer system as an instrument for the bourgeoisie's social adaptation to the aristocratic and monarchical character of the military state.

The precondition for the destruction of the *Landwehr* was the existence of the system of indentured farm labor *(Instenverfassung)* on the East Elbian estates. The *Landwehr* was under the leadership of elected officers, who, by the nature of things, were small-town notables and hence likely to be politically liberal and opposition-minded. The indentured-farm-labor recruits were accustomed from birth to receiving orders from the estate owners and, therefore, provided the ideal human raw material for supporting the monarchy against the upward-mobile bourgeoisie. The three-year military service was maintained to transform indentured farm laborers into a technically trained force of superb quality and, at the same time, to weld resistant elements in the army as firmly as possible to this reliable nucleus. It was hoped that the introduction of equal and universal suffrage in the North German Federation and the Reich would also convert this class, which was loyal to the king and supplied the elite of the army, into shock electoral troops for the Conservatives and the monarchy in their struggle against the bourgeoisie. The destruction of the *Landwehr,* notwithstanding its popular appeal, the struggle against the bourgeoisie, and the maintenance of the three-year military service are closely associated with the introduction of universal suffrage.

However, this system was based on a serious psychological miscalculation: it assumed that patriarchal conditions still prevailed in reality, while in fact they had been crumbling fast since the middle of the century. Within half a generation, the system consolidated in the sixties by William I and Roon[e] was in a crisis, as German industrialization gave birth in the cities to a politically tightly organized and radical proletariat. This was even more radical than the petty bourgeoisie, which was ill-suited for political action. The authoritarian state thus found itself confronted with the problem of the internal political reliability of its army, which inevitably included a growing number of Social Democrats, as a result of the East Elbian plain's stagnant population, which could not keep up with the demands of the enormous army expansion. This crisis in reliability was caused by the fact that, at a time when the army was increasing in size, the rural population was dwindling in relation to total population, whereas the proletariat was increasing rapidly. Even more important was the simultaneous disintegration of the indentured farm-labor system accompanying the second agrarian crisis after 1875. The population stratum on which the Royal Prussian Army had been tailored was now being wiped out.

The army failed to adapt its structure to the change in composition of its recruits. Old Moltke had created the framework for the army that was taken over by his successors, who developed and transformed minor aspects without introducing major changes.

Schlieffen,[4] in contrast to Moltke, clearly recognized the destructive effect of war on the economy and therefore urged that war should lead up to decisive battles at the earliest possible moment. He nevertheless sought the Cannae[f] that was demanded by the vital needs of an advanced capitalist state, with the help of an army that had been technically modernized by Moltke through the incorporation of railroad transportation into the mobilization process and the acquisition of heavy artillery for the field army, but whose social composition was, until the end, incompatible with these technical expedients. The engineering corps and the heavy artillery were not considered prestigious units, and their officer billets were left to bourgeois elements; the field artillery with its predominantly aristocratic officer corps[5] looked askance at these heavy pieces of ordnance, which conflicted with their ambition to ride as elegantly as the cavalry.[6] General von Schlichting's[7] training regulations for the infantry, which discarded the traditional system of ranked lines (*Treffensystem*) and in the face of vigorous protests by the career officers, sought to adapt military tactics to the mental capacity of the two new army strata, the proletariat and the reserve officers, still illustrated by its compromise between skirmish lines and mass fire, an awkward grafting of modern technology on an army not geared to this technology.

The simultaneous proletarization of the cities and the dying out of the indentured farm laborers deprived the Prussian army of its politically and socially reliable recruits and led to their replacement by elements that were politically and socially unreliable. The most obvious way out of this difficulty was to curtail the size of the army; at least, this solution was in keeping with Prussian tradition dating

4. Walter Elze, *Graf Schlieffen* (Breslau, 1928).

5. On the basis of the 1913 rank lists, aristocratic staff officers filled 87 percent of the cavalry billets, 48 percent of the infantry billets, 41 percent of the field artillery billets, 31 percent of the army service corps, 13 percent of the Navy (all officers), and 6 percent of the foot artillery, the engineering corps, and the transportation corps.

6. The fine article by Franz Carl Endres, "Soziologische Struktur und ihr entsprechende Ideologien des deutschen Offizierkorps vor dem Weltkriege," *Archiv für Sozialwissenschaft und Sozialpolitik,* vol. 58, 1927, is very informative on these questions.

7. E. Freiherr von Gayl, *General v. Schlichting und sein Lebenswerk* (Berlin, 1913), pp. 120 ff.

back to 1819. It could not be implemented, however, because the second agrarian crisis put an end to Russo-Prussian friendship. In view of an external situation that made a two-front war seem likely, it would have been suicidal for the ruling classes to persist in their tactic of setting a ceiling on new military formations for fear of the political unreliability of the *Landwehr* and its officers, a policy that was still plausible enough in 1870 in the face of the numerically much weaker French forces. The army laws of 1887 and 1888 were predicated on the formation of very strong reserve troops in time of mobilization.

But the existing officer corps, which had already exhausted all half-way suitable resources from the nobility, was too weak a framework for this vastly expanded army. The remedy lay not so much in reaching down into the bourgeoisie for the expansion of the officer corps—up to the last years before the war, bourgeois officers in the higher ranks declined even more markedly than aristocratic officers—but rather, conversely, in assimilating the bourgeoisie to the army by transforming the bourgeois mentality into a military mentality and conferring a social nimbus on this bourgeois stratum that would in turn enhance the dignity of the reserve officer. The limiting factor in the expansion of the German army before 1914 and in Germany's role as a protagonist in the international armament race was the extent to which the German bourgeoisie could be feudalized. The point was finally reached where both the lower nobility and the newly feudalized bourgeoisie had exhausted their capacity for providing homogeneous officer material. Only "altogether unsuitable elements" were available to replace the officers needed for the three new formations requested by the General Staff in 1913, thereby "exposing the officer corps to the threat of democratization, quite aside from other dangers."[8] Only then, out of inner necessity, did the expansion of armaments come to a halt. The willingness of the Reichstag majority to approve the requested army increase carried no weight against the threatened democratization of the royal Prussian officer corps.

The destruction of the *Landwehr* represented a victory of the

---

8. The Prussian Minister of War von Heeringen to the General Staff, 20 January 1913, in Hans Herzfeld, *Die deutsche Rüstungspolitik vor dem Weltkrieg* (Bonn, 1923), p. 63.

monarchy and its aristocratic officer corps over the bourgeoisie with its outspoken tendency to encourage the *embourgeoisement* of the army, which could have been accomplished without political upheaval. The development of the reserve-officer system, beginning with the eighties and nineties, implied a final capitulation of the German bourgeoisie, which had renounced political revolution and was striving to attach itself as firmly as possible to the existing state power structure, for fear of an overthrow of the propertied classes. The dying out of the indentured farm laborers impelled the state to win over the bourgeoisie as a mainstay for its army, and fear of the proletariat in turn impelled the bourgeoisie to gain the state's support as a safeguard for its property.

Once this alliance, which one cannot find anywhere in recorded form, had effectively guaranteed the pacification of the state, and once the bourgeoisie had begun to supply manpower for the feudally infected reserve officer corps instead of for the liberal *Landwehr* officer corps, the state could serenely make a few concessions that it had previously refused: the transformation of the septennial military budget into a quinquennial budget and the introduction of two-year military service. The liberal parties had objected to the septennial budget, because it tied the Reichstag's hands in determining the proper army size, and because—given the system of triennial legislative sessions—it limited the two subsequent Reichstag sessions in their constitutional right of budget approval.

An agreement was reached in 1893 to restrict the approval of army strength to a five-year period, a liberal gesture without real significance. More significant was the introduction of a two-year military service, whose technical-military effect was to increase the number of trained men. Indentured farm laborers were dying out, and the more intelligent urban recruits needed no more than two years to be trained as technically usable soldiers. The decisive social factor, however, was the elimination of the danger that the aristocratic career officer corps might lose control over its men in times of internal crisis without the help of the three-year conscripts; the bourgeoisie with its reserve officers had replaced the indentured farm laborers conscripted for three years' service as the monarchy's military guard. The introduction of a two-year service was anything but a successful implementation of a long-standing bourgeois and liberal demand; in formally acceding to the demand, the victorious government actually accomplished the opposite from what had been expected of it. This measure did not represent a step in the direction of nationalizing the army, but it was a step in the direction of militarizing the nation by shifting from a reliance on the three-year conscripted farm laborers to a reliance on the feudalized bourgeoisie with its one-year military service.[g] It reflected an abandonment of the hope that the troops could be tied by an internal allegiance to the state in whose army they were serving, and it represented an increased emphasis on the Reich's class character by the assimilation of the military and the bourgeoisie. The shift in the social background of the recruits marked the end of the army's patriarchal system (which had included resort to corporal punishment), and as a result, beginning with the eighties and nineties, Prussian lieutenants, formerly modest fellows in general, turned into the insufferable prigs of the Wilhelmine era. The rulers severed the patriarchal ties that had bound them to the people and more than ever thought of themselves as those "in command."

4

The price the bourgeoisie had to pay for obtaining the help of the state in protecting its property was the sacrifice of specifically bourgeois concepts of honor and traditions. Before 1870, such traditions were beginning to take shape in the Hanseatic cities and in the Rhineland, and, purged of small-state peculiarities, they might have served as foundations for a middle-class German national sentiment and a seignorial, authentically upper-middle-class life style that was not copied from the nobility. In the harsh struggle between heavy industry and commerce, it was the more strongly feudalized heavy industry that gained the upper hand socially. In the Rhineland, old bourgeois traditions receded without a struggle before the new sources of power, iron and coal. Even in the Hanseatic cities, the success of the protective tariff and the colonial policies and the enthusiasm sparked by the fleet somewhat later cast a pall of social opprobrium on the old traditions, which had been associated with the free-trade opposition. It was not the army that was forced to adjust to bourgeois traditions under the pressure of social realignment; on the contrary, bourgeois traditions were the victims of the reserve-officer system. The objective of the tariff and fiscal reforms of 1879 and of Miquel's *Sammlungspolitik* after 1897 was to find compromises between real interests; the reserve-officer system was the principal tool for engineering the compromise between the bourgeoisie and the military monarchy in imperial Germany, and it was instrumental in creating the neo-German life style with which we are only too familiar even today from daily experience, the ridiculous nature of which has been so brilliantly exposed by Max Weber.[9]

The *Landwehr* officer had had little contact with the line officer, but the reserve-officer candidate's qualifications were scrutinized in the officers' mess by the officers of his regiment, who would later have to vote for him: Jews were disqualified *a priori* for the honor of "maneuver uncle," and Social Democrats were even more rigidly excluded, not only because of their adherence to a revolutionary party, but because their socialist allegiance was equated with a deficiency in "moral qualities." They were even barred from one-year service.[10] Anyone who failed to become a reserve officer lacked a decisive ingredient of social respectability. The academician who had not been promoted beyond the rank of noncommissioned officer was treated in civilian life like a second-class soldier in the barracks. "Loyalty to the King" was not the crux of the matter; the Progressive judges of the sixties had been loyal to the King too, and under William II lamentations abounded, particularly in legitimist circles, about this "King." What was at stake was the alliance between bourgeoisie and state power, which afforded mutual protection against the proletariat.

With a sureness of instinct rarely displayed in imperial Germany, the futility of trying to win the inner allegiance of the Socialist-infected troops for the ruling regime was recognized from the start. Irrespective of their proletarian origins, recruits were subjected to the discipline that had been designed for the cottagers. William II's notorious words at the dedication of the Alexander Barracks were

9. *Wahlrecht und Demokratie in Deutschland, Ges. Politische Schriften* (2nd ed., München, 1958), pp. 277 ff.

10. Decision by the Ministry of War, 18 February 1914, less than half a year before the outbreak of war! See Retired Major Erich Otto Volkmann, *Der Marxismus und das deutsche Heer im Weltkriege* (Berlin, 1925) p. 49.

nothing more, psychologically speaking, than an unfortunate rhetorical slip of the uninhibited monarch's tongue,[h] but, from a sociological point of view, they reasserted the objective of maintaining the traditional Prussian discipline in an age where the proletarian masses provided the bulk of the army's recruits. On the other hand, the tension between tradition and the newly emerging type of recruit sparked innumerable Reichstag debates, initiated by the parliamentary representatives of this new class, about mistreatment of soldiers and finally led to a strange half-victory of social democracy over the army.[11] The formal discipline intended for indentured servants was upheld, but the practice of thrashing recruits to turn them into good soldiers, a practice that was an intrinsic element of this discipline (in the authentic German tradition, Baron von Stein himself had in 1807 defended thrashing and denied that it was an affront to honor),[12] was gradually abandoned for fear of triggering Social Democratic debates in the Reichstag. Yet even today the proletariat's hatred of the military is largely based on a sure instinct for the anachronistic nature of formal discipline, which was designed for indentured farm laborers but still lives on.

The Prussian reserve officer disappeared with the collapse of the empire, but the unrealistic and arrogant attitude toward social and intellectual problems that was fostered by this institution has not disappeared and still characterizes a large part of our bourgeoisie. And if one identifies the period from 1890 to 1914, with some justice, as Wilhelmine, then this word signifies that inherently misguided outlook which, in its weakness, mistook bravado for an expression of strength, arrogance and conceit for a manifestation of dignity, and swagger for sensibility: in this life style William II was at one with his officers.

11. *Ibid.*, p. 47.
12. Delbrück, *Gneisenau* (Berlin, 1882) I, 134.

CHAPTER VI

The Social System of Reaction in Prussia under the Puttkamer Ministry

1

Imperial District Officer *(Bezirkspräsident)* Albert von Puttkamer's biographical sketch of his father, Robert von Puttkamer, the Prussian Minister of State,[1] makes it painfully apparent that the latter has not yet found a biographer capable of treating as fully as it deserves and on a level that could do justice to its complexity and significance the great problem whose successful resolution constituted the substance of his ministry.

When Robert von Puttkamer, after having filled the posts of County Councilor *(Landrat)* in Dennim, councilor for the Ministry of the Interior, District Officer *(Regierungspräsident)* in Gumbinnen and Metz, and Provincial Governor *(Oberpräsident)* in Breslau, scaled the highest rung in the career of a Prussian official by being appointed minister in 1879,[2] this appointment coincided with a major turning point for the Reich, which was to determine its political and social configuration until the collapse of 1918. Under the triple pressure of the transition to an industrialized state, the early stages of the agrarian crisis, and the swelling of the factory proletariat, the whole range of domestic policies was revised within the next few years to contend with these social and economic

1. *Staatsminister von Puttkamer: Ein Stück preussischer Vergangenheit,* ed. by Albert Puttkamer (Leipzig, 1929).
2. First as Minister of Public Worship and Education, later as Minister of the Interior.

developments. The most important legislative measures reflecting this revision were the tariff legislation in the capitalist and agrarian sphere, the anti-Socialist law and social-welfare legislation in the proletarian sphere.

But the full significance of this turning point has to be sought elsewhere than in these laws, because the anti-Socialist law was repealed after Bismarck's fall, social-welfare legislation failed to serve its political purpose, and the protective-tariff legislation did not prevent bitter conflict between industry and agriculture in the nineties; and not until Miquel's *Sammlungspolitik* was the issue settled finally—at least until 1918. [3] The true significance of this turning point lies in the transformation of bourgeois society; and it is in this area that Minister von Puttkamer intervened so incisively that his importance for the internal shaping of the new German empire was nearly as great as Bismarck's.

The reason for Puttkamer's appointment as minister in these circumstances was the reliability of his political and also his religious convictions. He was an orthodox conservative and had become accustomed from his youth to view the growth and victories of Prussian military power as a sign of a special divine dispensation.

"It seems to me that where the limitations of human wisdom and foresight are as apparent as they are in the impending European developments, there can be no question that the final decision lies in the hands of God, and that nations are merely unconscious executors and instruments of God's decrees. And I persist in believing that *Prussia is the good Lord's special favorite*, [4] and that He still has great things in store for it and will prevent its star from fading." [5]

It was with this faith in a Prussian God that Puttkamer embarked upon his crusade against social democracy.

The liberal bureaucracy, which had stood firm against reaction in Prussia since the reform era, was still identified in its official religious attitude with a vaguely pantheistic or deistic idealism. This was the idealism in whose name the reforms had been won, but in the course of administrative efforts extending over two generations,

3. See Eckart Kehr, "Englandhass und Weltpolitik," *Zeitschrift fur Politik*, XVII, 500. [See also above, Chapter II.]

4. Italics mine.

5. Letter to his father, May 1859, p. 15.

it had gradually exhausted its vigor and had in the daily routine of office suffered the same fate that befell bourgeois liberalism on an intellectual plane under the onslaught of the cultural criticism of the intelligentsia: it fell prey to inner dissolution. Under the influence of Bismarck's victories, more than one liberal privy councillor had come to venerate the bitch goddess success. And the question arose whether after 1870 this liberal bureaucracy in the administration, the law courts, and the universities still had the capacity to surmount the new problems of capitalism, the proletariat, and the agrarian crisis. The truth was that it did not, as a result not only of its internal disintegration but of the new threat of socialism, which attacked it with its own weapons. Socialism had used the "academic freedom" offered by the bourgeois universities to develop its own system, and it used the institutions and privileges of the bourgeois *Rechtsstaat*—parliament, the right to vote, free expression of opinion—to propagate its own social ideals. It developed a world view whose consequences seemed to be objectionable from the point of view of humanitarian idealism, but which humanitarian idealism had to tolerate and permit to exist under all circumstances if it wanted to remain true to itself. One of the intellectual leaders of the rising reaction, the Leipzig historian of jurisprudence Rudolf Sohm, among the most brilliant and inventive German jurists of his time, tersely stated the reason why existing institutions were incapable of defending themselves by liberal methods against a proletarian revolution:

It was within the third estate itself that the ideas originated that are now serving as firebrands to rouse the masses of the fourth estate against the third. The things that are written in the books of the educated class and the scholars are now preached in the streets. It is nineteenth-century education that is preaching its own destruction. Like eighteenth-century education, nineteenth-century education carries revolution in its womb. Once the offspring that it has nourished with its own blood is born, it will murder its own mother.[6]

Liberalism was in fact incapable of protecting against socialism

6. Rudolf Sohm, *Kirchengeschichte im Grundriss* (Leipzig, 1888), pp. 192–193. The book is a collection of essays taken from the *Allgemeine Konservative Monatsschrift*. See also Sohm's lecture, *Die Gegensätze unserer Zeit* (Heidelberg, 1883), particularly pp. 24–36.

Bismarck's power- and military state, which had reluctantly and for tactical reasons allied itself with national and liberal tendencies. The power state had to search out other "spiritual" support. This it sought and found in Christian religion and the Church. "But if the state wanted to accept the help of the Church in subduing social democracy—and its need for the spiritual support of an ally was indisputable—it was an untenable contradiction to continue to wage an all-out campaign against the firmest and most disciplined of the churches"[7] and to persist in the *Kulturkampf* against Catholicism, which had dominated the empire's first decade of existence.[a] The *Kulturkampf* was discontinued, and the liberal minister, Falk, who had waged this campaign, was dismissed when the proletarian danger became acute. He was replaced by Robert von Puttkamer, in whose eyes God was Prussia's ally, for whom the struggle "in favor of Christendom and the monarchy"[8] fulfilled an inner need, and who earnestly attempted to provide the Bismarckian state with the ideological support that it lacked by building Christianity into the system. Puttkamer's efforts were not directed toward restoring simple piety, but rather toward reestablishing a "purely external, purely formal, bureaucratic religiosity"[9] under state control. Old Emperor William coined the notorious saying: "The people needs its religion," but what he meant by this is clearly revealed by his reaction to the proposal that Luther's four-hundredth anniversary be turned into a national holiday: he was "simply stunned," because even free thinkers would be able to take part in it.[10] Religion was divested of its autonomous "religious" character and converted into a worldly weapon wielded by the ruling imperial regime against democracy and socialism. What characterized Puttkamer's reactionary stand was not so much his restoration of Church control over the elementary schools, but rather his exploitation of Church and religion in his anti-Socialist campaign. He was anxious to preserve the Christian character of elementary schools, but he wished to "accept the collaboration of the Church only within the

7. Fritz Hartung, *Deutsche Geschichte 1871–1919*, 2nd ed. (Bonn, 1924), p. 93.
8. *Ibid.,* p. 203.
9. Max Weber, *Verhandlungen des 8. Evangelisch-sozialen Kongresses vom 10. Juni 1897,* p. 110.
10. To Puttkamer, September 1, 1883, p. 138.

framework of the state's constitution and the state's laws."[11] The trend set in motion by the Reformation, which had broken up a unified Christendom into individual state Churches, found its logical climax here when the royal *summus episcopus* of a nation-state deployed his country's Church as an instrument of propaganda and aggression in the class struggle.

The official encouragement of religion was one way of undermining liberal idealism in the bureaucracy; another way was to reshape it and adapt it to the new circumstances. Idealism had been the *Weltanschauung* of the Prussian ministerial bureaucracy in its struggle for governmental power against the aristocracy. The feudalization of the bureaucracy in the eighties robbed idealism of its original meaning, although it continued its official existence notwithstanding its actual demise, and although "Goethe and Bismarck" became a popular way of characterizing the essence of Germanness, while Kant was reinterpreted as the precursor of the ideal of an absolutist state. This official idealism is clearly revealed when we examine Wilhelm von Humboldt's three biographies: the one by Rudolf Haym (1856), the one by Eduard Spranger (1908), and the one by Siegfried Kaehler (1927), which parallel this change in outlook. Where religion fell short as an intellectual foundation, idealism was expected to fill the gap: in a positive sense, by using this great intellectual movement as the cornerstone of Bismarck's version of the power state, and in a negative sense, by exploiting it as a weapon against "materialism," in that it "affirmed the leading role of natural science in the world of phenomena, but recognized the primacy of moral law for the world of action."[12] Idealism was assigned the task of erecting a formalistic scaffolding for Germany's *Weltanschauung* in general like that which Laband[13] had provided for constitutional law *(Staatsrecht)*.[b]

2

It could not be expected, however, that a "spiritual" transformation like the replacing of humanitarian idealism by religion, would

11. Address by Puttkamer, p. 48; see also p. 51.
12. See Gustav Schmoller's *Jahrbuch,* (1883) p. 1037, for his discussion of Sohm's *Die Gegensätze unserer Zeit,* in which he misunderstands Sohm, from whose standpoint, significantly enough, this formalism is insufficient.
13. See discussion in following section.

by itself assure the state of a solid foundation. From a practical point of view, religion could be propagated only in the elementary schools; the secondary schools *(Gymnasien)* were already beyond its reach—in contrast to Russia, where the curriculum in the *Gymnasium* faithfully mirrored periods of exacerbated and attenuated reaction by the proportional share of philology and the natural sciences—and universities were even more impervious to such intervention. But social transformation proved highly effective where "spiritual" transformation failed. It made its influence felt even in the universities, as is apparent in the disciplines with the greatest impact on political ideology, that is, constitutional law and history.

Laband's constitutional law, which became the constitutional law of the empire, is characterized by two seemingly contradictory tendencies: on the one hand, the development of a "method of jurisprudence," in which constitutional law is treated strictly as a field of law rather than as a field of politics and political theory and is subjected to a stringently logical and absolutized formalism, and, on the other, the interpretation of the state as the source of commands and the compeller of obedience, in disregard of its subjects' constitutional rights, as well as the notion that "in all state action, the genuinely political *(staatlich)* aspect lies in the ruler's power of command over the subject, and the guarantee of its implementation by coercion."[14]

But there is nothing accidental about this apparent discrepancy between the logical autonomy of the law and state power: by obscuring the connection between political life and constitutional law, Laband was able to construct a coherent and logical framework bereft of any positive content. He preferred to deprive his constitutional law of any historical or philosophical foundation rather than be forced to inject something of substance into the frame.

The old natural law has been given a new lease on life in a positivistic garb; it has been mysteriously resurrected in all its shabby bareness, but without its former grandeur. Or are we wrong in recognizing long outdated patterns of the doctrine of natural law hiding behind the most fashionable mummery? Are we not faced with the same underlying rationalistic

14. Otto Gierke, "Labands Staatsrecht und die deutsche Rechtswissenschaft," *Schmollers Jahrbuch* (1883) VII, 1151.

features, the same empty formal abstractions, the same barren, all-engulfing logical induction? The same mechanistic, individualistic, civil-law model of the state? The same superficial interpretation of jurisprudence idolizing law but giving coercion the last word? The same violent sundering of the spiritual bonds through which law and state are deeply entwined and intrinsically unified? The only missing element is precisely what originally constituted the fertile nucleus of natural law, its great historical content, its claim to immortality: the mountain-moving faith in the idea of justice! But in its absence, nothing remains. In as much as positivism could not reawaken the soul of natural law when it revived its formal apparatus, it could do nothing but resurrect a semblance of life. In place of a formalism invisibly guided by an idea, all we have is a formalism supported by dead matter.[15]

Laband's formalistic constitutional law in fact created the legal framework for state coercion, within which it could be given free rein without marring the appearance of the *Rechtsstaat*.

"For inasmuch as this method is entirely based on a purely juridical approach, which cannot eliminate the pervasive influence of hidden prior judgments with respect to basic general issues, the whole juridical construction is rooted not in the realm of science but in the realm of mere opinions and beliefs."[16] At the same time, it provides the magistrature with a methodical framework within which it can execute all governmental orders without the risk of internal conflict or the need to uphold "justice against law."[17] The constitution affirmed the independence of judges; with its formalism, Laband's constitutional law created the spiritual dependence on the part of the judges required by Bismarck's crypto-absolutism.[18]

"If one goes to the heart of the matter, Laband's 'state' is identical with the 'government' as the active subject of the law, while

15. *Ibid.*, pp. 1191–1192.
16. *Ibid.*, p. 1120.
17. F. Freiherr Marshall von Bieberstein, *Vom Kampf des Rechtes gegen die Gesetze: Freiburger Universitätsrede 18. Januar 1925* (Stuttgart, 1927). See particularly material on p. 40, footnote 132 and p. 83.
18. The administration of the examination for the post of assistant judge was likely to strengthen this tendency too. The 1869 instructions for the examination, which provided a thorough treatment of general legal and political problems, remained in effect after 1879, but the examination gradually was restricted to purely professional topics. See Albert Lotz, *Geschichte des deutschen Beamtentums* (Berlin, 1909), p. 612. For the remolding of the judicial administration, see section 3.

elected representatives appear merely as an extraneous consultative committee on state interests," a "preferred stockholders' meeting convened according to the statutes to approve certain decisions and to keep an eye on the administration."[19]

Laband's constitutional law was attuned not only to Bismarck's police state but even more specifically to a police state organized along capitalist lines. It therefore served as a framework both for the bureaucracy's power drive and the aspirations of economic interests.

There is good reason to be afraid that such a formalized jurisprudence, which has so completely cut itself off from the central idea of justice, will be unable to cope with the tasks confronting it. . . . For by abandoning any ideal substance of law, jurisprudence undermines its power of resistance against the onslaught of political, religious, social, and economic forces and interests. . . . The technical strength of its apparatus will not indefinitely guarantee its rule. Whatever it may gain in precision and in serviceability as a tool, historical experience warns us that such improvements increase the danger of different forces and interests exploiting it as a mere tool and destroying it internally by the subservience forced upon it. . . . At no time, and least of all in our own time, when public life is in a state of deep turmoil and torn by a multitude of conflicts, can the law dispense with its unceasing struggle to reassert and reshape itself. . . . Surely the fate of the law is not a matter of minor concern for us. In the last analysis, the preservation of our culture is at stake.[20]

The victory of the idea of the power state in historiography was as typical of the new era as the victory of formalism in constitutional law. The historiography of the fifties and sixties, with its libertarian and national outlook, was laid to rest with the founding of the Reich. A man like Theodor Mommsen,[c] who had the courage publicly to brand the policies of the eighties as a "big fraud," stood for a whole generation as a solitary figure in the rising tide of chauvinism,[21] while among the younger generation, a gentle and delicate man like Friedrich Meinecke turned away from the mainstream to the history of ideas.[d] The military and the bourgeoisie knew power exclusively as victors and beneficiaries: domestically, from a

19. Gierke, *op. cit.*, p. 1148.
20. *Ibid.*, pp. 1189 and 1193.
21. Ludo Moritz Hartmann, *Theodor Mommsen: Eine biographische Skizze* (Gotha, 1908).

political and social standpoint, as the class ruling over the proletariat, and externally as the class ruling over Europe's most powerful state, particularly in relation to vanquished France. It is hardly surprising that the glorification of power and the mystic cult of the state won general acceptance. It was Treitschke's[e] five-volume work on German history that had the greatest political propagandist influence. He was a proponent of the personal approach of modern historiography: "Men are the shapers of history"—a singular mixture of liberal individualism and submission to the strong leader. He was the most influential propagator of the official idealism, lavishly applying the word "ethical," the highest praise idealism could bestow, to all basic values of the Bismarckian empire, shrinking not even from the monstrous blasphemy: "The justness of war is based quite simply on the consciousness of an ethical necessity."[22] He and his vastly inferior disciple Dietrich Schäfer[23]f had a persuasive and seductive effect on the masses of "educated persons," who in the late seventies came to accept more and more wholeheartedly the new attitude that denied intrinsic value to economic achievements and intellectual accomplishment, which they reduced to mere expressions of governmental and military power. Gustav Schmoller's[g] *Acta Borussica* were a much more significant and respectable scholarly achievement in which the best of the time is reflected. This work sets out to describe the power of the absolute state and its influence on economic and social developments, "to prove at last to the world that Frederick William I was the greatest king of the Hohenzollern dynasty . . . and that Frederick the Great excelled not only as a diplomat and military leader but as a ruler in times of peace."[24] Treitschke projected his partisan feelings and emotions onto the period between 1807 and 1848, while Schmoller used his *Acta Borussica* to clarify the problem of the eighties, how the power state should deal with economic and social development, by his scholarly account, based on documentary evidence, of the relationship between the state, its administra-

22. Friedrich Meinecke, *Die Idee der Staatsräson in der neueren Geschichte* (München, 1924) p. 509.
23. *Ibid.*, p. 497.
24. Prussian Academy of Sciences to the Minister of Public Worship and Education, April 21, 1887, *Acta Borussica,* Silk industry, I, xiii.

tion, and grain, tariff, currency, and fiscal policy during the period of absolutism.

3

Reactionary efforts to integrate the bourgeoisie within the state were even more significant for the struggle against socialism than attempts to remold religious and intellectual attitudes.

On the one hand, Bismarck's Prusso-German state was a military state, but on the other, the Prussian army, which had not hesitated to fire on the nationalist German bourgeoisie in 1848, had fought in 1866 and 1870 to implement the political ideas of the progressive bourgeoisie. However, relations between the army and the bourgeoisie were generally tense, precluding any social contact,[25] and the bourgeoisie's antigovernmental mood had been further exacerbated by governmental violations of the constitution during the period of military conflict. While victory over Austria and France doomed the bourgeoisie to defeat and impotence, incipient industrialization was making it wealthy. Even though the conservative agrarian nobility had retained its power over the state, the onset of the agrarian crisis eroded its generally modest wealth. The landed nobility's position with respect to the bourgeoisie had become nearly as precarious as the liberal bureaucracy's helplessness with respect to socialism. The state needed the joint support of the military and the bourgeoisie. In a situation in which one of these old antagonists was increasing its political power but losing its wealth, whereas the other was increasing its wealth and social standing but losing political power, the state had no choice but to act as peace maker between them lest one of them allow this discrepant development to threaten the foundation of the regime. It was under the pressure of the proletarian threat that an intermeshing of the army and the bourgeoisie developed, for which the reserve officer served as a connecting link,[26] and which was instrumental in creating the neofeudal type of German bourgeois. There arose a new society, a

25. Felix Priebatsch, *Geschichte des Preussischen Offizierkorps* (Breslau, 1919), pp. 44–45.

26. See Eckart Kehr, "Zur Genesis des königlichen Preussischen Reserveoffiziers," *Die Gesellschaft*, 1928/II, 492 ff. [See also above, Chapter V.]

bourgeois-aristocratic neofeudalism,[27] which sealed itself off against the proletariat and the isolated remnants of the liberal bourgeoisie that resisted feudalization, just as the officer corps and the liberal bourgeoisie had at one time mutually excluded one another; a "coalition of joint interests was formed to exploit those that refused to ally themselves with it"[28] and a "mass corruption of organized economic groups took place in which entire professions gained wealth in an organized and impersonal way at the expense of other groups, a process the Wilhelmine era viewed as perfectly unobjectionable."[29] It was left to the Social Democratic movement to take over the legacy of the German-nationalist bourgeoisie's opposition against the army and the class state.

The state was not content with fostering neofeudal attitudes and convictions compatible with reserve-officer status but gave at least equal priority to a comparable remolding of the administration. A way had to be found to eliminate liberal privy councillors from the ranks of public servants, and in fact their elimination took place with remarkable dispatch. Albert von Puttkamer paints a pretty picture of this neofeudal bureaucracy:

The nobility formed the nucleus of the Conservative party, and in keeping with its tradition, insisted on a considerable measure of loyalty to the king. The whole younger generation of public servants was impregnated with these views. Bourgeois elements vied with their aristocratic colleagues in openly displaying their convictions. Anyone familiar with personnel conditions in Prussian government offices must know that liberal political views had almost no exponents among government officials. The younger generation was conservative in its political views.[30]

It is regrettable that no further information is available on this transformation of the bureaucracy and the technical measures by which it was carried through. Albert von Puttkamer mentions as a matter of course that an official with politically unacceptable views

27. Carl Brinkmann, *Die Aristokratie im kapitalistischen Zeitalter, Grundriss der Sozialökonomik,* IX, 1.
28. Theodor Mommsen's speech of 24 September 1881, quoted in L.M. Hartmann, *op. cit,* p. 120.
29. M.J. Bonn in the collective work *Internationaler Faschismus,* ed. by Carl Landauer and Hans Honegger (Karlsruhe, 1928), p. 140.
30. *Ibid.,* pp. 80–81.

was not reprimanded but simply blocked in his promotion; he only hints at the large number of public servants who were former members of the student leagues *(Korpsstudenten)*[31] and he never specifies what were the results of this peculiar selection principle that made promotion to the higher echelons of the bureaucracy contingent on—having been chosen reserve officer by an officer corps. If we are to believe Ludwig Bernhard,[32] who had a good chance to observe the bureaucracy's effectiveness in the East, half a generation after Puttkamer's departure from office, by the time all assistant judges *(Assessoren)* had reached top positions, the Prussian administration was a shambles.

The biographical sketch fails in one respect, which was crucial in Robert von Puttkamer's own eyes and remains crucial in assessing his accomplishment: an account of how the remolding of the administration was effected.[33] To gain some idea of the external manifestations of this transformation, we shall draw on a few facts from the sphere of judicial administration[34]—a choice that is particularly apt, inasmuch as the higher-ranking personnel in the judicial administration was noted for its liberal tendencies.[35]

The rationalization of judicial procedure through the court reorganization law that went into effect in 1879 coincided with the beginning of reaction. The promotion of the Reich's Superior Commercial Court *(Reichsoberhandelsgericht)* in Leipzig to the status of Imperial Tribunal *(Reichsgericht)* as well as the dissolution[36] of the Prussian Superior Tribunal *(Obertribunal)*, which had acquired a bad reputation through its politically biased adjudication in the years of conflict,[37] was still the product of the liberal era, but socially the restructuring of the judicial machinery played into the hands

---

31. *Ibid.*, p. 82.

32. Ludwig Bernhard, *Der Hugenbergkonzern* (Berlin, 1928), p. 5.

33. The extent of this remodeling can be seen in a letter of William I to Puttkamer of January 22, 1886, after the actor Barnay had been excluded from further appearances in the royal theaters because of his speech at an "oppositional" (and not even a Social Democratic) meeting, as quoted in Puttkamer's biography, p. 140.

34. *Cf.* Friedrich Holtze, *Fünfzig Jahre preussische Justiz* (Berlin, 1901), p. 40.

35. Johannes Ziekursch, *Politische Geschichte des Neuen Deutschen Kaiserreiches* (Frankfurt, 1927), II, 385.

36. Friedrich Holtze, *Geschichte des Kammergerichts in Brandenburg-Preussen* (Berlin, 1904), IV, 239.

37. *Ibid.*, II, 385.

of the impending reaction. The curtailment in the number of tribunals deprived many judges of their office and the ten oldest age classes were retired—thereby in a single blow relieving of their positions the progressive judges from the conflict period, who were approaching retirement age. By another provision, lawyers as a group were exempted from state control, so that many of the most capable younger liberal judges, who were anxious to escape political pressure, became lawyers, a profession where their promotion would not be held back for political reasons. And a third factor in this almost idyllically smooth restructuring process was the freezing during the entire eighties of the number of judges' positions, irrespective of the growing need for judges. This freezing process coincided with the retirement of the ten oldest age classes and therefore prevented any position from becoming vacant through superannuation.[38] The process offered not only a perfect opportunity for lowering administrative costs—the unpaid assistant judges were overburdened with substitute work and were constantly being asked to serve as auxiliary judges—but also for the rigorous political sifting of the rising generation. Notwithstanding the paucity of available material, which makes methodological caution imperative, it is safe to assume that the rapid increase in positions beginning with 1889[39] was not a consequence of Miquel's fiscal reform but was the government's way of rewarding the rising generation, which had been subjected to stringent tests and found to be politically reliable. The entire magistrature of the Wilhelmine era was headed by these assistant judges of the eighties. But that was not all: only those assistant judges reached top positions who had gone through a second sifting insuring their political reliability, the office of public prosecutor.[40]

It would be a fundamental error to associate the restabilization of society too closely with the revival of the monarchy under William I. Although monarchist feelings of the bourgeoisie were heightened during his reign, this phenomenon is of secondary significance com-

38. *Ibid.*, IV, 286 for further details, such as p. 292: "Rarely has a change been introduced under such inauspicious circumstances for the higher-ranking officials."
39. *Ibid.*, IV, 321.
40. See also Ernst Fraenkel's excellent work *Zur Soziologie der Klassenjustiz* (Berlin, 1927), p. 14 f. for further discussions on these problems.

pared with the importance of social realignments. Monarchism did not constitute the highest principle of the Prussian aristocracy and officer corps but should be conceived instead—to use Gneisenau's[h] expression—as a "poetic feeling" that was an integral part of the military profession; and if the nobility had rarely manifested open resistance toward the monarchy, it had in secret and because it consistently held the highest positions in the bureaucracy been all the more successful in making the monarchy bow to its social will to power.[41] The Prussian nobility could therefore easily maintain its feudal loyalty to the king, as the king was powerless to eliminate its privileges. It would be a mistake to envisage Puttkamer's reactionary system as a means of safeguarding the "monarchy" against "republican" proclivities.[42] Instead it should be viewed as a form of social Alexandrianism, a planned sealing off from the proletariat of the bureaucracy, the officer corps, and those strata from which they recruited their personnel, as well as an exclusion of all those who had any ties with the proletariat from positions of influence over the state machinary and from social respectability. Although the liberal bourgeoisie had already, under the impact of the empire's military successes after 1864, reasserted its loyalty to the king, the durability and solidity of monarchism was a consequence of the social realignment. Friedrich Julius Stahl[i] observed, concerning the motivation of the French bourgeoisie of the thirties and forties: "It is fear of internal convulsions that basically motivates the propertied segment of the population, for whom the French Chambers do not offer as much reassurance as does the English Parliament, and who therefore, by an eternal natural law, gather around the sheltering banner of the monarch."[43] These observations are just as valid for Germany fifty years later, and they

41. This conflict between aristocracy and monarchy needs to be stressed, in contrast to the usual insistence in Rightist circles on their identity of interests, a view shared by Puttkamer.

42. Puttkamer's claim that the Progressive party *(Fortschrittspartei)* was a proponent of republicanism, though based on Bismarck's well-known remarks, is untenable. The Progressive party was so tame after 1870 that it did not even dare to celebrate the twenty-fifth anniversary of 18 March 1848. See F. Falkson, *Die liberale Bewegung in Königsberg* (Breslau, 1888), p. 198.

43. Stahl, *Das Monarchische Prinzip* (1845), new edition 1927, p. 25; see also p. 48.

explain the development of an artificial "tradition" that expanded from decade to decade.

Within the aristocracy, at the time that its estates were changing hands with increasing frequency—and the protective tariff legislation inevitably led to sales prices in which the tariff was capitalized in advance—the institution of entailment became entrenched. Similarly, the continuity of army tradition from the days of absolutism was stressed with equal intensity, and it was forgotten that in reality the "Prussian army" was either the army of Frederick William I and Frederick the Great, of Scharnhorst[j] and Gneisenau, or of Moltke and Roon, and that these different armies were separated from each other by intervals of the most marked disintegration, so that they shared little besides geography. This mistaken belief in historical continuity found its most visible expression in the bestowal of artificial "traditions" on individual regiments, but also manifested itself invisibly in the officers' blindness to the social revolution in the empire, despite their daily confrontation with the new types of army recruits.[44]

Although this neo-German traditionalism stressed the Frederician aspects of the Prussian military state and disregarded Stein's[k] reforms[45] as far as possible, for all practical purposes a reversion to Frederician aristocratic despotism was out of the question. No matter how ruthlessly and systematically conservative officials were shifted to nonconservative districts, Puttkamer's personnel policy in civilian administration paralleled the military administration's practice of setting up reserve-officer corps and of integrating exclusively aristocratic and exclusively bourgeois regiments.[46] Those parts of the bourgeoisie that were susceptible to feudalization were drawn into the conservative administration and placed as far as possible on an equal footing with aristocratic officials—though not beyond the level of *Regierungspräsident*.[47] The highest post in the provincial administration that of *(Oberpräsident)* was still reserved to the nobility.

44. Otto Erich Volkmann, "Die sozialen Missstände im Heer während des Weltkrieges," *Wissen und Wehr,* March and April 1929.
45. Max Lehmann, *Freiherr vom Stein* (Leipzig, 1902) I, p. vii.
46. Pribatsch, *op. cit.* p. 58.
47. Puttkamer, p. 82.

4

The internal contradiction of this system lay in the fact that, while it could no longer do without the bourgeoisie, quantitatively speaking, for filling administrative and military positions, it refused to allow the promotion of bourgeois public servants and officers unless they shed their bourgeois convictions and assumed a neo-feudal outlook.

In the army, this new structure was organizationally reinforced by separating the personnel division from the Ministry of War, dissolving it as a budgetary entity so as to remove it from parliamentary control, and reconstituting it in the form of the Military Cabinet, as an army ministry of personnel responsible only to the king.[48] The General Staff was also liberated from its previously subordinated position in the Ministry of War and given an autonomous status as an agency directly accountable to the emperor.[49] The new personnel ministry was to have a free hand in maintaining the army's social homogeneity without the least parliamentary intervention; the General Staff, for its part, was to have an equally free hand in the conduct of warfare without having to submit to indirect parliamentary influence exerted through the Minister of War. Constitutional theory, with a commendable submission to the will of the government, gave its blessings to the privileged organizational status of the military, justifying this stand on the basis of the army's technical need for some elbow room. It really was trying to give a logical underpinning for a redistribution of power that strengthened semiabsolutism and weakened parliamentary influence in the face of the proletarian threat. Officers were in effect exempted from constitutional provisions and tied to the king by special relations of feudal loyalty, from which ordinary citizens were excluded. Officers were under the jurisdiction not of civilian but of military tribunals and of

48. Cabinet order dated 8 March 1883, quoted in Fritz Freiherr Marschall von Bieberstein, *Verantwortlichkeit und Gegenzeichnung bei Anordnungen des Obersten Kriegsherrn: Studie zum deutschen Staatsrecht* (Berlin, 1911), pp. 161 ff. For background of this Cabinet order, see Lucius von Ballhausen, *Bismarck-Erinnerungen* (Stuttgart, 1921), p. 259. From a psychological standpoint, this reorganization was attributable to General von Albedyll's urge for power, but sociologically its significance is greater than its concrete motive.

49. Cabinet order of May 24, 1883. Printed first in Günther Wohlers, *Die staatsrechtliche Stellung des Generalstabes in Preussen und dem Deutschen Reich* (Bonn, 1921), p. 32.

the court of honor with its duel-fighting obligations—and reserve officers remained subject to this court of honor even in civilian life. The establishment of a dueling code[50] incompatible with the generally valid criminal code was psychologically made to measure for the bulk of the officer corps. The aristocracy's monopoly in the officer corps had been a technical necessity in absolutist Prussia, because no other class capable of providing competent officers existed. Officers could indeed treat other classes with contempt, but in some conditions they were themselves treated by tradesmen, artisans, and even common soldiers as good-for-nothings.[1] Under Prussian neo-feudalism, a purely aristocratic officer corps was no longer technically needed. It now became a social weapon, whose purpose was to seal the army off from those serving in its ranks, thereby counterbalancing the threat of democratization implicit in universal military service. The most rigorous scrutiny of the social status of officers' parents and wives offered a positive method of maintaining this self-contained ruling class, and the systematic exclusion from promotion to the rank of officer of all noncommissioned officers who had been recruited through conscription[51] was an equally effective negative method.

In civil administration, the Cabinet orders of 8 March and 24 May 1883 have their organizational counterpart in the Imperial Decree of 4 January 1882. In the first part of this, the Prussian constitution was interpreted to mean that the countersignature of the competent minister did not invalidate the autonomous character of royal decisions—a statement that amounted to nothing more, from a constitutional standpoint, than a royal proclamation about the privileges that the King had retained in the constitution promulgated by him.[m] The second part of the decree had a more important function. It proposed to accomplish what had been impossible in the period of conflict and in the wake of the victories of 1866 and 1870: the purging of the liberal, progressive-minded bourgeois officials from the administration as a public warning to the rising generation

---

50. The official duelling theory summarized in Walter Elze, *Tannenberg: Das deutsche Heer von 1914* (Breslau, 1928), p. 21.

51. It was also impossible for an officer to give his word of honor to a noncommissioned officer. Cf. G. Rotermund, *Kommentar zum Militärstrafgesetzbuch für das Deutsche Reich,* 2nd ed. (Hannover, 1911), p. 456.

of officials that the government would employ only politically acceptable officials. Technically the decree concentrated on an area where political attitudes were most explicitly expressed, to wit, voting behavior. While official pressure was not applied as forcefully as on military officers, who were subjected to the dueling obligation, the king demanded insistently that "those officials to whom the execution of my governmental measures is entrusted, and who can therefore be relieved of their duty in accordance to disciplinary law, are bound by their oath of office to support the policies of my government in the elections."[52] The counterpart to the feudal loyalty of the officers was to be the public servants' oath of office. Public servants were expected to be not only servants of the state—as a result of which they were quite properly subject to their special disciplinary code, which made more stringent demands on them than the general criminal code did on citizens at large. But, beyond that, they were expected to be servants of the regime and even servants of the government in power and of its determination to feudalize the bourgeoisie. The recalcitrant were clearly threatened with disciplinary action.

We have already discussed how brilliantly this policy succeeded. But despite Puttkamer's greater power, which was the basis for this success, there were two areas in which his hands were tied. For one thing, he was only Minister of the Interior for Prussia, not for the Reich as a whole. The Reich's federal institutions prevented the extension of Prussian reaction to the rest of Germany. Hessen and Baden maintained a liberal body of public servants, the South German states adopted universal suffrage after 1900, and shortly before the outbreak of the war (1912), Bavaria effectively shifted to a parliamentary form of government.[53] In the second place, municipal self-government offered persecuted political liberalism a sphere of action in which patronage was exempt from the pressure of reaction. Great as was Puttkamer's inclination to smoke liberalism out of municipal governmment—a purpose he tried to accomplish through

52. Puttkamer, p. 143. Bismarck also toyed with the idea, at the end of 1881, of giving a substantial salary raise to all public servants or at least to the county officers (*Landräte*) and political officials. "That would gain the public servants' favor!" as quoted in Lucius von Ballhausen, *op. cit.,* p. 219, December 22, 1881.

53. Fritz Hartung, *Deutsche Verfassungsgeschichte vom 15. Jahrhundert bis zur Gegenwart,* 2nd ed. (Leipzig, 1922), p. 183.

more stringent communal supervision—[54] here his efforts were frustrated.

5

Puttkamer's biographical sketch is uninformative about his personality. The only significant information concerns the contrast between his harsh public stance against progress and social democracy and his basically peaceable private outlook. We discover that he was not combative by nature, and that he did not fight his way to the top of the bureaucracy by ruthless energy or insist on pursuing a policy of his own in his ministerial capacity. He was, in a technical sense, a competent public servant, whose frictionless adaptation to the pattern of his environment carried him upward to ministerial rank. When, in this capacity, he had to carry out a policy of harshness and coercion, because Bismarck ordered him to do so, he executed it with the same exactitude and efficiency that he would have employed in implementing a policy of reconciliation, if that had been prescribed. Like many other high-ranking Prussian officials, he was capable of "doing someone else's bidding." His inner convictions were not totally fused with the external task—public service for him was a technical assignment carried out with virtuosity; he kept his inner life to himself and was reluctant to put it on display. His intellectual interests were limited—classical drama was the only form of art that appealed to him. Notwithstanding the technical significance of his interventions for the internal development of imperial Germany, his actions were solely a function of his position as Prussian Minister of the Interior and of the orders he had received to carry them out.

We have had to be satisfied with sketching briefly the background for Robert von Puttkamer's ministerial activity and regret that the biographical sketch concentrates on partisan political attacks[55] against the current situation of the Reich and Prussia instead of elucidating this background and reporting significant new details. Two

54. *Ibid.*, p. 77.
55. It would have been more useful for Mr. von Puttkammer to leave out these superfluous remarks, which have no bearing on his father's activities and to have been more careful in copying the reproduced letters. Comparison of the facsimiles with the actual text shows countless instances of careless copying.

of these attacks are an amusing contribution to the sociology of conservatism and bourgeois neo-feudalism, which feed on sheer opposition to the values and conditions of their own time and systematically applaud and glorify the past.

Minister von Puttkammer was in despair about the moral decay of the eighties:

"Our political customs and political morality have not progressed since the introduction of the secret ballot for the Reichstag; on the contrary, things have been going downhill since that time."[56]

"In the large centers of commerce and industry, teachers' moral conduct has suffered a most flagrant decline. . . . It must be accepted as a proved fact that in response to the cycles of industrial expansion and decline, moral conditions in the teaching profession are registering similar fluctuations."[57]

This period of moral decline is the one which, in the eyes of his son, represents the flowering of German parliamentary institutions:

"If we closely examine the reports of this memorable day in the German Parliament,[58] we are inevitably made aware of the inferior level of parliamentary government in our own days. We need but look at the names of the speakers in the debate of that day."[59]

"Various parliamentary party groups included in their ranks men who raised the level of representative government to a height that was hardly surpassed by the Frankfurt Parliament (sic!) This was true of all parties, including the Social Democrats."[60]

This is how a spokesman for the German-National (*Deutsch-national*) party evaluated the level of the German Reichstag in the days when it was tightly held in check by Bismarck, lest parliamentary government lead to Germany's collapse, and when contemporaries vied in bewailing the decline of the parliamentary level and gloomily pointed to the high level attained by the parliament in the Paulskirche. It is a shame that in 1848 it was impossible to deplore the decline of parliamentary government, not because this parliament represented the acme of perfection but because there existed

56. Reichstag address, 1883, p. 157.
57. Reichstag address, 1880, p. 53.
58. Reichstag debate of January 24, 1882 concerning His Highness's decree of January 1882 (see above).
59. Puttkamer, p. 151.
60. *Ibid.*, p. 75

no previous German parliament to be idealized. If we only wait another thirty or forty years, the "spiritual" heir of Mr. von Keudell will use his father's biography to praise the glories of German politics—in the days when his reactionary father defended the opposite view.

6

In conclusion, we would like to touch upon a highly controversial and still unclarified problem, which has methodological significance for the practical application of the theory of the supra- and infrastructure: the question of liberalism among the East Prussian nobility, a problem with which Robert von Puttkamer had to contend as district officer in Gumbinnen. In the biography,[61] this East Prussian liberalism is summarily traced back to the agrarian reforms of Stein and Hardenberg,° which resulted in driving a part of the East Prussian large landowners into "a principled opposition to the Prussian government. Resistance to the government in monarchist Prussia in most other cases was equivalent to making common cause with the Progressive party [*Fortschrittspartei*]." Aside from the fact that the concluding sentence is a German-Nationalist catch phrase, this thesis in no way accounts for the fact that opposition to agrarian reform persisted in East Prussia and nowhere else, although it was originally just as vigorous in the other provinces: the Pomeranian nobility viewed the emancipation of the peasantry as a destruction of private property; the Silesian nobility predicted the collapse of the state and was not ashamed to requisition soldiers from the French occupation army in order to force the peasants to resume the performance of services from which they had been freed; in Brandenburg, opposition leaders—the arch-reactionary von der Marwitz[P] among them—had to be taken to Spandau. Political historiography is inclined to account for the liberalism of the East Prussian nobility in terms of foreign-policy factors; it envisions the liberal as well as the national opposition to the government in the threatened border provinces of East Prussia and the Rhineland as a natural response to the reactionary regime's lack of nationalist fervor after 1819. However, this explanation too is obviously inade-

61. *Ibid.*, p. 27

quate. The decisive basis of the liberalism of the East Prussian aristocracy was actually social and economic.

In the seventeenth century, internal political developments in the northeastern German states centered on the struggle between *dominium* and *domanium*, that is, on the contested ownership of the estates (*Rittergüter*) between the absolutist ruler of the principality and the landed nobility. The sooner the nobility capitulated to the prince, the more likely was the victorious ruler to leave it in control of a substantial proportion of the contested estates. In East Prussia the opposition of the estates proved to be more unyielding than elsewhere, and it was therefore the last to be suppressed. The following statistics reflect the final outcome: in 1800, the Crown was in possession of 326,000 hoofed animals, the aristocracy of a mere 164,000.[62] The East Prussian aristocracy never forgave the victorious Crown for this drastic curtailment of its possessions, and estatist opposition manifested itself at every conceivable opportunity. For this reason, Frederick the Great, rightly from his absolutist standpoint, refused the East Prussian aristocracy the privilege of establishing a rural credit organization comparable to the one that had been founded in Silesia: "They are unwilling to serve the Crown or to do anything for it, so his Highness will not do anything for them either."[63] And after his successor finally gave his approval to the credit organization, under the pressure of his own high-level bureaucracy, which was personally interested in developing agrarian capitalism, this credit cooperative (*Landschaft*) became the focus of estatist opposition to the monarchy. The German nobility took the lead in the general reluctance to pay taxes between 1807 and 1815,[64] and in 1813, at the height of the war, it was the East Prussian nobility that carried things to the point of refusing to transmit to Berlin the monies collected to finance the war.[65]

There is no intrinsic reason why this estatist opposition could not

---

62. Max Lehmann, *Freiherr vom Stein* (Berlin, 1902), II, 40. Theodor von Schön once referred to the Gumbinnen district as "this domain province" in *Briefe und Aktenstücke aus dem Nachlass Staegemanns* (Leipzig, 1899), I, 156.
63. Cabinet Order of June 1, 1781 in Hermann Mauer, *Das landschaftliche Kreditwesen Preussens* (Strassburg, 1907), p. 10.
64. Lehmann, *op. cit*, II, 201.
65. Karl Mamroth, *Geschichte der preussischen Staatsbesteuerung im 19. Jahrhundert* (Leipzig, 1890), I, 756.

have been conservative and reactionary. Its liberal and progressive features must be attributed to economic factors rather than to the opposition to the Hohenzollern dynasty.

In the eighteenth century, East Prussia was the most backward of all backward Prussian provinces; it had no factories and no kind of capital market, but it did have a highly developed trading system. Its location on the sea encouraged grain export to England and Holland, and its proximity to the Polish and later to the Russian border gave rise to a profitable transit trade in textiles, which were brought in by sea and shipped to Lithuania and Poland. The textile transit trade and the grain export gave its distinctive character to the East Prussian upper class in the later mercantilist period and set it off from the rest of protectionist Prussia: this upper class was in favor of free trade, since its existence was predicated on free trade with England and Poland.[66] The decisive factor was that the economic group that had a stake in this trade, besides the merchant class, was not composed of factory owners producing the export items but of estate owners and domain tenants producing grain for export. The overseas export of grain turned the East Prussian aristocracy into liberal free traders, won general acceptance for Adam Smith's theory in East Prussia, and thereby created the atmosphere in which Kant's moral philosophy could take root and influence the leaders of Prussian reform.[67] It was only in the reactionary period of the eighteen eighties, epitomized by Robert von Puttkamer, that East Prussian liberalism, which had gradually developed into a peasant liberalism, was carried to its grave: after 1900, in the same voting districts that had still elected liberal deputies in the seventies, liberals received only 10 percent of the victorious Conservatives' votes.[68]

66. Characteristically, there was a strong irritation about England in 1807–1808, because its ambition to rule the seas was perpetually leading to war and causing trade to be cut off, thereby provoking sympathy for the French cause in commercial circles, in contrast to official policy.

67. Arnold Oskar Meyer's essay "Kants Ethik und der preussische Staat" in *Festschrift Erich Marcks zum 60. Geburtstag* (Stuttgart, 1921) makes short shrift of the theory taken for granted in imperial Germany that Kant's sense of duty could only have originated in Prussia, but unfortunately limits itself to Kant's own thinking and neglects his surroundings. See also Carl Brinkmann, *Die preussische Handelspolitik vor dem Zollverein* (Berlin, 1922), p. 8.

68. Arthur Rosenberg, *Die Entstehung der deutschen Republik 1871–1918* (Berlin, 1928), p. 263.

CHAPTER VII

The Sociology of the *Reichswehr*

A chasm yawns today in Germany between the unwritten constitution of the army on the one hand and, on the other, the written constitution of the Reich and the also unwritten constitution of its society. The Social Democratic party is a major party, which controls the largest state within the state and from whose ranks the President of the Reich and many of its ministers have been and continue to be selected; it has the greatest numerical strength and can exert as much influence as this numerical strength warrants. And yet the Social Democratic party is not in a position to prevail on a single one of its party members to serve in the enlisted ranks of the army, and certainly not in its officer corps. And I am not even using the term party membership in its narrow sense of formal party affiliation, but simply to denote the broader circle of Social Democratic voters. Conversely, the German-National party is in a doubly favorable position, in that its members can participate in the Reich government and take over the office of Reich President, and at the same time fill all positions in the army, thereby giving the party simultaneous access to political and military influence. The army of our present state is recruited almost exclusively among the adherents of a single party and is isolated from all other parties.

Whenever one talks with officers about the isolation of the army in our democracy, the point is immediately raised that the Peace Treaty of Versailles is to blame for this, because it foisted a mercenary army on Germany. But the Versailles treaty is merely being used here as a social whipping boy, and it is unjust to blame it for this state of affairs. Although the mercenary army is a contributing factor in the isolated position of the Reichswehr, its impact is different from what the officers imagine; in any case, it does not play a decisive role. Far more important than the method of recruiting the troops is the makeup of the officer corps and the relations maintained between it, that is, the possessors of military power, and the possessors of political power. The sociological composition of the rank and file can safely be disregarded. "It never makes any difference when the officer corps functions as it should, that is, when it is authoritative. The officer determines the character of the troops, and the troops will be a reflection of his own character."[1] This relationship between the military and the political leadership is at the root of the discrepancy that constitutes the decisive problem of today's Reichswehr.

If a state maintains an armed force of any sort, there is no way it can avoid the central problem of bringing the structure of this armed force into harmony with the structure of society and political power. Prussian absolutism brilliantly solved this problem from its own point of view and kept the two sides balanced. Of the three major social groups, the aristocracy, the peasantry, and the bourgeoisie, each had a place assigned to it in the military hierarchy, respectively, officer corps, rank and file, and people exempt from military service. The aristocracy was handsomely rewarded for its military management, and the company commander could use his men as farm laborers on his father's or brother's estate when they were not in training. The army's organization was perfectly adapted to the country's social structure and the economic requirements of the ruling class. The Prussian reform era altered those features of the army that were geared to the aristocracy's economic requirements, but left intact those that corresponded to the social structure. The only modification was that the bourgeois was now also subject to military service, but, if he had a modicum of educa-

1. Franz Carl Endres, "Soziologische Struktur und ihr entsprechende Ideologien des deutschen Offizierkorps vor dem Weltkriege," *Archiv für Sozialwissenschaft und Sozialpolitik,* LVIII (1927), 308.

tion, he quickly passed into the new class of militia *(Landwehr)* officers that had been created for him and that commanded the new militia force, now placed alongside the standing army.[a]

The establishment of the militia was an attempt to perpetuate the separation of the estates that dated from the absolutist era: aristocracy and peasantry were to remain in the line army, and the bourgeoisie was to consider the militia its own army. As long as the bourgeoisie and hence the bourgeois army, the militia, raised no political demands, this experiment could safely be pursued, but once the bourgeoisie began to show signs of political activity, the Prussian state realized that by maintaining the separation of the estates in the army, it was laying the groundwork for an armed civil war and pressing weapons in the hands of its political and social adversary. The militia was dissolved, and its regiments incorporated into the regular regiments; at the same time, the elimination of the militia's officer corps put an end to the organization of the bourgeois opposition's military leaders. The newly established reserve-officer corps,[2] which from the eighties on conferred social prestige upon its members, was by means of the supervision provided by the officers' mess kept closer to the spirit of the career-officer corps than had been true of the militia's officer corps. The bourgeoisie was reintegrated into the army on condition that it resume its former status, just as it was reintegrated into the state as a whole on condition that it accept its spiritual subservience to the military monarchy.

The Hohenzollerns were as brilliantly successful in coming to terms with the bourgeoisie and liberalism as they had been in dealing with the aristocracy in the eighteenth century. It was a different story with the working class and social democracy, with which they were unable to cope from the eighties on. The middle class was given a share of state power, though not the lion's share, but the Social Democrat was barred from any participation in the state and could not even serve in the army as a one-year volunteer.[b]

The system reached this critical state even before the outbreak of the World War, when the army reached the million mark. The famous 1913 proposal for an additional three army corps was rejected because the Minister of War felt that the social homogeneity

2. [See above, Chapter V.]

of the officer corps could not withstand this strain and would threaten a democratization of the officers.[3] The army's upper limit was determined not by the amount of money approved by the Reichstag but by the possibility of preserving the homogeneity of the officer corps and by its ability to put the troops through their paces in a sufficiently authoritarian manner. This upper limit had been reached, if not exceeded, by 1913. France, on the other hand, was able to build up a larger army than Germany because after the failure of the Commune experiment,[c] that is, after the final stabilization of the social and political structure of the Third Republic in the eighties, it could afford to disregard such social considerations in the composition of its army.

Prussian militarism was responsible for blocking the unlimited expansion of the army. This is not as paradoxical as it sounds, for militarism is not a function of numerical army strength but of the existence of a class of officers who segregate themselves from the rest of the nation as a specially honored warrior caste and of a bourgeoisie that accepts the superiority of this caste and is willing to submit to it.

The World War resulted in the destruction of this social system of the old army, even before the outbreak of the revolution. The heavy losses at the beginning of the war called for a greatly expanded new officer corps and the establishment of new formations. The number of reserve officers had been kept at a minimum before 1914, to maintain the social level at any price. Even in wartime, efforts were made to select the temporarily commissioned lieutenants according to the old social stereotype, but almost invariably one had to resort to militia officers rather than the old-style reserve officers. And by then it was too late to worry about the internal political reliability of the troops in this gigantic army. The standing army of prewar days, which had been a pliable instrument in the hands of the Supreme Military Commander, had changed into a citizens' army, which was useless for internal political action.

This development was not a harbinger of future solutions. Had Germany been victorious, the old tendencies would have reasserted

3. Prussian Minister of War von Heeringen to the General Staff, 20 January 1913, quoted in Hans Herzfeld, *Die deutsche Rüstungspolitik vor dem Weltkrieg* (Bonn, 1923), p. 63.

themselves with a vengeance. As things turned out, the trend toward a citizens' army culminated during the revolution in conditions of anarchy among the troops, and the militia officers (that is, the lieutenants with temporary commissions) left the army to look for civilian employment. From the start, the new army that was set up after 1919 lost the militialike elements of the army of the World War, and it therefore retained, or rather attracted once more, the same elements as the prewar army: career officers and, through recruitment, troops who had the same rapport with their commanders as the prewar officer corps had had with the Supreme Military Commander. The residue of the old army's private and intimate character, based on the special bonds between officer and king, was intensified in 1919/20 with the creation of the free corps,[d] private organizations that at first relied on personal and extragovernmental commitments and were supported only to a minor extent by loyalty toward the state. The ties with the monarch were projected on the leaders of the free corps and, after the consolidation of the Reichswehr, were shifted once more to the chief of the army command, or, more specifically, to the man who served in this capacity, General von Seeckt.[e] The Reichswehr was loyal to Seeckt in the same way that the mercenary *Landsknechte* were loyal to their captains: they were ready to fight at the orders of this supercaptain of the *Landsknechte* but not at the orders of the state. There developed a relation of loyalty that coexisted with the oath to the constitution and perhaps surpassed it in fervor. Although the World War had led to a disillusionment with both political and military leaders, the military could not shed their belief that men were the shapers of history.

There is a serious weakness, however, in this faith in the leader, the great man; its danger lies in times of crisis, when the leader is determined to strike out and carries out this intention. In quiet times this faith is harmless, because of its passive character; the Reichswehr waits for orders, and, if none are given, it remains quiet. That is why the Reichswehr uncomplainingly accepted Seeckt's fall and contents itself with waiting until he returns.[f]

With Seeckt's dismissal, the visible surrogate for the supreme military commander disappeared, but even in retirement Seeckt has retained this role. The Reichswehr is incapable of getting along without this fiction of a supreme military commander, and for this the officer corps must bear the blame. The *ancien régime's* officer corps represented a social class, a social power, an institution conferring a social nimbus, which was even reflected on the bourgeoisie through the reserve-officer system. The Reichswehr officer corps today is a purely professional class; in contrast to prewar conditions, officers now receive adequate pay from the start. However, there are no longer any social advantages connected with this profession; it has just become a profession like many others. From the point of view of their social position, officers have been converted into military technicians pure and simple, just as there are aviation and postal-service technicians. This shift from a social to a professional status has resulted in the disappearance from the army of the wealthy bourgeois officer, a figure that was common before the war and thanks to which more than one cavalry regiment was nicknamed "Association of Mounted Merchants." From a technical military standpoint, the disappearance of this group of officers is to the Reichswehr's advantage, but socially it reflects the fact that Reichswehr officers no longer occupy their former place on the social ladder and have had to accept the fact that they had fallen in the social scale. It is not surprising that this demoted professional class still has the same pretensions as the former social class and tries to maintain them artificially. It is encouraged in this tendency by the Reichswehr's praetorian character, which was taken over from the old army. It was the king's command, the orders of the Supreme Military Commander, that activated the royal Prussian army, which was, for all practical purposes, the king's private property. Although Seeckt could at best be viewed as an ideological surrogate for this supreme military commander who no longer existed, behind him there was nothing but an ill-defined mass of political and social influences that vacillated this way and that and were incapable of producing a unified military policy. In the absence of any personality that could leave its mark on the Reichswehr, for lack of a political party bold or strong enough to shape the army according to its own will, the Reichswehr withdrew into itself and isolated itself from all tendencies that determine the modern state.

However much it complains about this state of affairs, it is social democracy that has been the major culprit in isolating the

Reichswehr. Neither before 1914 nor after the war was it able to agree on a half-way coherent stand on armament policy. It was unsure itself concerning what it had in mind with its demand for a citizens' army (Julius Deutsch[g] openly admitted this), and its attempts after 1918 to democratize the army by fine-sounding decrees and the introduction of military "stewards" *(Vertrauensmänner)* did not prevent its own adherents from keeping away from the army and leaving a free field to the old officers. Carnot[h] had a free hand in building up a new army from the rank and file after the desertion of the old officers during the French Revolution. Noske[i] had no choice but to build up the new Reichswehr on the basis of its officers, because no regular soldiers wishing to give the republic positive support could be recruited in its ranks. If the objective had been to establish an army whose relation with the new state was like that of the old Prussian army to its state, that would have implied giving as many special privileges to the workers, as the old army had given the aristocracy in the officer corps and the upper bourgeoisie in the reserve-officer corps. But this solution was out of the question; the working class did not win single-handed; the proportional strength of the different groups in 1919 was reflected by the Weimar coalition. And even if the workers had won single-handed, they were tired of the war, they had been pacifist in principle before the war and had hated the state that made them join the army by the coercion of universal military service. Why should they now serve as soldiers under exactly the same officers as before the war? The result was that they failed to enlist. The soldiers' councils did their best to prevent new formations from being established, thereby giving officers the opportunity to recruit men they considered reliable for these new formations. The Social Democrats' pacifist inclinations and their faith in the possibility of internal disarmament collided with their interest, as members of a revolutionary movement, in protecting by force the power position they had just won. It was the pacifist tendencies that prevailed, thereby dooming the German revolution to failure and assuring the rebuilding of an army unaffected by the revolution.

The fact that it was possible to rebuild the Reichswehr on the basis of its officers rather than its rank and file was initially due to the abstention of the workers, but the continuation of this policy up to the present must be attributed to a different cause, which has nothing to do with the military. The Reichswehr is the first mercenary army that is in a position to screen its recruits, because the supply is bigger than the demand. There is no need for the Reichswehr to look for recruits; it is flooded with requests for admission and can turn down anyone that it deems unsuitable. What has brought about this enviable situation is the high level of unemployment, thanks to which the Reichswehr can secure reasonably well-qualified manpower for its troops. The devaluation of the old one-year-service certificate *(Einjährigenzeugnis)* as a condition of employment leads many *Gymnasium* students in their second-to-last year to enlist in the Reichswehr, where they are eagerly welcomed.[j] These recruits largely belong to the lower middle class, which was in opposition to the state before the war and is now again in opposition to the new state, then as Social Democrats and now as German Nationalists, and which today feels a natural affinity with the officer corps.

But though it is true that the Social Democratic movement and the Weimar coalition[k] in the broader sense suffered a catastrophic defeat in bringing the military constitution into harmony with the political constitution, partly through their own fault and partly through the force of circumstances, the Reichswehr's victory in the long run will prove to be a Pyrrhic victory and will lead the Reichswehr into a blind alley.

The officer corps of the Reichswehr is always on the lookout for a leader, for a great man; the officers want to be given orders like praetorians, without wishing to be informed of the purpose of the command. The prewar army, notwithstanding its name of people's army *(Volksheer)* "was an instrument of the dynasty, whose raw material was provided by the people."[4] As a mercenary army, it is easier for the Reichswehr in a democratic state to maintain this tendency of serving as the instrument of some individual, be it a monarch, as in former days, or a dictator, as might happen in our time. The army of the *ancien régime* had at least, in addition to the dynastic cadre, a force of 100,000 men passing through its ranks every year, men who came from civilian life and returned to civilian life, whereas today's Reichswehr, as a mercenary army, is self-

4. Endres, *op. cit.*

contained. The dictated Versailles treaty, by forbidding universal military service, certainly shares the blame for the social isolation of the Reichswehr, but not in the way the officers had in mind. In a conscripted army, the maintenance of prodictatorial elements in the officer corps would not be feasible. Just try to visualize what would happen if a leftist government wanted to set up a leftist militia and thus to eliminate the Reichswehr as an internal political threat. But the Reichswehr is a mercenary force, and therefore its social structure, despite its incompatibility with the Reich's political structure, is protected by the Treaty of Versailles.

There is a second link between the present structure of the Reichswehr and foreign policy. Let us disregard all current foreign political assumptions for a moment. If one is concerned with the question of the German military situation, the problem inevitably arises: is Germany capable of raising a large army with this military structure in case of war? The Treaty of Versailles forced the Reichswehr on us because the Big Four regarded this military structure as a way of preventing the raising of an army in time of war. This plan misfired. The Reichswehr has been developed as a cadre army to the point that it can easily be expanded to many times its present strength in time of war. The Treaty of Versailles has deprived Germany of technical military weapons, but it could not prevent the establishment of a new army. But Germany's incapacity to exploit this possibility of fleshing out the professional core of the Reichswehr is a function of the Reichswehr's nature. A grave crisis would immediately break out if the working masses were to be fitted into this socially alien framework. The danger lies not so much in their refusal to do military service as in the incapacity of this officer corps to lead large masses of workers. We are reminded of old Theodor Mommsen's remark that something is rotten in any state with an army in which a soldier cannot become an officer.

When one deplores Germany's inability to defend itself, one must not always put the blame on the Versailles treaty with its prohibition of technical means of war but should also blame the Reichswehr, which itself obstructs the road to victory through its social attitude, which is vividly expressed in its policy of recruitment.

CHAPTER VIII

The Genesis of the Prussian Bureaucracy and the *Rechtsstaat*

A Contribution to the Dictatorship Problem[1]

1

The birth of the modern state coincides with the rise of absolutism. The state is a product of two factors:

1. The ruling prince's struggle against the private monopolistic power of the money lenders in the early capitalist period, of whom Fugger and Welser are the best known examples.[a] These monopolists extended credit to the prince, by which he could satisfy his politically generated pecuniary needs, which had outstripped his economic resources. Concentration of capital in the hands of these financiers stemmed from a few large, lucrative enterprises. The loans enabled the prince to carry out his policies without founding them on a broadly based tax revenue regularly collected by a bureaucracy. At the same time, this arrangement confronted the ruler, in his never-ending financial straits, with economic powers that were their

1. Ernst Fraenkel's article in the October 1931 issue of *Die Gesellschaft* raises the question of the demise of the *Rechtsstaat* resulting from the blurring of the distinction between laws and administrative regulations. His contribution sheds further light on Dessauer's brilliant and highly original exposition in his *Recht, Richtertum und Ministerialbürokratie* (Mannheim, 1928). My own essay attempts to explain this demise of the *Rechtsstaat* by a sociologically oriented analysis of the genesis of the distinction between laws and administrative regulations in Prussia. I shall also analyze the reasons why this distinction could be maintained until now and clarify where we are at this juncture by retracing as unequivocally as possible how matters have evolved in the last hundred years. In view of the large number of problems raised and the inadequacy of scholarly works on which I could draw, I will have to limit myself to sketching in the lines of development.

own masters and openly flaunted their strength. Jakob Fugger, who had financed the election of Charles V to the imperial throne,[b] had no qualms about mentioning in one of his later letters: "Your Imperial Majesty could never have won the Roman crown without my assistance."

2. The prince's conflict with the legally sanctioned power positions of the estates, which were upholding the claim that public authorities depended on the consent of the social strata supporting them, a medieval tradition that is the feudal counterpart of democratic ideas.

Absolutism requires a transfer of power over the state from the tripartite condominium exercised jointly—or competitively—by the estates, the monopolists, and the prince, to the prince's exclusive private possession. To use Jellinek's expression,[2] this transfer represented a grandiose expropriation process, inaugurated in northeastern Europe by the confiscation of noblemen's estates, and in southwestern Europe by a series of state bankruptcies; the end product of this expropriation was the transformation of the state into a trust under the sole management of the prince, who could freely dispose of all financial, military, and human resources.

In the military realm, this transformation was embodied in divesting the armies of their private character. They ceased to be the private property of the "captains," whose last and most brilliant representative was Wallenstein,[c] and came to be the property of the prince. As a result of the compromise reached with the estates, the common people became more strictly subjected to princely authority. The estates were excluded from political power, but their economic position was left intact, and the peasantry was placed at their mercy by more stringent forms of serfdom. Independence from monopoly capitalist loans was won at the price of establishing a fiscal apparatus: the state bureaucracy.

The first timid approaches toward a bureaucracy date back to the twelfth and thirteenth centuries and become more evident in the fifteenth and sixteenth centuries. Nevertheless, Western bureaucracy is a product of absolutism. Even so, it was not the Hohenzollern monarchy that initiated Prussian bureaucracy in its nineteenth-

2. Georg Jellinek, *Der Kampf des alten mit dem neuen Recht. Ausgewahlte Schriften* I, (Berlin, 1911), 406.

century guise and in the form in which it persists today as the Reich's bureaucracy. If bureaucracy is more than an arrangement whereby routine business is carried out by menials, we must conceive it not in symbiosis with monarchy but in opposition to it. Absolute monarchy was incapable of tolerating an autonomous bureaucracy at its side. The bureaucratic machinery elaborated by the two great eighteenth-century Hohenzollern did not operate autonomously. It functioned on a merely technical level (and inefficiently at that), its sole purpose being the execution of the princely director general's will. To reinforce this dependency organizationally, nobody was allowed to gain any insight into the operation of the apparatus as a whole. The dictatorship of Frederick the Great was predicated on the maintenance of rivalries between the different pseudo ministers in charge. His cabinet government (in contrast to the state of affairs in the last years before 1806) remained a mere technical improvisation for expediting the performance of public services.

Absolutism in its prime had a powerful weapon to ward off possible engulfment of the absolute monarchy by the absolute bureaucracy it had spawned. This was to place members of the aristocracy in the highest administrative echelons, although the bureaucracy, which had been recruited from "bourgeois," that is nonaristocratic, elements, had been set up in the first place to act as a weapon against the aristocracy. The resulting cleavage in the administration into two classes would then inevitably generate social rivalry between them and eliminate the danger that the apparatus might unite in its opposition against the monarch at its head.[3] Such a danger might well arise otherwise, for although the nonaristocratic functionaries, being exclusively dependent on their salaries or their officially sanctioned[4] bribes and not having won any pension rights as yet, could be manipulated as easily as salaried personnel can be today,

3. *Cf.* a lecture by Otto Hintze published in an abbreviated version in *Forschungen zur Brandenburgischen und Preussischen Geschichte,* IX (1897), 339–340. The issues involved here are barely adumbrated in his essay "Die Hohenzollern und der Adel," *Historische Zeitschrift,* V (1914), 112, since the thrust of his polemics is directed against Maurenbrecher's "Hohenzollern legend" and social democracy.

4. This applied only during the reign of Frederick William I. Frederick II, for his part, introduced fantastically high salaries to eliminating this corruption. These high salaries still persist here and there under the stamp of traditional Prussian frugality.

employees in the top echelons of the expanding apparatus inevitably gained positions of power equivalent to those of the "expendable" top managers in today's private firms. No precaution could prevent the consequences of this expansion of the apparatus, which culminated in the situation characterizing the last decades of Frederician rule. During that time the personal wishes of the monarch were constantly at odds with the opinions of the ministers in their role as technical experts. The king had no way to avoid subjection to his own bureaucracy except resort to expedients that would be hard to justify objectively—like the institution of self-governing economic agencies (analogous to the practice common in exotic or semiexotic states of calling in American experts for financial advice) or alternatively, the throwing of any privy councillor bold enough to criticize his economic policies into jail.

Even the recruitment of the aristocracy into the bureaucracy and the concomitant paralyzing conflict between it and the bourgeoisie failed in the long run to safeguard the prince's position at the top of the hierarchy. By exploiting the positions of power it had been officially granted, the aristocracy was able to organize agrarian credit societies (*Landschaften*) as early as 1770 and to lay the foundations of speculative agrarian capitalism,[5] thereby pursuing and eventually succeeding in a policy of independence from the absolutist economic policy from which it derived its subsidies: a policy of reemancipation from absolutism that found its ideological superstructure a generation later in the Romantic movement.[d]

The administrative apparatus that had been created by an absolutist state whose main basis was agrarian, in spite of some industrial pretensions, could not cope with the problems generated by incipient capitalist developments in northern Germany in the final third of the eighteenth century. Textile production, which was presumably managed rationally by the king's orders to the Cabinet, and which was at the core of all absolutist welfare politics, turned into a center of corruption, in which the bribing of ministers, privy councillors in the General Directory, and Cabinet councillors

5. Moritz Weyermann's *Zur Geschichte des Immobiliarkreditwesens in Preussen* (Karlsruhe, 1910) has attracted little attention, though his material is indispensable for understanding the early stages of Prussian conservatism.

became a common and effective practice.[6] And the absolute state, in its fear that a joint-stock bank *(Aktiennotenbank)* might foster a "dependency" on the financial requirements of the private sector of the economy, was left no choice in the end but to encourage a monopoly capitalism in the hands of Jewish silver merchants alongside its own administrative machinery. The bureaucracy could keep this monopoly capitalism in check only temporarily. Shortly before 1806, the government's economic policy became subservient to the profit interests of these monopoly capitalists,[7] a glaring evidence, during this final stage of absolutism, that its tendency to paralyze conflicting class interests by a compensating *pouvoir neutre* could lead to absurd consequences.

2

Even Frederick the Great, all his personal gifts notwithstanding, succeeded only formally and superficially in restraining the inflationary pressure of agrarian capitalism to increase the price of land. His control over the continually expanding bureaucratic apparatus was equally precarious. When he died, agrarian capitalism gained the upper hand; the silver monopolies acquired positions of great power shortly thereafter. The bureaucracy's first victory over the new monarch consisted in its securing the irremovability (tenure) of public servants, or at least the principle of making them removable not according to the monarch's whim but in response to the findings of disciplinary authorities composed of the peers of the accused official. Of the two time-honored rights of public officials taken for granted today, tenure and pension rights, tenure came first. Retirement pensions as a right rather than an act of charity were not secured until 1820. The important thing, it was felt, was to protect the bureaucracy from royal intervention, rather than securing a comfortable life for public servants.

The successful struggle for tenure marks the beginning of the

6. *Cf.* Otto Hintze, *Die Preussische Seidenindustrie im 18. Jahrhundert* (Berlin, 1892), II, 646, footnote 1.
7. Friedrich Freiherr von Schrötter's *Das Preussische Münzwesen im 18. Jahrhundert*, 4 vols (Berlin, 1904–1912) is uninformative with respect to questions that do not concern the technical aspects of coins. Social and economic problems regarding the silver monopoly are treated superficially.

overt takeover of the monarchy by the bureaucracy. Baron vom Stein, the man who led the bureaucracy to victory, never failed to express his opposition to bureaucracy in words and convictions. Yet in his administrative practice he proved himself a typical bureaucrat of the declining *ancien régime*. He was appointed minister in 1804 in the wake of the revolt of the privy councillors of the General Directory against the king's commands, un unprecedented event in Prussia. The king never forgave Stein for having been imposed on him by the bureaucracy. Even three years later, in the order for Stein's dismissal on January 3, 1807, the king was to say: "I gave in."

In 1805 and 1806, as the decisive stage of the bureaucracy's struggle was approaching, Stein was a champion of this dictatorship, which was about to replace the power structure of absolutism in its waning years. With a total lack of perspective, he simultaneously attacked the various positions of strength that blocked the progress of bureaucratic absolutism. He attempted to eliminate the aristocracy's tax-exempt status and its privileged position generally. This first attack misfired even before Jena.[e] He then sought to destroy the power of the monopoly capitalists, who were making the economic ministers dance to their tunes, but here too he misjudged the great strength of his opponents. He achieved nothing positive, and, on the negative side of the ledger, the financial collapse of Prussia, which took place long before that fateful 14th of October,[f] must be attributed to his actions. In conjunction with his attack on the nobility and monopoly capitalism, he was also waging a struggle against the "Cabinet," to which Frederick the Great's Secretariat had been converted after his death, and which the weakened monarchy had inserted as a buffer between itself and the power-hungry bureaucracy. Between April and December 1806, he waged a relentless smear campaign aimed at having the cabinet councillors thrown out of office—in the hope of taking their place himself. This campaign miscarried and led to his own dismissal. Stein's case is an example of the use of ideologies for purposes of obfuscation, not only during the actual events of 1805/6[8] and during his second ministry, 1807/8, a time that was rife with false issues,

8. For a scathing criticism of Stein the politician, see Georg Winter's *Die Reorganisation des Preussischen Staates unter Stein und Hardenberg,* vol. 1 (Publikationen aus den Preussischen Staatsarchiven, vol. 93), (Leipzig, 1931).

but also in the writings of later historians, who fell under their spell and tried to use them politically as tools of antiabsolutist liberalism. The commemoration for Stein held in 1931 amply demonstrated that even many Socialists are so conformist in their historical views that they uncritically accept the bourgeois Left's ideological elucidation of the past, even where it is incompatible with a materialist interpretation of history. Baron vom Stein was a conservative and defender of the estates, a man in whom an irreconcilable contradiction prevailed between high-minded convictions, vague, incoherent programs for political reforms, and reactionary interventions, a man who inadvertently cleared the way for the dictatorship of the Prussian bureaucracy and who, by destroying monopoly capitalism and aristocratic privileges, also triggered the disintegration and levelling of the rigidly structured estate-type society of the eighteenth century. Yet he was acclaimed as a liberal democrat (as that term was understood by the *Deutsche Staatspartei*)[g] and credited with such notable contributions as the unleashing of ethical-individualist forces, the sponsoring of administrative reforms, and the fostering of self-government.

Local self-government became significant only in the second half of the nineteenth century, when it rescued urban development from the unitary administration of a semifeudal military monarchy by converting towns into islands of self-government. In 1808/9 the towns fought bitterly against self-government, which in practice meant the transfer of heavy financial burdens from the bureaucracy onto the shoulders of its social competitor, the despised and yet fear-inspiring bourgeoisie, which had gained a measure of autonomy and wealth, at least in its upper strata, as a consequence of the war. This was the net outcome of Stein's ideology of self-government. Stein's administrative reform—the merging of the State Council with the ministries—never worked. What is more, it amounted at best to a reshuffling of the upper administrative levels, a reorganization whose social foundations had been laid earlier. For it was during Hardenberg's three-months' rule as Prime Minister, April through July 1807, that the dictatorship of the bureaucracy first manifested itself as a substitute for both the monarch and his surrogate, and that the ministerial bureaucracy intervened as an activating, independent, and crucial political factor. Hardenberg surrounded himself with a small clique of highly qualified young privy councillors—Staegemann, Schön, Altenstein, Niebuhr.[h] These men were the first to operate in the guise of secretaries of state and ministerial directors, serving as "experienced aides"—in the official jargon of the time—to the minister in charge of "policy" and making decisions for him. The typical bureaucratic structure, which Karl Twesten[i] once defined in these terms: "Hermetically closed toward the outside, torn by strife and animosities within,"[9] emerged at that time rather than under Stein. The triumph of the clique of ministerial directors was not simply a matter of replacing the king's influence by that of the privy councillors. Beyond that, the clique launched ruthlessly brutal and slanderous attacks on its opponents, showing openly its determination to entrench itself in office and expand its influence. In the end, the opponents were expelled from office, and the clique succeeded in stabilizing its sovereignty *comme un rocher de bronze* like that of Frederick William I,[j] toward the outside and within the bureaucracy itself.

Beginning with the spring of 1807, when Hardenberg's clique had its first taste of the sweetness of power, and more markedly after Hardenberg's 1810 appointment as State Chancellor, the Prussian bureaucracy offered a homogeneous board of regents *(Regentenkollegium)* with a broad republican base and a monarch at the helm, whose members were selected by cooptation, just as happens in modern parliamentary party delegations. Having secured the right not to be removed except through disciplinary action and the right to a retirement pension, the bureaucratic dictatorship was invulnerable to any challenge either by the king or, in later years, by the bourgeoisie. Since no political regime could survive without a bureaucratic executive apparatus, every Prussian regime wishing to replace this bureaucratic dictatorship was first compelled to come to terms with the persons previously in power, who were at the same time the only available administrative experts. In the end, the new regime had to guarantee the bureaucracy's privileges and power for the sake of its own survival. The power still held by today's bureaucracy can be traced back to the intermeshing and fusing of administration and politics in the first half of the nineteenth century,

9. Karl Twesten, *Was uns noch retten kann: Ein Wort ohne Umschweife* (Berlin, 1861).

which was a by-product of the supplanting of the monarchy by the bureaucracy.

3

No bloody revolution was required in this displacement process. All action took place inside the ministries with the countersigning of Cabinet orders, with speeches, debates, proposed laws and enacted laws, that is, with typically parliamentarian methods. The condition indispensable for a bureaucratic political regime in the eyes of modern political theory, namely "the conduct of state affairs, on the whole, within a solid framework,"[10] could not have been met at that time, nor was there the stability on the basis of which things could be left to the bureaucracy. On the contrary, all lines of development were still shrouded in mist, not only with respect to foreign policy, but also in terms of social and economic realignments within the country.

In the course of this realignment process, the bureaucracy was obliged to come to terms with existing politico-social forces. The monarchy, from which it formally took over most of its attributes, presented the least difficulties. The reigning monarch, intellectually handicapped as he was, relinquished his power willingly, seeking only to retain the Cabinet Council as a buffer against Baron vom Stein's unpredictable political actions. Stein's intolerable behavior served to limit his own authority power, but with the exception of the period of his government, Frederick William III actually flung his power at the feet of his ministers. When a minister proved incapable of exercising this power for personal reasons, as happened in Altenstein's case shortly before his dismissal, a transitional state might well arise in which the king would insist on ministerial guidance, and the minister in turn would devoutly beg the king to take charge of the political orientation.

Coming to terms with the aristocracy was more complicated. Between 1807 and 1812, the foundations were laid, disrupted, and smoothed over once more for an understanding that might be characterized as a firm alliance against all outsiders and a struggle between allies wherever their individual interests came into conflict.

10. Hans Nawiasky, *Die Stellung des Berufsbeamtentums im Parlamentarischen Staat* (München, 1926), p. 7.

The first act of reconciliation between the bureaucracy and the nobility, which was foisted on the reluctant privy councillors by Stein, was the October 9 edict, followed by the November 24, 1807, moratorium.ᵏ The latter was a more crucial factor in the outcome of the struggle and was imposed by landowning interests within the bureaucracy. This three-year moratorium applied to all repayments on land adversely affected by the embargo on grain export and the resulting collapse of the land prices that had been inflated by speculation.⁽¹¹⁾ The emancipation of the serfs meant that the bureaucracy relinquished its right to regulate peasant conditions at its own discretion and in every detail. Such minute regulation was becoming more untenable and absurd in the face of the growing complexity of property relations induced by the spread of agrarian capitalism. Although the nobility, out of misapprehension, first opposed the introduction of this reform, the measure placed the peasantry at the mercy of the manor owners without the mitigating protection that bureaucratic supervision had provided in the past. The absolute monarch had prevailed over the aristocracy partly because he was willing to expose the peasantry to a harsher serfdom. In its bid for power over the aristocracy, absolute bureaucracy was equally willing to resort to the contemporary version of selling out the peasantry: by the emancipation of the serfs. The destruction of the aristocracy's political power position by a revolutionary attack on its private-economy base was never even considered. Stein and Schön, with their absolute respect for the sanctity of private proper-

11. To preclude misunderstandings: this moratorium was the outgrowth of an economic system that was already doomed and on the verge of collapse, and even this desperate expedient was incapable of reviving it. Baron vom Stein, with his lack of sophistication in concrete economic matters and his precapitalist ideological outlook, succumbed to the influence of a notorious swindler, Heinrich von Beguelin, who later presided over the *Oberrechenkammer* (Court of Accounts) when he foisted this moratorium on his antiagrarian privy councillors, who subsequently sabotaged it in the finest style. From the attitude of the reformist bureaucracy it can be seen that the 1807 land moratorium should not be counted among the measures intended to eliminate the capitalist economy, in contrast to the 1931 moratorium of the *Osthilfenotverordnung* (emergency decree for aid to the East). Rather, it was a measure backed by that part of the nobility whose interests lay in early capitalist land speculations, and it was passed against the wishes of those bureaucratic forces which were eager to clear the way in Prussia for liberal nineteenth-century mercantile and industrial capital. See also Hilferding's comments in *Gesellschaft* (January 1932), p. 10.

150]

ty, did not even have the courage to refuse the moratorium, which might have accomplished the same thing in a less belligerent way. Instead, the bureaucracy came to share political power with the landed gentry at the expense of the unrepresented third party, the "emancipated" peasantry,[12] which, while nominally securing its human rights, was in fact plunged into even greater misery than it had suffered under the Frederician policy of "peasant protection."

The bureaucracy's efforts to undermine the capitalist foundations of the agrarian manor economy ran parallel to this sellout of the peasantry. The 1807 moratorium led to the breakdown of the entire real-estate market and agricultural-credit system. When the nobility finally realized in 1809/10 that the moratorium had only worsened its position, it undertook a proinflation campaign to reduce the burden of its indebtedness by a rise in the price level as a whole—a campaign erroneously categorized by political historians as a manifestation of estate-type opposition to Hardenberg. Under Marwitz's leadership,[1] the ideological cover used in the years of agrarian pressure in favor of inflation was retroactively transformed into the cornerstone of Prussian conservative ideology, so that the irrational agrarian capitalism of pre-Napoleonic years grew into an irrational mystique of the state. A candid avowal of favoring inflation was unthinkable after the shocking experience with the French *assignats,* which had the same traumatic effect upon contemporaries as the German inflation has had upon today's generation.[m]

4

In the 1790's, the bureaucracy had already invoked the ideology of the *Rechsstaat*[n] in its attempts to limit the monarch's power. Ten years later, in the confrontation between bureaucracy and nobility, this ideology was even more frequently used in a self-serving manner: it was brandished as a weapon when it served the purposes of the wielders of political power, and it was set aside when it would have favored the opponents' position. In its struggle against the nobility, the bureaucracy invoked the very legalistic arguments that it found detrimental in its dealings with the bourgeoisie. In the absolutist state, the only private property receiving full legal pro-

12. Georg Winter, "Zur Entstehung des Oktoberedikts," in *Forschungen zur Bran-denburgischen und Preussischen Geschichte* (1924), XL, 33.

tection was that of the ruling landed gentry: "Only aristocratic privileges are fully guaranteed the protection of the courts."[13] It was discovered in 1807 that "perhaps less than half the nonaristocratic landowners were protected in their property rights."[14] The extension of formal legal property guarantees to strata not previously benefiting from them through legal provisions enacted by the administrative bureaucracy put an end to the privileged status of the ruling class as an island of legal sanctity in a sea of effective lawlessness. The bureaucracy, in its legislative capacity, with the support of its presumably dependent judicial branch, could then assume the role of social arbiter between all classes, which were now all subject to the same legal provisions.

The monarch's power position had cemented the coalition between the administrative and the judicial bureaucracy. Once he relinquished this power, it was inevitable that administration and judicature would confront each other in the new power vacuum. The conflict between administrative and judicial authorities coincided with the breakdown of the previously accepted principle of subordination to the will of the prince and its superseding, on the one hand, by political expediency, which ruled the administrative bureaucracy, and, on the other, by the abstract legal formalism of normative "law," to which the judicial bureaucracy owed its allegiance.

The exemption from the demands of political expediency on the part of the judicial bureaucracy is a specific feature of nineteenth-century life and of the *Rechtsstaat,* whose existence is contingent on this exemption. Until that time the demands of political expediency had governed all parts of the bureaucracy. The exemption was a result of the social and economic order's growing dependence on normative law. Once the capitalist economy had evolved from the stage of "early capitalism, with its patriarchal merchants, who might personally be either honest or dishonest," to a stage where the "objectively calculating wholesaler of modern times"[15] held sway, the need arose for a legal order which, although not categorically ex-

13. Edgar Loening, *Gerichte und Verwaltungsbehörden in Brandendenburg-Preussen* (Halle, 1914), p. 332.

14. First-hand report by Chancellor Baron von Schroetter, December 25, 1807. Preussisches Geheimes Staatsarchiv.

15. Carl Brinkmann, *Die Preussische Handelspolitik vor dem Zollverein* (Berlin, 1922), p. 27.

cluding shady but lucrative deals, was not based on singling out specially privileged groups; instead, it gave all individuals freely competing in the market an equal and calculable opportunity for profit. It required a "complete calculability of the functioning of public administration and the legal order and a reliable formal guarantee [for contracts] by the political authority."[16] Capitalist development hinged on a two-phase evolution:

1. Formalization of the law, that is, a limitation of arbitrary royal intervention into legal procedure, since absolutism in its decline had only renounced direct intervention into the reaching of the verdict, but had persisted in all other forms of intervention. This formalization required the development of a bureaucratic power that could counter-balance the will of the monarch, whose "reverence for the law" could hardly be counted upon as sufficient to give up his omnipotence.

2. Limitation of this mediating position of the bureaucracy, once it had taken over the monarch's role, by entrenching capitalist interests directly in positions of political power, so that they would be able to block the intervention of the overpowerful bureaucracy in economic activities or, if necessary, make the bureaucracy responsive to the capitalists' interests. All "political" demands of the nineteenth-century German bourgeoisie were in fact economic demands. All that was demanded was a political guarantee for economic interests, but there was no "political" motivation.

All these "political" demands of the bourgeoisie are predicated on the existence of formal law. The bourgeoisie demanded and finally secured the application of the formalistic mathematical standard of majority rule in company law and in parliamentary voting procedure, on the basis of which modern legislation took shape. The specific provisions of the electoral franchise guaranteed that this formal criterion of majority rule would never jeopardize the bourgeoisie's own interests. It is apparent that in this respect too the issue of guaranteeing individual liberty, which was given rhetorical priority, served as a mere tactical facade, for as soon as the bourgeoisie's

16. Max Weber, *Wirtschaft und Gesellschaft: Grundriss der Sozialökonomik* (Tübingen, 1922), III, 94. [The English text is quoted from the recent translation *Economy and Society: an Outline of Interpretive Sociology*, ed. by Guenther Roth and Claus Wittich (New York, 1968), I, 162.]

economic demands had been met, it retracted its earlier political demands. The political activity of the German bourgeoisie collapsed out of inner necessity once it had imposed its economic demands on the old political ruling groups; these former opponents now became its allies. The German bourgeoisie's basic lack of political backbone must be attributed to the headlong growth of the capitalist economy. Why would anyone wish to reduce satisfactory earnings by political opposition—which might well be dangerous? The most effective weapon of the nineteenth-century authoritarian state *(Obrigkeitsstaat)*—a weapon it wielded, however, without realizing its effectiveness—was the liberalization of the judicial bureaucracy. The latter came to adjudicate according to formalistic principles and to reject with increasing vigor any influence by the government on its attitude, feeling itself exclusively responsible to normative law. It thereby satisfied the interests of the bourgeoisie, diverting it from its preoccupation with politics.

This normative law, as we now understand it, had not yet taken shape under monopoly capitalism as it existed under the absolutist state, or at least it manifested itself only in an incipient and fragmentary guise. Absolutism could not conceive of a generally valid law that might interfere with the monarch's task of arbitrating between class interests. Whenever absolutism allowed formalism to prevail anyway, the latter quickly gained the upper hand and cracked its political structure. The first time a formal regulation of capitalist legal relations occurred in Prussia was in 1748 and 1750, when mortgage regulations were issued by which the position of creditors was protected against retroactive priority of privileged mortgages. As a result, short-term capital investment could be expanded into long-term investment, and the foundation was laid for the first modern, privately financed capitalism in Prussia: agrarian capitalism. Industrial capitalism, outside Silesia, where it had taken root under Austrian rule and where it was gradually suppressed again, existed only in the form of a corrupt state capitalism with vastly inflated prices. The concurrent jurisdictional regulation of 1749, by setting general administrative norms rather than going by individual precedents, also left traces within the bureaucracy of a formalization of administrative practice by increasing standardization. And the Prussian *Allgemeines Landrecht* of 1794 already paid tribute theoretically to the concept of legislation by insisting that, since in the absence of a parliamentary body both administrative regulations and laws emanated from the king, laws could be valid only if they had been "properly publicized." But this "lawfulness" *(Gesetzlichkeit)* had no practical implication except for mortgage regulations, which had cleared the way for some economic developments. In other respects, its significance was limited to the ideological realm. Administrative practice disregarded even this modest request of legal theorists and attributed full force of law to whatever opinion was expressed by the king without prior review by the courts. It insisted on this interpretation of royal prerogative not only before 1806, but even after the bureaucracy had replaced the monarch as *de facto* ruler. In this way, administrative practice sought to limit, if not to prevent altogether, judicial efforts to replace royal regulations based on expediency by the formality of the law, whose abstract validity, invulnerable to administrative intervention, was recognized as supreme by the bench. The bureaucracy hoped thereby to protect its recently acquired power position. For this bureaucratic opposition to the formalism embedded in the new capitalist economic doctrine was founded on its determination to preserve the autonomy of its political leadership, which it had just taken over from the monarch. This instinctive bureaucratic response reflected an eminently political way of thinking. The bureaucracy was hampered by "the inevitable conflict between an abstract formalism of legal certainty and their desire to realize substantive goals. Juridical formalism enables the legal system to operate like a technically rational machine. Thus it guarantees to individuals and groups within the system a relative maximum of freedom, and greatly increases for them the possibility of predicting the legal consequences of their actions,"[17] thereby eliminating the bureaucracy's opportunities for intervention in matters that were of crucial importance to the state's economic policy and finances.

We must nevertheless reject the opposition's claim that between 1808 and 1848 the dictatorship of the bureaucracy was characterized by the arbitrary despotic frenzy of conceited privy councillors. For this the development of an autocratic bureaucracy was too closely meshed with the development of capitalism in Prussia: its leading

17. *Ibid.*, p. 468. [For the English text, see above translation, II, 811.]

bourgeois members were linked by family ties with the free-trade sector of the economy, especially in East Prussia, while its aristo-cratic members maintained intimate links with the remnants of speculative agrarian capitalism, on the verge of collapse after the precipitous drop in grain prices of 1808. The irrational desire for politically discretionary decision-making power was frustrated ideologically by the rationalism of legal formalism and organiza-tionally by the expanding judicial bureaucracy, which was deter-mined to be subservient only to the law, although this asserted independence could be implemented only sporadically until its for-mal recognition by the constitution promulgated in 1848.

Prussian foreign loans after 1818 were among the major attempts by the bureaucracy to circumvent the recognition of an independent magistrature. In the decade between 1808 and 1818, the Prussian state was mired in endless financial plight and was forced to muddle through from one short-term loan to the next. The bureaucracy could not ignore reiterated demands from bankers, for legally unex-ceptionable guarantees for their loans and were often enough forced to comply with these demands. They therefore sought a way to short-circuit all political consequences of further demands from bankers, whose ultimate objective of controlling state finances was becoming increasingly clear (and once such control was conceded under emergency conditions, it could be legally upheld by the courts). The solution was to replace short-term domestic loans with long-term foreign loans from the Rothschilds, an operation that stood in part on shaky legal ground. This large-scale transfer abroad of a sizable portion of the state debt prevented domestic creditors from exerting any political influence. "Prussia would have had to draft a constitution much earlier, had the House of Rothschild not given it a breathing spell,"[18] the mayor of Bremen, Johann Smidt, wrote home from the Diet *(Bundestag)* in 1820.

The exemption of the judicial bureaucracy from submission to royal commands proceeded in two stages. We may as well ignore the puncturing of administrative justice in a few isolated areas under ab-solutism; these were mere paper victories for the Minister of Justice. In the few instances where more substantial victories were obtained,

18. Egon Caesar Conte Corti, *Der Aufstieg des Hauses Rothschild 1770–1830* (Leipzig, 1927), p. 284.

they were implemented only in the newly acquired Polish territories and not in the industrial districts of the more highly developed West. Minister of Justice Beyme, whom Stein had denigrated as morally inferior in the course of his struggle for admission into the Cabinet,° took the first major step in 1809. It involved an improvement in judicial procedure, whereby the vast number of complaints addressed to the king regarding the inadequacy of the judicial system was reduced, as was the king's continuous intervention in the course of justice.[19] Beyme succeeded thereby in strengthening the judicial bureaucracy's independence from the king. But, once the absolutist bureaucracy had taken over the absolutist monarchy, it was in the former's interest to seize control of judicial institutions, whose independent judgment would limit its power, and to strengthen its political position by imposing on its subjects a system of justice that was geared to the bureaucracy's own needs. The Cabinet order proclaiming that "the courts should be bound in their decisions by no other considerations than the prescriptions of the law"[20] must not be taken at face value, and we must distinguish between its wording and its sociological significance. For in practice, the Ministry of Justice became a formal authority to which appeals could be addressed and which was entitled "to alter and rectify the substantive content of the tribunals' prescriptions, so far as it is not subject to the judge's decision, in response to complaints by the parties involved."[21] At the same time, the bureaucracy's formal appeal structure assumed the function of petitioning for the king's grace. The bureaucracy, though keeping its hands off the immediate sentencing process, freely ordered the courts to turn down anticipated lawsuits or to reject cases that had already been accepted. If the Ministry of Justice refused to challenge the independence of the courts, the administrative bureaucracy could appeal to the king to reach a decision, thereby instituting a sort of Cabinet justice. Although the term "Cabinet justice" coincides with the one applied under the *ancien régime,* its function was different. It was no longer a manifestation of the fact that the entire state, including the judicial

19. Clearly expressed in the first-hand report of July 8, 1809. In Edmund Heilfron, *Die Rechtliche Behandlung der Kriegsschäden in Preussen nach den Freiheitskriegen* (Mannheim, 1916), p. 12.
20. Cabinet order of 6 September 1815.
21. First-hand report by Minister of Justice of 7 August 1815.

machinery, was conceived as the prince's private property. On the contrary, it was now viewed as a tool in the administrative bureaucracy's arsenal in its fight against the emancipation of the judicial bureaucracy, which inevitably accompanied the state's development into a bourgeois-liberal constitutional *Rechtsstaat.* Another weapon in this struggle was the repeated transfer of lawsuits against the Treasury from the regular tribunals to a variety of administrative-settlement procedures. The decree of 3 January 1849 is characteristic: four weeks after the promulgated constitution assured the independence of judges, the courts were relieved of their responsibility for initiating criminal proceedings, and all indictments were centralized in the public-prosecutor's office, which was under the jurisdiction of the Minister of Justice.

It should not be assumed that judicial independence, the judge's right and duty to adjudicate in accordance with his conscience, is an inalienable conquest of human progress. In Germany it was in fact the reflection of the bourgeoisie's emancipation from the dictatorship of the bureaucracy. The true meaning of an "independent" judicial system in a country whose judicial bureaucracy did not belong to the same social class as its administrative bureaucracy was lucidly pointed out by Prussian Minister of the Interior Schuckmann in his 1825 memorandum: "In my opinion, the idea that judicial boards should themselves determine the limits to their own jurisdiction is totally unacceptable and would result in the Prussian state's ceasing to be a monarchy and turning into a bureaucratic republic, in which sovereign power would rest in the hands of judicial boards."[22]

In the absence of any acute political threat, even dangerous ideas may be allowed to circulate freely. Before 1806 the bureaucracy was more sympathetic toward the concepts of the *Rechtsstaat* than after 1815. Before 1806, the *Rechtsstaat* represented nothing but a theoretical demand; in fact, it was a demand which was useful as a weapon in combatting the monarch's influence over the bureaucracy. After 1815, the implementation of the bureaucracy's own ideals served to restrict its power; only the judiciary persevered in its efforts to establish a *Rechtsstaat.* The administrative bureaucracy

22. Schuckmann's statement of opinion of 6 October 1825. Mentioned in Loening, *op. cit* p. 214 and quoted *verbatim* in Heilfron, *op. cit,* p. 27, footnote 12.

took timely countermeasures to confine the jurisdiction of the courts as narrowly as possible[23] and to limit to the utmost the legal weapons against the state available to the capitalist bourgeoisie (which could be eliminated only if capitalism itself were also done away with). By these measures it was hoped that state rule by a homogeneous collegial leadership could be saved from disintegrating into a parliamentary bureaucratic dualism, as in fact did occur in the middle of the century. The administrative bureaucracy's efforts were greatly enhanced by the professional training of the future members of the magistracy: whenever the question of extending judicial procedures into public and administrative law arose, the specialized experts within the bureaucracy had a strong case in countering these suggestions by stressing the lack of specialized knowledge on the part of the judges. Naturally, nothing was done to reform the professional training for young barristers so as to increase their competence in public law.

5

The independence of the bench remains unproblematic only as long as the judge represents the same social interests as the administrative bureaucracy and the ruling strata of the state. When judges do happen to represent other interests, two possibilities arise: the political rulers may feel compelled to limit this independence in case of conflict and thereby incur the responsibility for an act as repugnant to bourgeois ideology as the infringement of the sanctity of private property; the alternative is a political despotism exercised by the tenured judicial bureaucracy and by the social strata it represents. The conflict revolving around the judicial bureaucracy's social composition in the nineteenth century parallels the legislative fight for budget control: both the demands for budgetary legislation and the demands for formal judicial procedures in the hands of judges subject only to the law are political manifestations of the property-owning bourgeoisie's determination to allow only members of its own class and sharing its own class ideology to have a decisive voice in the disposal of its own money: in parliament through public law and in the courts through contractual law. These political manifestations of the bourgeoisie's will, which had such an impor-

23. Loening, *op. cit.,* pp. 154–155.

tant place in the nineteenth century, were contingent on a relatively prosperous bourgeoisie, that is, on a large number of independently employed professionals and businessmen with a vital stake in these issues. Once the formerly independent middle classes had been transformed into employee groups, under the double-pronged onslaught of cartels and trade unions, these issues became more ambivalent.

Developments in Germany since the 1880's demonstrate that although the independence of judges is a key element of liberal ideology, it was actually tied not so much to liberalism as an idea as to individualistic capitalism as an economic system.

The independence of liberal-minded judges remained the bourgeoisie's main weapon against the bureaucracy as long as the latter wielded all power. In the 1880's, however, an alliance took shape between the state's established social ruling classes and the bourgeoisie, which had been victorious in the economic realm (by the passage of the mining law, the company law, the commercial code, and the deregulation of interest rates). But it had suffered political reverses (the outcome of the constitutional conflict, indemnity, the septennial army budget renewal),[p] and in consequence the perspective toward the independence of the magistrature underwent some changes. The bourgeoisie was less concerned about the conversion of the previously liberal magistracy to a more conservative outlook[24] than it was reassured by the maintenance of this independence and the preservation of existing methods of recruitment. The only source of future judges were young men whose parents were wealthy enough to finance the cost of education first in the *Gymnasium* and then at the university, and who had the means to keep on supporting them during their years as unpaid junior barristers and their equally unremunerated service as assistant judges, which in the 1880's was likely to extend up to ten years. As long as the liberal principle that wealthy parents should pay for the cost of education remained unchallenged, there could be no social threat in the institution of independent judges, who reached judicial decisions on the basis of their consciences, since financial interests in

24. For the ministerial handling of this transformation, see Eckart Kehr, "Das soziale System der Reaktion in Preussen unter dem Ministerium Puttkamer," *Die Gesellschaft,* 1929/II, 253 ff. [See also above, Chapter VI.]

their broadest sense had become more completely intermeshed with political life. This was true with respect to the stock exchange, where the stocks of the mining and armament industries were gradually overtaking banking and railroad stocks.[25] It was also true for the Reich as a whole, because the state was giving the wealthy classes a positive stake in its prosperity by financing armaments through the sale of bonds rather than through taxation. Neither chance nor poor political leadership should be blamed for the collapse of liberalism in the five years following the inauguration of the armament loan policy. In line with this new political attitude of the bourgeoisie, even the still "independent" magistracy acquired almost automatically a bourgeois-neofeudal attitude and, in the confrontations between the expanding proletariat and the ruling classes, generally decided in the latter's favor. However, legal formalism continued to prevail and so remained in force as a basis of all judicial decisions, because the bourgeois-capitalist classes could not conceive of basing their law suits on any other juridical model. Besides, isolated legal decisions resulting from a strict formalistic interpretation of the law and favorable to groups not participating in the control of the state could be viewed as harmless and without political implications, in the face of the state's power position. The older English judicial tradition of applying different legal methods for dealing with different social classes did not suit the German situation: a formal procedure for conflicts within the ruling classes and the arbitrary methods of the justice of the peace for conflicts between the ruling classes and the common people.[26] The German judicial system had been constructed in the nineteenth century on a unitary model and was not susceptible to subsequent fragmentation.

As a result, legal formalism, which both philosophically and practically served as the underpinning for an independent magistracy and for the *Rechtsstaat,* did not collapse with the end of political liberalism. The collapse occurred only in the wake of the crisis that accompanied capitalism's decline from its prime. The demise of legal formalism can be traced through a whole series of interlinked manifestations. The first evidence was the *Reichsgericht's* adoption of law-finding based on the principles of "good faith" *(Treu und*

25. Felix Somary, *Bankpolitik,* 2nd ed. (Tübingen, 1930), p. 101.
26. Max Weber, *op. cit.,* p. 470.

Glauben) introduced in September, 1920, by the famous decision on the *clausula rebus sic stantibus.*[27] Another sign of the collapse of legal formalism is the headway that has been made by the so-called Free Law movement. From a sociological perspective it might be said that this movement advocates extending the principles of expediency that govern the conduct of the lawyer at the service of a private client to the decision-making of the publicly employed judge. This extension is predicated on some conditions that have been masterfully described by Ernst Fraenkel in his *Soziologie der Klassenjustiz.*[28] It can occur only when the image of the judiciary declines from that shared by the ruling bourgeoisie in the prime of capitalism to a view of it held by a helpless and resentful petty bourgeoisie locked into "false" combat against the proletariat rather than against monopoly capitalism. A parallelism emerges between the dissolution of the inevitably unitarian formalistic legal thinking into mutually exclusive but simultaneously valid "good faith" decisions and the dissolution of the unified judicial system of the nineteenth century into a set of juxtaposed judicial organs, each with its own specific judicial procedure. The administrative tribunals were a first manifestation of this trend, whose full impact made itself felt after 1918 in the financial and labor courts. Another manifestation of the decline of legal formalism is the blurring of the distinction between statutory law and administrative regulation, a distinction of vital importance for the *Rechtsstaat.* This blurring was an outcome of the discontinuation of parliament, the legislating element in the nineteenth century, and the simultaneous transfer to the bureaucracy of the task of emergency legislation. Among these measures may be cited the abrogation of legal guarantees for equal opportunities for all individuals competing in the economy, which is exemplified by the introduction of special in-house rates on the *Reichsbahn,* which violate the prohibition against secret rate agreements. Another instance is the order of the Foreign Exchange Department to the city of Frankfurt am Main not to pay the legally

---

27. Friedrich Dessauer, *Recht, Richtertum und Ministerialbürokratie: Eine Studie über den Einfluss von Machtverschiebungen auf die Gestaltung des Privatrechts* (Mannheim, 1928).

28. Berlin, 1927. See also his comments on Dessauer's book in the *Archiv für Sozialwissenschaft und Sozialpolitik,* LXIII, 409.

recognized bill of exchange debt of 200,000 marks to the English bank of Kleinworth, Sons and Co.[29] Other instances of this blurring are the "law" concerning the Danat bank and the recent emergency decree on aid to the East. It is not so much a matter of subverting capitalism altogether as of challenging it from within and *ad hoc*, in accordance with the respective power of the social groups, each of which is hoping to save its own skin by such means.[q]

On the surface, it might seem as though matters had returned full circle to where they stood in the first half of the nineteenth century, when the bureaucracy was striving to preserve a relative political independence from the capitalist economy, whose existence it never attacked on principle. It was simply a case of temporarily reinforcing the position of the bureaucracy, which could exercise a technically required substitute rule at a time of acute crisis. But this crisis has undermined the foundations of the bourgeoisie as it existed in the nineteenth century and has led to its cleavage into two groups: a big-business patriciate of general managers and a mass of petty-bourgeois employees. The *Rechtsstaat* has thereby lost its social foundation: the patriciate, on the one hand, can better exert its leverage through its political strength than through lawsuits fought in the courts according to formal legal procedures; the petty bourgeoisie, on the other hand, has never based its legal doctrine on formalism but only on equity, the consistent application of which, if it did not do away with capitalism, would at least eliminate calculability, the cornerstone of the capitalist economic system.

---

29. The point is not whether this court decision was based on unrealistic assumptions. Until that time it was unthinkable for an administrative authority to invalidate even the most insane court order.

CHAPTER IX

The Dictatorship of the Bureaucracy

The foundations of bureaucratic dictatorship in Germany can be traced back to two different sets of causes, a narrower and a broader one. The narrower relates to the paralysis of class forces and the gains made since about 1923 by economic pressure groups, as a result of which bureaucracy was cast in the role of arbitrator between these conflicting interest groups. We will attempt in our discussion to situate this narrower set of causes within a broader context, to explain how this bureaucratic power organization persisted at the end of the inflation.

The school of historiography that paid intellectual homage to the socially powerful at the end of the nineteenth century and shrouded historical problems in a cloak of ideological obfuscation was responsible also for absolutizing the ideology that the Prussian bureaucracy had evolved as a class-linked interpretation of politics. It arbitrarily extended to all society the supervision bureaucracy exercised, intellectually, morally, socially, and politically, over a small sector, asserting that there was real substance to the bureaucracy's formal power of arbitration between the two great economic forces, the bourgeoisie's commercial and industrial capitalism and the big landowners' agrarian capitalism. It transformed the seemingly firm power position of the bureaucracy, which in fact and in the long run teetered precariously between the paralyzing class forces in Prussia-Germany, into an ideology of public service. The theory that bureaucratic rule should be equated with an authentic governmental policy *(Staatspolitik)* was based on two elements: the attestation of loyalty to the monarch—whether rooted in byzantine intrigues, tactical considerations, or sincere conviction—and a spurious rationale whose claim to universal validity was an attempt to obtain from this buffer position between classes what could never be secured in this fashion, namely an invulnerable ideology solidly rooted in class interests. This theory implied that governmental policy in the hands of the bureaucracy was not only technically but ethically superior to the "fragmentary" policies (to use Bismarck's phrase) laid down or pursued by political parties in parliament. It was conveniently forgotten that the bureaucracy had come to life not as an instrument of the "state" but as an instrument in the prince's struggle for political and economic power against the estates and as his tool for expropriating feudal property and turning it into royal property. The Prussian bureaucracy never actually denied that it had been originally designed to impose a specific social order at the expense of a different order, but ideologically the social and political structure on which it was based was equated with the state as such.

There is no need to attack the bureaucracy or to denigrate its "objective accomplishments" in order to show the fallacy of identifying bureaucracy with dedication to the state *(Staatsidee)*. When one shifts the discussion from what is essentially a problem of class conflict to a defense of bureaucratic rule on the strength of the decisive role played in its ranks by highly trained personalities carefully selected for their extended practical experience, lack of bias, and devotion to the public good, several points are overlooked: First, the bureaucracy will either refuse to employ or expel from its midst persons who have indisputable technical qualifications but are unwilling to submit to the bureaucracy's political and social will. A case in point is that of Assistant Judge Eugen Richter, who was finally dismissed even from his modest position as mayor of Neuwied.[a] Second, the objective achievements of the bureaucracy have never resulted from its own capacities but have prevailed only if they were compatible with the relation between class forces. The bureaucracy's achievements can never be attributed to its own merit but are a product of the class situation. It is not within the power of the judicial bureaucracy to guarantee that its members act according to their honest conviction on the basis of their best knowledge and conscience; it is the society in which they adjudicate that will ultimately determine whether this is possible. Even if we disregard the shaky foundation of the *Rechtsstaat,* unsalaried assistant judges *(Assessoren)* who are counting on obtaining a permanent position and who for years function as judges, are in no position to risk verdicts that might antagonize their superiors, on whose evaluation their livelihood depends. And even if the formal judicial procedure is left in the hands of the judicial bureaucracy, at least in those areas to which it was confined in the nineteenth century, it is still possible for those exerting political power to grant pardons and to upset just sentences.

Today's bureaucracy is more qualified technically than the bureaucracy of the first part of the nineteenth century, during which it held unlimited sway in Prussia. In the same way, insight into the social struggle was greater in the bureaucracy of the German empire than in that of the war of liberation, and actions like the cold-blooded and cynical sacrifice of the small peasantry in the so-called emancipation of the serfs of 1807 never recurred before 1914. For anyone who has thumbed through hundred of volumes of documents from that period, the halo of many a privy councillor pales, for even in those days privy councillors and ministers did not neglect their personal and financial interests during their service in the state administration. The fact that the bureaucracy's big corruption scandals failed to find their way into the press and must be slowly dug out of a mountain of files is not to deny their existence. It is a major methodological error to conclude that the greater publicity surrounding corruption today necessarily implies its greater, or rather, relatively greater, scope compared to earlier times. The integrity of the bureaucracy is in any case less significant than is popularly assumed, not only because it is quite possible to be beyond reproach as an individual and still to be corrupt as a member of the ruling class, but even more because the documents show that the Prussian bureaucracy never was beyond reproach, the only difference being that we are less familiar with their individual and social corruptibility in those days than in our own time. One might go even a step further and say that inner conviction, the feeling of class honor, the sense of decency, are relatively secondary. Frederick the Great, no more the founding father of bureaucracy as it took shape in the nineteenth century than his father was, always, in theory and practice, gave ministers of questionable honesty but indisputable intelligence preference over men who were honest and beyond reproach but had limited intelligence. Every large apparatus, whatever its degree of integrity, can only accomplish as much as the class situation permits. The bureaucracy needs the ideology of a special class status not to enhance its accomplishments but to maintain its political and social self-confidence. For from a sociological point of view, the bureaucracy is not made up of the aggregate of public servants with guaranteed life-long employment and pension rights, but of a small group of high-ranking officials in decision-making positions; in fact, it is identified with the ministerial bureaucracy. It is self-evident that this is the group which determines administrative policy in all countries and that in view of its position, it does more than attend to routine matters. What is different in Germany is that this technical-administrative influence is buttressed by a second influence stemming from the historical situation of the Prussian bureaucracy in 1807. This second influence is political and social and explains the ideology of the genesis of bureaucracy as a special class, an ideology which persists even today.

Prussia-Germany is the only place where the bureaucracy is a coopted republican board of regents, that is, where the members of the board choose their fellow members, and only in Germany does this bureaucracy constitute a self-contained power organization, notwithstanding the highly visible conflicts within it. Although the bureaucracy had to yield its governmental power temporarily in the wake of the so-called revolution of 1918, in the long run this experience increased its strength. The right to dismiss political appointees offered no effective corrective for this power, because it was applied sparingly to reassure the successors of those who took over from the dismissed officials, and because the appointment of persons not coopted by the bureaucracy on ministerial orders was such a rare occurrence as to make no real difference. In fact, bureaucratic rule is not affected by the nature of the regime, as long as the government is not in the hands of a ruthless group that sets itself above all classes but attempts to keep a balance between the classes, as was true in Prussia after 1807 and even more visibly in Germany since

[167

1918. Even at present it makes no real difference whether the bureaucracy exercises its power by advising parliamentarians to whom it submits the material needed for reaching decisions on concrete questions or whether it proceeds by issuing on its own emergency decrees over which parliament has no control. The nature of the political regime has little impact, as can be judged from the rapid disappearance of the propaganda campaign against "political" and in favor of "technically competent" ministers waged in the first years of the republic; the bureaucracy quickly recognized that its opportunities for intervention were far greater under a parliamentary minister than under a minister with technical expertise chosen from its own ranks.

This power position dates from the period of the collapse of the absolute monarchy, when the capitalist bourgeoisie had not yet gained sufficient strength to take over political power in the state, which it was keeping afloat with its loans, and when the aristocratic landowners had lost their capitalist footing through the collapse of agricultural prices in the wake of the continental blockade and were turning to romantic conservatism. The power-hungry bureaucracy, which had just displayed its power over the king by ruthlessly forcing him to appoint Stein as minister (1804), seized the reins during this power vacuum, never to relinquish them to this day. It was able to retain power by playing the aristocracy off against the bourgeoisie at a time when these two classes were their only dangerous opponents and, since the eighties, by playing both these classes off against the new adversary, the proletariat. These changes of position throw light upon the problem of homogeneity in the bureaucracy. In fact, the bureaucracy at no time achieved social homogeneity. The political rulers never failed to make room for their own favorites. Under Frederick the Great, there was no definite policy after the war; it was all a matter of influence. Hardenberg, the real founder of Prussian bureaucracy, brought in figures from outside the ministries in line with his political objectives, which he could not implement with the privy councillors at hand. The only unifying social factor within the bureaucracy as it evolved in nineteenth-century Prussia was its segregation from the lower strata.

The members of the bureaucracy are required to have completed their university education. Outsiders are excluded on principle, the only exception being made for posts as district officials *(Landratamt)* for which estate owners are also eligible.

Lower-ranking public servants are as consistently barred from promotion as promotion from these ranks was consistently encouraged in the administration under absolutism, which had no experience as yet with bureaucracy as a social class. The new group of "middle-level public servants" was therefore recruited from the cities, which developed their own administrative procedures in self-government. The only remaining instances of a homogenous bureaucracy without distinction between upper and middle-level officials are technical agencies like the *Reichsbank*. The very thing which, from the perspective of moral philosophy and the history of ideas, may have seemed as the incarnation of unhampered individual advancement and the amalgamation of individual freedom with the ethical requirements of the state as a whole, is recognizable by anybody whose vision is not befogged by German idealism as the basis of bureaucracy's power position; it was a bureaucracy, precisely, which never absolutely blocked ascent from modest circumstances and which, like the wealthy bourgeoisie, always replenished its ranks from the owners of small or no property, but which never permitted this elevation to take place in a single generation. Typically, the son whose father had partially worked his way up from modest beginnings would, by his own university education, acquire a certain intellectual, social, and political style, and, having repudiated his class origins, could then freely pursue a career in the higher ranks of the bureaucracy.

The exact nature of this style changed with the modifications in the social distribution of power and the need for allies. However, the characteristic feature of the bureaucracy was not the content of this outlook but rather its form and the equating of this form with the nonexistent but proclaimed content. The bureaucracy's feeling of class loyalty finds its formal expression in its "sense of duty," which implies no substantive position with respect to any specific social or political question. This sense of duty, which is the ethical counterpart to nineteenth-century legal formalism, can justify any kind of political face-about and expediency. The concept of "loyalty," another formal characteristic, is inapplicable to the bureaucracy, because the apparatus continues to operate smoothly even after the replacement of top-level officials by their most virulent opponents. And how else could the system operate if academic, middle-level, and lower-level public servants are not to be deprived of their job security and pension rights? Allegiance to the monarch was never formally violated, but the major feature of the Prussian reform was precisely the social redistribution of power in Prussia through the replacement of the monarch by the increasingly powerful bureaucracy as the determinant and decisive factor. The bureaucracy is perforce a power apparatus for well-defined predetermined ideologies, and is similar to the Center party among political organizations. It remained liberal in its orientation as long as the bourgeoisie functioned as a junior partner in the alliance against the aristocracy. This liberalism was discarded and replaced by conservatism when the bourgeoisie concluded an alliance with the aristocracy against the proletariat. This attitude was maintained after 1918, because class relations were not altered except that the proletariat was yielded a small measure of political power in the wake of the monarchy's collapse. In the face of bureaucratic reluctance, the proletariat could make only half-hearted advances into the capitalistic power structure. At the same time, the paralysis of class forces fostered the power of interest groups that carried on the class struggle in its new form, in which instruments of the state, namely, the army and the bureaucracy, were engaged on both sides, not as objects of this struggle but as subjects. Both of these were already in control of the state machinery before 1918 and failed to be expelled from this position after 1918. They continued to apply their traditional system of cooptatation along the same lines as the former ruling classes and thereby became political power factors alongside the political centers of power established by the Weimar constitution. Their political influence grew even stronger than before 1918 as a result of the fact that their structure differed from that of the real political leadership.

The paralysis of class forces therefore constitutes one element in the growth of the bureaucracy's power in the republic. The second element is the development of governmental, that is, bureaucratic interventionism. State interventions in the economy in the early nineteenth century were always technically motivated, and even communal monopolies for gas, electricity, water, and transportation should not be interpreted as onslaughts on free enterprise. It was only when capitalist society in Germany, in contrast to the situation in England and France, proved unable to cope with the labor movement that a radical reversal took place and the attempt was made, with the typical impetuosity of a military state, to annihilate the proletarian movement on the one hand by police intervention and on the other by sanitary and hygienic measures. Modern bureaucratic interventionism in Germany, with its many brilliant achievements in social-welfare measures, which were later taken over by other states, is an outgrowth of these tactical measures. The war economy, viewed at the time as a form of state capitalism or state socialism, failed to leave its mark on the postwar economy, but it did arouse the bureaucracy's consciousness of its vast capacity for intervention.

The capacities for intervention are further reinforced by restraints on mobility. These are caused on the international level by the blocking of international migrations, and domestically by housing shortages and unemployment; they induce ever closer ties between the population and the state it inhabits, to which it is now tightly linked, even if this link has an oppositional character. And if this same population is out of work or without resources as independent property owners, there is an increased interest on its part in the state and in the way the state is administered, because the decision how much food is to be distributed to the unemployed and which class is to be subsidized by the state lies in the hands of the top-level bureaucracy.

The third basis for the current power of the bureaucracy is the support it receives from the higher judicial bureaucracy and from the *Reichsgericht*. In the era of individual capitalism it was indispensable for the state to guarantee each individual competing in the free market an equal chance to get ahead and to eliminate the privileges of a feudal or semifeudal era standing in the way of this chance, in short to develop a *Rechtsstaat*. The fiercest conflicts between the bureaucracy and bourgeois individual capitalism took place during the first three quarters of the nineteenth century. Ranke[b] once designated these conflicts as a struggle between royal and popular sovereignty, though we view it today as a confrontation between the bureaucracy's drive toward a power monopoly and the

[171

bourgeoisie's desire for as rational a regulation as possible of free competition, that is, a regulation based on consistent and hence accurately calculable judicial procedures. At the time of the bourgeoisie's political capitulation in the eighties, it had already succeeded in implementing its economic demands and in securing the establishment of the *Rechtsstaat*. From then on a united front was presented by the administrative bureaucracy, the judicial bureaucracy, and the bourgeoisie in Germany, spearheaded against the numerically increasingly powerful industrial proletariat.

Since 1918, when the proletariat received a concrete share in the government of the state, this alliance has expressed itself in the fact that, under the cloak of the *Rechtsstaat* ideology, which is still upheld, the judicial bureaucracy, which is unscathed and keeps being recruited consistently from the bourgeoisie, offers its support wherever possible. The lower middle class, fully expecting protection on the part of the magistrature with its middle-class tendencies, was partly thwarted in its fight against the inflation and monetary revaluation only because it was paralyzed by the upper bourgeoisie's capitalist proclivity for taking advantage of inflation to reduce its indebtedness.[c]

A clearer instance of class posture is the inclusion of public law in the training of the oncoming generation of jurists. In the nineteenth century, judges received no training in public law, lest they be tempted to intervene in the bureaucracy's sphere of competence for the benefit of the bourgeoisie. Now that the exercise of political power has been partly shifted to nonbureaucratic elements, the political bureaucracy needs the support of the magistracy, which in turn requires training in public law to be able to evaluate political power interests and to make its verdicts conform to this knowledge. Only on this basis can it offer support to the political bureaucracy. The "independent" judicial bureaucracy thus acquires a higher supervisory authority over the "policy-making" of nonbureaucratic groups. It can thereby paralyze whatever social changes this policy is attempting to induce in the administrative bureaucracy by extending the jurisdiction of the regular courts to administrative questions, a tendency that has steadily increased during the past decade.

An even more characteristic instance of this transfer of major power positions to the judicial bureaucracy—and one that is more in the limelight and crucial in important cases—is the gradually assumed supervision by the *Staatsgerichtshof* over all political matters and the way in which its verdicts have varied depending on the groups under consideration. Otto Braun's attempt to carry out the Young Plan referendum without adhering to the provisions of the Reich constitution's Article 130, in line with the practice established during the past decade, was rejected by the *Reichsgericht*, and Prussia was compelled to abide by the formal wording of the constitution.[d] The Brüning government, with its Christian-Conservative orientation and with a policy of emergency decrees strongly influenced by the bureaucracy, was not deterred from using Article 48, which had been designed to apply to street rioting, as a basis for unquestionably unconstitutional legislation.[e] The *Reichsgericht* acted to limit the power of the "red" administration in Prussia, while leaving intact the power of the bureaucratic Brüning government, with its ties to the old ruling social classes, using mutually exclusive arguments to justify each of these interventions. And the refusal of the *Staatsgerichtshof* to thwart von Papen's *coup d'état* of 20 July 1932[f] by issuing a temporary decree, which could easily have been handed down and justified in view of the primitive legal issue at stake, was motivated by the purely formal argument that the temporary decree should not anticipate the final settlement of the question. This effectively sanctioned von Papen's actions and is a perfect illustration of this sociologically inevitable collaboration of all branches of the bureaucracy. It also exemplifies the smooth operation of their alliance for purposes of evicting the working class from political power.

CHAPTER X

Modern German Historiography

The task of analyzing the present state of German historiography is fraught with difficulty because it is so closely bound up with, and determined by, the general social and political development of the empire and the republic. Since the middle of the nineteenth century German historiography has been an almost perfect mirror image of the political-social situation. Speaking of one of the most famous works of German history, Mommsen's *Roman History*, which was honored with a Nobel Prize in 1902, fifty years after the first edition, the distinguished historian Eduard Meyer said that one could learn more from the book about German liberalism in the 1850's than about the whole history of Rome up to the death of Julius Caesar. The history of German historical writing is a part of general German history. It does not stand by itself, but touches at every point general social and internal relationships.

The decisive factor in this connection between historiography and political-social development is not the fact that German professors, in contrast to their American colleagues, have always been state officials. There was a time when German professors, despite their position as civil servants, dared to write books that resulted in their dismissal. But those days of opposition to authoritarian government lie far back, in the 30's and 50's of the past century, and that friction in the relations between the state and the university later disappeared. Even during the Wilhelmine period, it was possible on occasion for university professors to express free democratic criticism.

The administration of education in Germany's largest state, Prussia, was for more than twenty years in the dictatorial power of Ministerialdirektor Althoff,[a] whose wise policy it was to give capable intellectuals who had shown democratic tendencies since their youth, access to the universities, lest they turn away and become leaders of the political opposition. They were glad to receive good positions, for the German university professor enjoyed great prestige, and they were able to voice their opinions candidly from their lecterns, as long as they were not too radical. On the whole, they presented much less of a threat than if they had appeared as oppositional speakers and leaders in the Reichstag. At the same time, if their verbal opposition became too bold, fines for violating the disciplinary code of public servants were levied against them, as happened to Hans Delbrück, the author of the four-volume *History of the Art of War*, when he expressed the view that the oppression of the Danes in North Schleswig made him blush with shame.

In my opinion, the reason for the connection between historiography and politics lies not so much in the professor's position as a civil servant as in his affiliation with the bourgeoisie, an affiliation that is economically only partial, but ideologically complete. It is true that because he is a public servant with a fixed salary from the state, the professor only half belongs to the bourgeoisie, but even so, until his thirty-fifth or fortieth year, until he is appointed full professor, he usually has to support himself. As an unpaid lecturer *(Privatdozent)* or associate professor, he has to live as a private individual from his own resources, before becoming a civil servant. Ideologically, however, professors have identified themselves with the bourgeoisie and, from the beginning of the nineteenth century, were counted among its spiritual leaders. Their intellectual attitude from decade to decade reflected the same economic and social vicissitudes as the bourgeoisie, swinging from radical to moderate liberalism, from alliance with the military monarchy and support of the suppression of the labor movement to imperialism and now [1933] to fascism.

From the 1830's onward the German professor of history was a representative of middle-class liberalism in its two forms: its belief that the individual should have the possibility of free economic development in order to be able to support himself; and its belief that the state should have the same kind of freedom in order to make its existence secure. Freedom for the individual and power for the state were the fundamental tenets of the historians until the year 1870, and their writing was guided by these goals. This so-called political school of historiography finally collapsed because the German empire was founded, not by the bourgeoisie, but by the military, the aristocracy, and the Prussian state. All economic demands of the middle class were fulfilled, but the political ones, so far as they were not purely rhetorical, were ignored. All political power remained in the hands of the old ruling class. The bourgeoisie submitted to this distribution of power, and bourgeois historians no longer appeared as advocates of the two facets of liberalism, freedom and power, but only of the latter. As theoreticians of power, however, they were acquainted with it only from the standpoint of those who wielded it. Germany was the strongest state in Europe, having vanquished France; in their hearts, the theoreticians of power belonged to the ruling and not to the oppressed class; they consistently enjoyed power and saw only its advantages and charms. Of all his generation, Bismarck had the most skeptical view of the uses of power in the international sphere; but at home, in the class struggle, he exploited all its possibilities, and his supporters followed him unconditionally. The swelling of the proletariat, with its threat to private property, led to an alliance between the bourgeoisie, the aristocracy, the officer corps, and the monarchy that was almost completely destroyed by the opposition in 1918–1919. It remained in force, however, until the end of the German empire and resurfaced in our own time in slightly altered form. Two names epitomize the bourgeoisie's change of front in favor of Bismarck and his state: Paul Laband and Heinrich von Treitschke.[b] Laband's constitutional theories won general acceptance among the jurists; the most prominent of the bourgeois-liberal historians who glorified power was Treitschke.

But there was also another line of development. Alongside the bourgeois-liberal historiography there was a conservative one, intellectually superior to its competitor, that of Leopold von Ranke. Ranke cannot be explained by simple formulas, like the liberals. In his works everything was expressed with greater delicacy and caution, and his scope was more universal than theirs. He looked at everything from a broader perspective, did not become personally involved in the issues raised, and did not intervene as arbiter in the conflicts he described. He observed the role played by power in history, but this did not move him to glorify it. He was a pious man, and to him historical scholarship was the means of contemplating a course of events in which God played a direct role. Ranke's writing was highly regarded for its literary qualities, but its impact on the historiography of his day remained slight. He had many disciples, but, when they saw how much care their mentor took in interpreting his sources, they came to believe that writing history and analysis of sources were the same thing. The grotesque result was that Ranke became the patron-saint of the "footnote historians" and only later, around 1910, came into his own again.

In the 1880's and 1890's, however, his restrained, conservative kind of history had no influence. His moderate outlook on political power, his religious approach to politics, fell by the wayside when, after Treitschke's death in 1896, that historian's historical view won general acceptance because the German bourgeoisie was swept off its feet by the giddy intoxication of power. The economic depression, which had lasted twenty years, was coming to an end, prices were rising, courage was reviving, and with growing wealth came political pride. At the end of the nineties, the expansion of the German fleet went hand in hand with the growth of German imperialism.

However, the bourgeoisie's intoxication with power coincided with an uncertainty and disquiet and a growing doubt as to the security of its wealth. Despite the anti-Socialist Law, the German labor movement was growing, and it developed into a power that increased with every Reichstag election. The nation gradually split into two parts that could no longer communicate with each other. The university stood completely on the side of capital and conservatism. No professor dared be a Socialist. Those who were called "Socialists of the Chair" had leanings toward social reform but had nothing to do with proletarian socialism.

The university's decision to side with the bourgeoisie confronted German scholarship with enormous scientific problems. Socialism was not just a political movement but also a scholarly discipline with its own problems, which, though rooted in liberal capitalistic political economy, had led to anticapitalistic results in the course of their development. I shall not dwell on the way in which the economists dealt with this dilemma. German historiography, for its part, chose to take a more comfortable way, namely, to ignore these questions. All historical scholarship that delved into the same problems as Marxism was branded as Socialist, Marxist, and revolutionary. Social history has to do with the history of social groups and classes. Since it shared this with Marxism, it was equated with the Socialist interpretation of history and, in the universities, was repressed. Karl Lamprecht, who, under the influence of West European positivism, dared to write history that went beyond the problems of the state and power (although it was not correct in its methodology and was ill-conceived, its author failing to see that it was impossible to write this kind of history within the confines of liberal historiography) was not only unrecognized but boycotted by his colleagues. As a result of this, there is still no adequate nineteenth-century social history of Germany, although huge problems remain to be clarified in this field. In fact, nineteenth-century German history should really be rewritten from scratch.

To take one example. In the United States, Prussian conservatism is usually defined as feudalism and brushed aside as obsolete, like the dinosaurs in the Field Museum. In the popular image, William II remains a figure in cuirassier uniform with helmet and soaring eagle, all very romantic and feudal. But actually this is quite secondary. The real significance of the Prussian aristocracy lies not in its feudalism but in its ownership of a large grain-producing industry and in its participation in the power struggle as an agrarian capitalist class against the industrial capitalist class. And it has survived not on the strength of its feudalism but as modern agrarian capitalism. And William II's significance does not lie in his bragging and saber-rattling—in reality he was one of the weakest and least influential monarchs we know, and all he did was to go along with what the two capitalist classes asked of him.

But official German historiography has never concerned itself with significant questions of this kind. And economic history is always relegated to the background. Economists do occasionally make contributions to economic history but, as far as historians are concerned, only the harmless problems of medieval economic history are within their scope, while modern economic history is out of bounds. In all Germany there is not a single professor of modern history with the slightest grasp of the way in which economic processes impinge on history. One might say that it simply cannot be admitted that economics has an impact on politics or that leading figures in the economy inevitably influence legislation. This fact is not recognized. And if somebody does allude to it anyway, he is immediately embroiled in political difficulties that are more serious than those that Delbrück encountered. They force the nonconformist into political and social opposition and perhaps even cause his ostracism from respectable society.

Just one example. Germany had one outstanding social historian, Gustav Schmoller, whose collected essays, *Umrisse und Untersuchungen,* represent one of the highest achievements of historiography. In various parts of his work, Schmoller could not help but reach the same conclusions as Marx. There are many things about which there is room for only one opinion, even for men of different political views. I have personally been attacked as a Bolshevik for introducing in one of my lectures half a page of Schmoller's *Umrisse,* because the attacker failed to realize that it was a quotation. Yet Schmoller was a conservative, a Prussian to the marrow. There is not a trace of Marxism in him. Nevertheless, he did not escape the penalty of the identification of social history with Socialist party propaganda. When the death of the director-general of the Prussian State Archives in 1896 led to a vacancy in a highly esteemed position among German historians, Schmoller's name appeared on the list of persons from whom the emperor was to choose a successor. Schmoller had written many essays, based on historical documents, expressing his love and admiration for Prussian absolutism. But William II crossed out his name with the comment that Prussian government documents could not be entrusted to a Social Democrat.

This grotesque identification of social history and Socialist history in the emperor's mind remained typical of German historiography in the empire and still survives today. Whoever writes social history is automatically called a Socialist, even if he is conservative and imperialistic. It is equally characteristic that Schmoller's death in 1917 led to the extinction of German social historiography. Whenever specialists take up problems that were studied by Schmoller, they accept theories that he developed in the 1880's, because he was regarded after his death as an honorable man and not as a Socialist. In the 1880's, Schmoller's theories were a great achievement. Today, of course, many new insights are available to us. It is, however, unthinkable to go beyond Schmoller. The only historian who has elaborated his conception of Prussian absolutism is an American, Professor Dorn in Columbus, Ohio,[c] who in Germany is almost wholly disregarded.

German historians in the days of the empire therefore wanted to have nothing to do with socialism either as a party or as social history. They were compelled to espouse the interests of the imperialist German bourgeoisie in every respect. Dietrich Schäfer made use of popular methods in his defense of imperialism and reaped much success as a teacher at the Berlin University. On a much higher scholarly level, Otto Hintze[d] argued in favor of the social and internal political considerations supporting Germany's *Machtpolitik.* He carried his studies on the constitutional aspects of absolutism nearly to the point where he might have been labeled a red revolutionary. But on the whole he was such a proud, honest, outspoken, and unobjectionable imperialist that he escaped this danger. When defeat in the World War led to the collapse of his *Weltanschauung,* he was more deeply affected by this blow than most other historians. This unrelenting imperialist of former days almost turned into a Social Democrat in the republic, not out of inconstancy but because Germany's defeat represented the most personal defeat for him, since he had honestly, openly, and unreservedly identified himself with the old power politics.

Notwithstanding Hintze's scholarly achievements, he was not the leading or the most typical German historian for the years between 1910 and 1925, because he was too outspoken as an advocate of power. The German bourgeoisie of this period could no longer—or not yet—accept such a stand. It could no longer accept the straightforward veneration of power, that Treitschke had taught. Of course people took pride in the growing fleet, the steadily expanding army, the mounting wealth. But grave political crises kept threatening Germany, and from the time of the first Moroccan crisis,[e] people no longer were optimistic about German foreign policy. Could its great power really secure victory? Was it a good idea for each major power to build *two* new ships for each ship built by its neighbor? Could any good come of this? Of course such qualms could not be publicly expressed; only Social Democrats said such things openly and predicted a catastrophe. But deep down one had to agree with them that this policy was bound to lead to chaos—only there was no way of preventing it.

There existed only two possibilities: to accept power politics openly and support it or to become a Social Democrat and attack it. For the broad educated strata of the German bourgeoisie, however, these were unpalatable alternatives. Since there was no positive third path available, they turned to a negative one, an escape into a weary, resigned contemplation of the evil and dirty world. The best was to look at this world from the outside, from afar, and to write about it as artistically as possible. Historiography was seen not only as a science but as an artistic achievement. Treitschke, the stubborn champion of might, became less congenial than Ranke with his cautious and skeptical attitude toward power. But Ranke's staunch and somewhat naïve piety could not be revived, so his work had to stand on its esthetic merits. Here we find the roots of German intellectual history, the history of ideas, and the extraordinary success of its founder, Friedrich Meinecke. Most of the younger historians belong to Meinecke's school; no other German historical school of any importance exists today.

The history of ideas is a German phenomenon that has risen in response to specifically German social conditions. This answers the question concerning its influence outside Germany. Practically nobody abroad pays any attention to it, and Meinecke is almost unknown in foreign parts. Foreign scholars who studied in Germany before the war are under the erroneous impression that other scholars, like Max Lenz, Erich Marcks, and Hans Delbrück are the leading German historians.[f] These men have, to be sure, made significant contributions to scholarship, but their ideas and historical methods were personal to them. No one took them up and carried them further; they have founded no significant school. This has happened only in Meinecke's case, because his history of ideas appeared at the right moment to show the intellectually disoriented bourgeoisie a way out of its difficulties. In the long run, it is a dead

[181

end. But temporarily those who enter it are strengthened and exalted. They feel as if they are on a high mountain from which they look down into a squalid valley where the mob, struggling for its daily bread, is penned in by the narrow horizon and cannot see the light beyond. The superiority complex of the mountain climber is highly developed in the intellectual historian and rightly so: he is not exclusively concerned with producing footnotes, as generally medievalists are. But is this feeling of superiority well-founded? The genesis of the German history of ideas amply demonstrates that it has not concerned itself with things that have had great and direct practical implications. It shies away from ideas that have revolutionized or attempt to revolutionize the world. Democratic ideas in America or France, Socialist ideas in Germany, Bolshevist ideas in Russia are all taboo, for they could only be treated by someone who has formed his own opinion about the social and political situation and has envisaged revolution and collapse in his own country. The historians of ideas are inclined to view such revolutions as repellent, because they force them to make hard choices for or against. Even if they are republicans and democrats, they are politically conservative. They take no interest in workers or employees. The problems of the latter are confined to the day-to-day struggle and are irrelevant at the lofty levels over which the historians of ideas hold sway. They are attracted by conservatives like Frederick William IV and Julius Stahl, particularly if their souls are complex.

This attraction explains the affinity between the history of ideas and the Freudian school. For Freud's school, and especially for the more influential one of his disciple Adler, which is usually confused with it, objective accomplishments and institutions are always the product of psychological complications. Their interest lies in dissecting the soul of the individual human being, not in describing objectively existing institutions. The success of Freud's school in Germany must be attributed to the same factors as those that account for the popularity of the history of ideas: a feeble evasion of the harsh decisions life brings and an urge for a narcissistic analysis of one's own precious soul. The combination of these two movements, the history of ideas and psychoanalysis, determines the situation under which many young German historians now write history. They like biographies, in which the protagonist, rather than leading a heroic existence as statesman, merchant, general, or explorer, simply develops his psyche. These biographies are invariably divided into two volumes. The first tome concludes with the hero's reaching the age of thirty and coming in contact with the real world, having "developed" himself until that time. The second volume, which is to contain the hero's claim to fame, never gets published. And for a good reason: the historian of ideas is by the very nature of things incapable of describing his hero's deeds and therefore gladly renounces the task of writing the second volume. Even in a work that stands far above the average, Gerhard Ritter's biography of Stein, two-fifths of the book are devoted to Stein's development before he took over his first ministry, although this has no real historical significance. Only the personal curiosity of the historian, concerning the way in which an interesting inner life has developed, justifies this procedure.

It is symptomatic of this inner weakness of German historiography that it tries with all possible means to protect its monopoly. Historical works written outside the academic orbit are ignored. Since both Catholic and Socialist historiography were still deficient from a scholarly standpoint until a few years ago, it was justifiable to pay no attention to them. A crisis arose, however, with the publication of "belletristic historical works," which appealed to a wide audience. These belletristic historians—whose leading exponent is Emil Ludwig[g]—consider history not as a subject matter on which to display one's erudition but something that must be made comprehensible to the masses and presented in simplified form. This responsibility was not assumed by the universities, where inner courage was lacking for such an undertaking, and so it was taken over by men outside the universities. The outcome was that these books were bestsellers, and that the historians in the universities furiously attacked the scholarship of these popularizations. The brunt of this attack was borne by the belletristic historians with a politically leftist outlook; those on the right, such as Beumelburg and his history of the World War,[h] were not molested.

This attack on historical works with a genuine appeal to a wide audience calls to mind how differently such things are handled in the United States. Beard's[i] two-volume work, *The Rise of American Civilization*, which appeared in an edition of 175,000 copies, has no equivalent in Germany, and it is unlikely that any such work will be produced by academic scholarship in the foreseeable future.

It was in the last years before the World War that German historiography shifted to the history of ideas, a disastrous development that resulted in the loss of Germany's influence on American historical scholarship. Prescot and Bancroft represent a prescientific stage of historical writing, but when American academic historiography began to take shape in the 1880's, when American universities were beginning to expand, most young American scholars were under Ranke's influence and attempted to follow his lead in historical research, in the hope of ascertaining "how things really were." They overlooked the weak points in Ranke's historiography, and for nearly a generation they did not notice Ranke's most serious flaw, though Americans should have been the first to recognize it, namely his failure to take into account the importance of business in politics. German historiography originated around the middle of the nineteenth century, a time when economic questions did not have such a vital impact on politics, or at least one that was easily demonstrable. It was unaware that things were changing and that economics was exerting a growing political influence. As for the Americans, the historiography they imported was as ill-suited for the early development of their country as it was for conditions in the 1880's and the 1890's. In the long run, this incompatibility between Ranke's historiography and American reality could not be ignored, and, shortly before the beginning of the World War, at the time when Germany turned to the history of ideas, America finally acknowledged the significant role of economics in history and political science. The initiators of this new historiography were Charles A. Beard with his *Economic Interpretation of the Constitution* and his *Economic Origins of Jeffersonian Democracy* and William E. Dodd with his *Expansion and Conflict.*[3] The former is now [1933] president of the American Historical Association, and the latter vice-president. In an undogmatic way, this new American historical writing seeks to avoid being associated with Marxist historiography. It is not necessary, one of its representatives has written, to accept Marx's view that the whole social structure is determined by economic circumstances; it is enough to recognize these forces as contributory to the formation of institutions.

The break had been accomplished. In America, the influence of economics on politics was now recognized by historians; in Germany, ideas became the guiding thread through the labyrinth of politics and the determining factor in political developments. Since official historiography now accepted the primacy of ideas, all those who believed that economics also played a role in politics were for all practical purposes excluded from the universities. What had been a grotesque farce when Schmoller was turned down as director of the Prussian State Archives exists as a reality today as it did thirty years ago. Such beliefs are still identified with socialism, and anyone who is considered to be a Socialist is automatically ostracized, even in the Weimar Republic, and loses any claim to influence. Anyone who tries to write social and economic history like Dodd and Beard accepts the risk of lifelong unemployment. Beard, Dodd, Craven,[k] and Walter Dorn in Columbus would never have become professors in Germany, even under the republic. If they had started to write social history before their appointment as full professors, they would never have been admitted to university faculties, and their only way of earning a living would have been as secretaries for local Social Democratic or Communist party organizations.

On the map of historical problems that still require further exploration some continents have already been fully charted, while others have been neglected. On the German map of historical problems, the continent "economic and social history" is as blank as the map of Africa before Stanley and Livingstone. But nobody is brave enough to undertake an expedition to these areas, where booty abounds at every step. Instead, hundreds of doctoral candidates every year choose as their hunting ground fields no bigger than a square inch, hunting for prey either in the history of ideas or in foreign policy. There is no great difficulty about writing a small doctor's dissertation of a hundred pages on a special problem and underpinning it with diplomatic documents. Interest in special questions of foreign policy has intensified since the publication of the large documentary collections, from which all economic factors have been carefully excised. But even this hunting ground has been overgrazed, in view of the large number of German doctoral candidates. The German doctorate is less demanding than the American Ph.D., and there are accordingly many more German doctorates awarded. Notwithstanding the rich pastures within such easy reach, one of the most eminent German historians told an American historian recently that, with the best of intentions, he could no longer think of any thesis topics. And he was quite right. The accessible fields have become exhausted and the others are protected by "Do not enter" signs.

Signs of this were apparent even before the war. The influence of the World War and the change of regime upon historiography was negligible if one ignores some emotional tendencies and concentrates on new methods and new ideas. The history of ideas reached the height of its influence. The German bourgeoisie as a whole was in flux, uncertain whether it should sympathize with socialism or go over to the new nationalism—until 1930 it had not yet opted for nationalism, or for socialism either—and, in this uncertain situation, historiography also suspended judgment, and the conditions that originally encouraged the history of ideas continued to prevail. Meinecke's *Idee der Staatsraison in der neueren Geschichte* mirrored this vacillating attitude, presenting the state and power simultaneously as white and black, good and evil, dirty and clean; hence no decision was conceivable either for or against the state, for imperialism or for pacifism, for capitalism or for socialism, since good and evil were inextricably intertwined. In short, the history of ideas came to a dead stop in a feeble and languid quietism and committed moral suicide by its failure to provide support for the present from the past. But the followers of history of ideas did not realize that they were already dead. In recent years a few attempts have been made to link the history of ideas with the political right and nationalism, for instance in books like Siegfried Kaehler's *Wilhelm von Humboldt und der Staat*[1] or Masur's Stahl biography.[m] But it is no longer possible, on the basis of the history of ideas, to build up a living historical discipline or to establish connections with nationalism or socialism, because it is rooted in an inner evasion from political choice.

For this reason the isolated attempt to elaborate a new fascist interpretation of history seems doomed to point the way toward the past rather than the future. This attempt was made in Hans Rothfels's[n] lecture "Bismarck und der deutsche Osten," which appeared in the *Historische Zeitschrift* (147, 1933). Rothfels, who is a professor at the University of Königsberg, near Germany's eastern border, has observed at first hand the convulsions created by nationalist ideas in this border zone between Eastern and Central Europe. He has observed how the combination of democracy and national identity, which had its origin in the capitalist countries of western Europe, has raised havoc with the political organization of the agrarian East. This leads him to the conclusion that an authoritarian and patriarchal regime is needed in order to permit *several* nationalities to coexist in peace within a *single* state. His starting point is justified; conditions in these border areas are untenable in the long run. But he fails to draw the logical consequences; the Soviet Union is the only state that has found a workable solution to the problem of having many nationalities coexist within a state. The only objective Rothfels pursues with his ideal of an authoritarian state is the preservation of a German, Baltic ruling stratum over these various Eastern populations. It is too late for that solution. These populations will not let themselves be ruled any longer by Baltic barons, and Germany's position in the East has been irretrievably lost. But as a historian of ideas—he too belongs to Meinecke's school—Rothfels is incapable of facing this harsh truth and takes refuge, like the romantics, in authoritarian, aristocratic forms of government. But for the time being Rothfels represents an exceptional case with his unambiguous slogan, "Back to the dictatorship of the barons!" Even where the new historiography is far to the right, it has never taken such a forthright stand.

During the half-generation of the Weimar Republic, history of ideas continued in its old form with its reluctance to look facts in the face. This position corresponded not only to the vacillation of the educated bourgeoisie, which shirked a choice between right and left, but also to the organization of German science, which after 1918 had to a large extent freed itself from the influence of the state and therefore from the danger of Socialist influence, and which had established two independent states within the state. These two autonomous scientific bodies in the German republic were the Kaiser-Wilhelm-Institut and the Notgemeinschaft der deutschen Wissenschaft. It is necessary in conclusion to say a few words about them so that the German historiography of the past decade can be better understood as a part of German scholarship and history in general.

Both organizations were set up privately and supported by endowments, an unusual procedure for Germany, where universities are state institutions; the Kaiser-Wilhelm Gesellschaft was established in 1913 and the Notgemeinschaft in 1920. But as a result of inflation, when the dollar was worth four billion marks, both these private endowments became worthless and the funding of the two organizations was assumed by the state, the Reich and Prussia. The state was not allowed to intervene in any way except to provide financial support. Both organizations maintained their autonomous administration, their trustees and governors, who were now administering state funds. Add to that the universities' tradition of self-administration, including the selection of their own professors, with the result that state appointments of professors against the wishes of the faculties have always been viewed as an infringement of academic freedom and have set off protest movements, and the complete picture of the situation of German scholarship in the Weimar Republic emerges. The fact is that 95 percent of its support comes from the state, with its pronounced Socialist, democratic, and liberal tendencies, but that it is 95 percent independent of the state in its organization. From a social point of view, there have been slight changes in the background of the ministers and a few political appointees, but there has been no social change in the composition of German scholarship. There are a very few cases where the government was able to impose its will against the wishes of the universities, but these are rare exceptions. The staff of the universities is still selected and promoted according to the prewar principles of political reliability; in historiography, social and economic history has remained precisely in the same position as before the war; it is still identified with socialism, and social history has remained Socialist history. This social distribution of power, which has persisted unaltered in the republic and which will be affected only on the political surface by the new changes, will block any attempt to apply the methods of modern American historiography in Germany and to replace the sterility, the Alexandrianism, of the history of ideas by a historiography that is alive and responsive to what is happening in the world around it.

Editor's Notes

Chapter I. The German Fleet in the Eighteen Nineties and the Politico-Military Dualism in the Empire

a. In old German law, the *Muntbezirk* was the area of jurisdiction belonging to the *Muntmannen* (the "protecting hand"), who watched over the ruler and his family, dependents, and retainers. The *Oprishchina* was the personal guard of Ivan IV of Russia. Both forces were free from the usual restraints and processes of law.

b. One of the half-way steps towards responsible constitutional government in Germany was the winning of the right of certain ministers to counter-sign royal orders. Marschall von Bieberstein's *Verantwortlichkeit und Gegenzeichnung bei Verordnungen des Obersten Kriegsherrn* (Berlin, 1911) discusses this complicated question.

c. Joseph Maria von Radowitz, a Catholic nobleman from Westphalia, became one of Frederick William IV's closest advisers almost immediately after that monarch's accession to the throne in 1840 and, in 1849, was the leading spirit behind the plan for a union of the states of northern Germany under Prussian leadership, which led to a sharp crisis with Austria, and, at Olmütz in 1850, to a humiliating Prussian abandonment of the scheme. Radowitz was always suspect in the eyes of the older Prussian conservatives, chief among whom were the brothers E.L. and Leopold von Gerlach. The latter was a prominent member of the camarilla that advised Frederick William during the revolutionary troubles of 1848 and encouraged him to oppose ministerial and parliamentary demands.

d. During the first part of the nineteenth century, the Chief of the General Staff was a mere subordinate of the Minister of War and had no direct access to the sovereign. Helmuth von Moltke, who became Chief of Staff in 1858, changed this by his masterly direction of operations in the last stages of the war against Denmark in 1864 and in the victorious war against Austria in 1866. In 1870, when Prussia went to war with France, Moltke was not only the king's most intimate adviser on military affairs but was also claiming the right to make decisions (about the terms of armistice, for example) which were essentially political.

e. Lorenz von Stein (1815-90), professor of national economy at Vienna after 1855, may be considered one of the founders of modern social science. His *Verwaltungslehre* (8 vols., 1865-84; reprinted, 1962) contains much that is still relevant to contemporary problems of constitutional government and administrative practice.

f. The "interlude of Prussian reformism" was the period 1807-19, following upon the defeat by France, during which basic reforms were effected in the areas of social organization, education, local government, and military affairs. On Kehr's view of these reforms, see Chapter VIII.

g. The left liberal and socialist members of the Reichstag wanted periodic reviews of the military budget, the more frequent the better; the military wanted no review at all. The issue was continually debated from 1867 to 1874 and regulated in the latter year by the Septennial Law which called for a seven-year review. In 1893, in order to make the Reichstag more amenable to an increase in the size of the army, the government reduced the period of review to five years, while also lowering the term of service from three to two years. See Chapter V.

h. The Kartell elections were those of 1887. In order to secure a conservative majority in the Reichstag, Bismarck took advantage of tension between the powers in the Balkans to create a war scare by means of inspired articles in the press, the calling up of reserves, and the announcement of a war loan. These tactics were successful, the Conservatives, Free Conservatives, and National Liberals, who formed the electoral alliance called the Kartell, winning 220 of the roughly 375 Reichstag seats.

i. The Chief of the Military Cabinet handled the king-emperor's correspondence with the commanding generals but, in his capacity as director of army personnel, was a subordinate of the Minister of War, as was the Chief of the General Staff. Since it was the custom for the War Minister to respond to questions in the Reichstag, and since the War Minister in 1883, von Kameke, was supposed to be a liberal who might be inclined to be too forthcoming about personnel policy or strategical planning or other sensitive matters, Bismarck agreed with the military's demand that the General Staff, and the Military Cabinet in all its functions, be made independent of the War Ministry and responsible only to the monarch. See Chapter VI.

j. Alfred Tirpitz joined the naval service in 1865. He became a protégé of Chief of Admiralty Ulrich von Stosch, who made him chief of the Torpedo Section in 1877. In 1892 he became Chief of Staff to the Chief of the High Command of the Navy, with special responsibility for the development of tactics for the High Seas Fleet. In 1896 he became Chief of the Eastern Asiatic Cruiser Division and was responsible for the choice of Kiaochow as a location for a German military and economic base. In 1897 he succeeded Admiral Hollmann as State Secretary of the Imperial Naval Office.

k. Ernst Levy von Halle, later professor of economics at the University of Berlin, was employed in the 1890's by the News Section of the Imperial Naval Office to provide scientific information and arguments in support of naval legislation for legislators and other interested groups.

l. The *Jeune École* comprised those theorists, mostly French and Russian, who believed that the Nelson type of naval combat was gone forever and that, in the age of steam, when the weaker adversary would seek to avoid major conflict and rely on raiding and commerce-destroying, speed was the first priority. Therefore, they favored the construction of fast cruisers and torpedo boats rather than of battleships.

m. In January 1896, under the influence of the Jameson raid against the Transvaal, which led William II to think about intervening on behalf of the Boer Republic, he insisted to his Chancellor that "cruisers must be laid down . . . in numbers corresponding to the capacities of our dockyards."

n. Gustav Freiherr von Senden-Bibran was Chief of the Naval Cabinet from 1889 to 1906.

o. The basic assumption of Tirpitz's "risk theory" was that Germany's fleet, while not so large as to be capable of defeating the British fleet, should be large enough to pose such a formidable threat that the British would seek a political agreement with Germany and be willing to make concessions in order to secure it.

p. Ulrich von Stosch was Chief of the Admiralty from 1871 to 1883.

q. Leo von Caprivi, who was Reich Chancellor in the years 1890–94, served as Chief of the Admiralty from 1883 to 1888. Like Stosch, he was a soldier by training and had reached general's rank.

r. The constitutional crisis that had resulted in Bismarck's dismissal in 1890 was still unresolved, and the Reichstag was in a refractory mood through the chancellorship of Caprivi and that of Hohenlohe (1894–1900).

s. The Civil Cabinet was a personal bureau of the emperor, analogous to the Military Cabinet, but handling the monarch's communications with civilian branches of the government.

t. When he became emperor, William II had increased the size of his personal suite of adjutants and reorganized it as an "Imperial Headquarters" under Generaladjutant Hans von Plessen. This added one more irresponsible agency to the number already dabbling in politics.

u. Dr. Ernst Maria Lieber was a Center party deputy in the Reichstag from 1871 to 1902 and was leader of the party after the death of Ludwig Windthorst in 1891.

v. Theobald von Bethmann Hollweg was Reich Chancellor from 1909 to 1917. In 1912 he was inclined to accept proposals for a naval agreement with Great Britain that were brought to Berlin by the British War Minister Lord Haldane. Tirpitz's opposition made an agreement impossible.

w. In 1912–13 the General Staff's demands for increases in army strength were opposed by the Ministry of War. See Chapter III.

Chapter II. Anglophobia and Weltpolitik

a. J.R. Seeley, professor of modern history at Cambridge University from 1869 to 1895, was the author of the influential book *The Expansion of England* (1883) and was an ardent advocate of British colonial expansion.

b. The *Sammlungspolitik*, or policy of concentration, was conceived by the National Liberal politician Johannes von Miquel as early as 1890, when he said that the "great task of the present is . . . to gather together all the elements that support the state and thereby to prepare for the unavoidable battle against the Social Democratic party." Implemented after 1897, particularly by Bernhard von Bülow during his chancellorship (1900–09), it took the form of a parliamentary alliance between the representatives of agrarian and industrial interests, based on the recognition and satisfaction of mutual economic interest.

c. Wilhelm Cuno was Reich Chancellor in 1922–23. His attempt to counter the French occupation of the Ruhr in January 1923 by a policy of passive resistance contributed to the runaway inflation without deterring the French from their purpose. His government was replaced by a government of the Great Coalition with Gustav Stresemann as Chancellor in August 1923, and his policy was abandoned.

d. Kehr's airy "everybody knows" is a typical instance of his slapdash way of dealing with historical references. What he means here is not clear. He may be referring to the feeling of resentment over Prussia's failure to go to Austria's aid during the Italian war of 1859, although this was more pronounced among Prussian conservatives and South German liberals than among Prussian liberals and progressives. He is probably thinking about those who opposed the proposed reform of the Prussian army in 1860 on the grounds that Prussia's foreign policy—specifically, its failure to support the cause of national unification—did not justify it.

e. Adolf Wagner (1835–1917), economist and leading member of the Union for Social Policy, was, paradoxically, also an étatiste, an anti-Semite, and a convinced supporter of agrarian life and values against industrialism.

f. "The Boers." The reference is to the government of Transvaal whose resistance to British pressure led to the Boer War in 1899.

g. After the restoration of Ferdinand VII of Spain in April 1823, the members of the Holy Alliance would have liked to restore Spanish power in the new world. George Canning made it clear that the British government would resist this, and his position was supported by the United States government in December 1823 by the promulgation of the Monroe Doctrine.

h. In the latter part of 1912 Col. Erich Ludendorff of the General Staff insisted that an increase of 300,000 recruits and the raising of three new army corps were necessary for Germany's security, despite the fact that sizable increases had already been made earlier in the year.

i. The government's interest in promoting a German-dominated railway system in the Middle East connecting Baghdad, Constantinople and the Persian Gulf ports was dramatized by a visit of the Kaiser to Damascus in 1898.

j. At the end of the century, Russia's growing influence in the Far East seemed to threaten the British with war, perhaps with the French on the Russian side. From this predicament the British extricated themselves by the Japanese alliance of 1902.

k. The upswing in world trade faltered in 1900, causing a sharp crisis in financial circles. See Chapter IV.

l. The passage of the protective tariff of 1879 was accompanied by a shift on Bismarck's part to a conservative anti-Socialist policy.

m. Felix Jules Méline, French minister of agriculture (1883–85), president of the Chamber (1888–89), prime minister and minister of agriculture (1896–98), played a major role in drafting protectionist legislation after 1890.

n. Eugen Richter (1838–1906) was the leader of the Progressive party; Rudolf von Bennigsen (1824–1902) of the National Liberals.

o. In 1891 Caprivi carried through the Reichstag a series of trade treaties with Austria, Italy, Belgium, and Switzerland that reduced duties on imported wheat and rye in exchange for favorable rates on German exports of manufactured goods.

p. Bismarck's program of social insurance, passed during the 1880's, had no apparent effect on the militancy of the working-class movement. The Subversion Bill *(Umsturzvorlage)* of 1895 and the Penitentiary Bill *(Zuchthausvorlage),* first proposed in 1896–97, were intended by the parties of the right to correct this. Both were rejected by the Reichstag.

q. The Reinsurance Treaty was concluded in 1887. Three years later, to the disappointment of the Russians, the German government decided not to renew it. Ivan Alekseevich Vyshnegradsky, Russian finance minister from 1887 to 1892, made protective tariffs a major instrument of Russian fiscal policy. His tariff of 1891 was the cornerstone of economic and financial policy until 1914.

r. S.Y. Witte, Russian minister of finance from 1892 to 1903, set out to develop industry by attracting foreign capital. Tariffs were used to create a reserve that would enable Russia to adopt the gold standard, thus enhancing the country's fiscal standing. By 1897 this policy was successful enough to encourage a good deal of French and Belgian investment.

s. "Between 1898 and 1901." These dates marked the high point of the negotiations for an Anglo-German alliance which, if consummated, the British would have used against Russia and its ally France.

t. After the collapse of the efforts to reach a German alliance, the British turned to Tokyo and concluded an alliance in 1902.

u. The Dawes Plan was an international arrangement negotiated in 1924, which relieved Germany's financial crisis by bringing foreign capital in the form of short-term loans into the country.

v. N.K. Giers, Russian foreign minister from 1882 to 1895. A believer in collaboration with Germany and Austria-Hungary, he was forced, by the German decision not to renew the Reinsurance Treaty, to reorient his policy toward France after 1890.

w. In 1887, in order to force a solution of the Bulgarian problem, Bismarck closed the German stock market to Russian government bond issues.

x. In 1891, the French and Russian governments agreed to consult in the case of threats to the peace; in the following year, they supplemented this with a military convention; and, in January 1894, they ratified a formal alliance.

y. In the preliminary stages of their *rapprochement*, the French and Russians exchanged visits of their fleets. The incident mentioned in the text occurred during the visit of the French squadron to Kronstadt in ~~1893~~. 1891.

z. In German history, the *Gründerzeit*, a period of frantic expansion and speculation, extended from the end of the French war to the crash of 1873.

Chapter III. Class Struggle and Armament Policy in Imperial Germany

a. Karl von Clausewitz (1780–1831) was Germany's most famous military theorist, author of the treatise *On War* and other studies.

b. The decisive battle of the war between Austria and Prussia took place at Königgrätz in Bohemia on 3 July 1866.

c. Alfred Count von Schlieffen, Chief of the General Staff from 1891 to 1905, was the author of the plan for invading France through Belgium, which was used in 1914.

d. Caprivi, who had negotiated a colonial agreement with Great Britain in 1890, was thinking of France and Russia as Germany's future antagonists when he made these calculations.

e. Hans Delbrück was professor of history at the University of Berlin from 1896 to 1921. Heinrich Dietzel (1857–1935) was professor of economics at Bonn after 1890 and was an ardent advocate of *Weltpolitik*.

f. The Prussian constitutional conflict ended in September 1866 with a settlement (the Indemnity Act) in which the Chamber accepted the army reforms it had opposed since 1860 (and, by implication, also accepted the king's right to command his army as he wished), while the Crown acknowledged parliament's budget right.

g. None of the major powers, except Russia, was anxious to accept any degree of disarmament or arms control at the first Peace Conference at The Hague in 1899, but the chief German delegate, Colonel Schwarzhoff, was brutally frank in rejecting all forms of international regulation.

h. In 1911, in response to French occupation of Fez, the German government sent the gunboat *Panther* to Agadir, ostensibly to force the French to

194]

withdraw or to grant extensive compensation to Germany. This forcing play back-fired, the Germans eventually having to back down in return for concessions that patriots found trifling, if not insulting.

i. Adolf Wermuth was Bethmann's secretary of treasury, a firm opponent of any increase of military expenditure. The tactics he and Bethmann followed here were only temporarily successful, and the endemic financial problem was rendered so hopeless by military demands that Wermuth resigned in disgust.

j. The Chief of the General Staff was Field Marshal Helmuth J.L. Count von Moltke, nephew of the Chief of Staff of the period of unification.

k. In October 1912, Serbia, Montenegro, Bulgaria, and Greece had launched an offensive against Turkish territory in Europe. The resultant confusion threatened to bring Austrian and Russian intervention and conflict, with unforeseen consequences.

Chapter IV. The Social and Financial Foundations of
Tirpitz's Naval Propaganda

a. The Reptile Fund was established with funds confiscated, after the war of 1866, from the exchequer of the King of Hannover and the treasuries of other deposed princes. Its purpose, Bismarck said, was "to pursue evil reptiles into their holes and observe their movements." In part, the fund was used to provide subventions to newspapers for articles the Chancellor wanted to see in print.

b. After his dismissal, Bismarck intermittently criticized the policies of his successors. The *Hamburger Neueste Nachrichten* willingly served as a kind of house organ for him, and he could have found others, if necessary.

c. Since the federal government was not constitutionally entitled to collect direct taxes, it was largely dependent for its financial solvency upon contributions from the separate states. These were called *Matriku-larbeiträge*.

d. August Keim was the founder of the *Wehrverein* or Defense Union, a potent pressure group for new armaments.

e. Karl Ferdinand Freiherr von Stumm-Halberg (1836–1901) was an industrialist and conservative politician with newspaper interests.

f. Adolf Woermann was a leading Hamburg shipping magnate who had been active in promoting German colonialism since the early 1880's.

g. The Frankfurt Assembly of 1848 had tried to satisfy the old dream of reviving the glories of the Hansa by founding a German fleet. This did not survive the collapse of the national experiment and, under the revived Germanic Bund (1850–66), naval construction was left to the separate states, which meant that the tiny Prussian navy was the sole German fighting fleet, apart from the Austrian navy, which was a respectable force.

h. Karl Peters, famous African explorer of the 1880's, was, while serving as Reich Commissioner for German East Africa in the 1890's, accused of misusing government funds.

i. Werdeck-Schorbus and Levetzow were Conservative deputies in the Reichstag, the latter serving as president of that body from 1888 to 1895. Kanitz was an agrarian spokesman who had proposed a plan (the *Antrag Kanitz*) for a government monopoly of all grain imports, the grain to be sold at a fixed price well above the 1880–1890 average. This transparent attempt to circumvent the Caprivi trade treaties the government refused to accept.

j. The Center party had two extreme wings, an aristocratic and a democratic one. While he was leader of the party, Ludwig Windthorst sought either to reconcile their differences or to steer a middle course between them. After his death in 1891, the relative unity he had achieved broke down for a time. In 1893 the party was split on the army issue, and the democratic wing helped to defeat it in its original form. In the 1893 elections the party lost ten seats, a result which doubtless influenced its subsequent change of direction.

k. The Colonial Society had had some influence in persuading Bismarck to seek colonies in 1884 but had not grown greatly since then. The Pan-German League had been founded in 1890 by Heinrich Class. Its influence was discernible in all patriotic causes. In 1897, for example, it was financing and publishing propaganda materials prepared inside the Imperial Naval Office.

l. The propaganda chief was Korvetten-Kapitän August von Heeringen, a persuasive writer and a talented public speaker.

m. The *Zentralverband Deutscher Industrieller* was founded by Wilhelm von Kardorff and other industrialists in December 1875 to fight free trade and to promote industry. It maintained close links with other trade associations, like the Union of Iron and Steel Industrialists and similar organizations in the textile and chemical industries. Emil Kirdorff of the Gelsenkirchen Mining Society served on several of its committees. Alfred von Krupp, the Essen steel maker, did not play a prominent role in its affairs but had great influence.

n. In 1894, Stumm-Halberg, who was one of the most passionate advocates of the Subversion Bill, attacked the economists Adolf Wagner, Gerhart von Schulze-Gävernitz, and Lujo Brentano by name, accusing them of using their university chairs to disseminate socialist doctrine.

o. Hugo Stinnes (1870–1924), by the end of his career, during the Weimar period, was a power of the first magnitude in virtually every branch of economic activity from mining, steel fabrication, transportation, and textiles to publications. The DAZ was the *Deutsche Allgemeine Zeitung*.

p. Alfred Hugenberg (1865–1951), newspaper publisher and conservative politician, who had been one of the founders of the Pan-German League, was to become the leader of the conservative German National Peoples party in the 1920's and to serve as Minister of Economics and Food in Hitler's cabinet in 1933.

q. Prince Chlodwig zu Hohenlohe-Schillingsfürst was Reich Chancellor from 1894 to 1900.

r. The bill for the construction of the North Sea Canal occupied the attention of the Prussian *Landtag* from 1894 to 1899. In August 1899 it was defeated by the votes of the two Conservative parties, supported by the Poles and the Center.

s. Max Franz Guido Freiherr von Thielmann, after two years as ambassador to Washington, served as Secretary of the Treasury from 1897 to 1903.

t. *Non olet:* It doesn't smell.

u. Emil Rathenau (1838–1915) was the founder of the *Allgemeine Elektrizitäts-Gesellschaft* (AEG).

v. Maximilian Harden (1861–1927) was the editor of the influential journal *Die Zukunft,* an admirer of Bismarck, and a persistent and damaging critic of William II's circle of advisers and friends.

Chapter V. The Genesis of the Royal Prussian Reserve Officer

a. When Kehr wrote this essay, the German army was limited by the terms of the Versailles treaty of 1919 to 100,000 officers and men, all long-term volunteers.

b. Oswald Spengler (1880–1936) was the author of *The Decline of the West* (1918) and an influential pamphlet, *Preussenthum und Sozialismus* (1919) which argued that Germany's hope of regeneration lay in the values of the Prussian past.

c. The *Landwehr* was raised in 1813 and participated in the liberation of Germany from Napoleon, becoming thereafter an important feature in liberal ideology.

d. See below, Chapter VI.

e. Albrecht von Roon, Prussian War Minister from 1859 to 1873, was the driving force behind the army reform.

f. In 216 B.C. Hannibal crushed the Roman army at Cannae in Apulia in a perfect battle of encirclement. This battle became the ideal model for Schlieffen's own strategy.

g. Candidates for a reserve commission normally applied after they had completed their *Gymnasium* education and received the *Abitur* certificate. They then served as *Einjährig-Freiwillige* (one-year volunteers) before becoming Reserve Lieutenants.

h. In the speech at the Alexander Barracks in Potsdam, the emperor sought to impress upon his uniformed auditors the necessity of obedience, telling them that, even if commanded to shoot their own fathers and brothers, they must obey.

*Chapter VI. The Social System of Reaction in Prussia
under the Puttkamer Ministry*

a. The *Kulturkampf,* or "battle for civilization" (the name was coined by the National Liberal deputy Rudolf Virchow) was the offensive that Bismarck had mounted against German catholicism in 1873, partly in the hope of breaking the independence of the Center party, partly because he honestly believed he was forestalling an international Catholic campaign against Germany.

b. Paul Laband (1830–1918) was professor of constitutional law at Königsberg from 1864 to 1872 and after that at Strassburg.

c. Theodor Mommsen (1817–1903), author of the famous *Roman History,* was professor of ancient history at the University of Berlin from 1858 until his retirement. He received the Nobel Prize for Literature in 1902.

d. Friedrich Meinecke (1862–1954) was professor of history at Strassburg, 1901–06, Freiburg im Breisgau, 1906–14, and Berlin, 1914–48. In 1948 he was the first Rektor of the Free University of Berlin.

e. Heinrich von Treitschke (1834–96), professor of history at Berlin from 1874 on. The first volume of *German History* appeared in 1879.

f. Dietrich Schäfer (1845–1929) was professor of history successively at Jena, Breslau, Tübingen, Heidelberg and, from 1903 to 1921, Berlin.

g. Gustav Schmoller (1838–1917) was professor of economics at Halle, Strassburg and, after 1862, at Berlin.

h. August Count Neithardt von Gneisenau (1760-1831) was a leading member of the Prussian reform party and was Blücher's brilliant chief of staff during the war of liberation. His definition of "love of one's ruler, love of the fatherland" as poetry was made in a letter to King Frederick William III in 1811.

i. F.J. Stahl (1802–61), philosopher of law. His *Staatslehre,* with its emphasis on legitimacy and prescriptive rights, had a strong influence on the constitutional practise of Prussia and the Reich.

j. Gerhard Johann David Scharnhorst (1755–1813) was the reorganizer of the Prussian army after its defeat at Jena in 1806.

k. Karl Baron vom und zum Stein (1757–1831) was the leader of the Prussian reform party.

l. What Kehr means by this is difficult to say. No examples spring to the mind.

m. The Prussian constitution of 1848 was promulgated by the king in a voluntary action and was amended conservatively in 1850 in the same way.

n. Robert von Keudell (1824–1903) was a diplomat and an intimate friend of the Bismarck family.

o. Karl August Fürst von Hardenberg (1750–1822), Prussian reformer and Chancellor after 1810, implemented, and in some cases modified, Stein's reforms, including the policy of turning feudal lands into freeholds, which stemmed from the abolition of serfdom in 1807.

p. F.A.L. von der Marwitz (1777–1837) was the most persistent and eloquent defender of the aristocratic-agrarian cause against the Prussian reformers.

Chapter VII. The Sociology of the Reichswehr

a. See above, Chapter V, note g.

b. See above, Chapter V, note g.

c. After the defeat of Napoleon III's armies by the Germans in 1870, a revolutionary government, the Commune, established itself in Paris and maintained itself from March to May 1871, when it was suppressed with great bloodshed and reprisals by troops of the National Assembly at Versailles. Since this left a heritage of bitterness that affected the French working class for years, Kehr's point is obscure.

d. The free corps were volunteer forces called into existence by former army officers in order to deal with threats to local order, the Polish and Bolshevik pressure along the eastern frontiers, and the possibility of the seizure of the central government by forces of the extreme left. The republican government that was headed by Friedrich Ebert relied upon them to suppress the Spartacists in Berlin in January and March 1919 and to overthrow the Soviet Republic in Munich later in the year; they were also used to restore the government's authority in the Rhineland in 1920.

e. Colonel-General Hans von Seeckt (1866–1936) had a brilliant record on the eastern front during the first World War, became head of the Troop Bureau of the new Reichswehr in 1919, and was Chief of the Army Command from 1920 to 1926.

f. In 1926 Seeckt invited a grandson of the former emperor William II to attend army maneuvers. Regarding this as an antirepublican demonstration and an action that would embarrass the state's foreign policy, the government dismissed him.

g. Julius Deutsch was an Austrian Socialist who appeared to have clearer ideas about military policy than his German party comrades. As State Secretary in 1918–20, he organized the Austrian Peoples Militia, which replaced the old royal and imperial army, and after 1920 he was the organizer of the so-called Republican Defense League.

h. Lazare Carnot (1753–1823) was the military genius of the wars of the French Revolution and the organizer of an army on the basis of the *levéee en masse*.

i. Gustav Noske (1868–1946) was Defense Minister in 1918–20 and had to deal with the threat of revolution from the extreme left in the first months of 1919. He found it difficult to recruit a defense force from the working class and had to make use of the free corps.

j. The one-year service certificate was available only to persons who had completed their *Gymnasium* education. See above, Chapter V, note g.

k. The Weimar Coalition was the basis of the governments in power from the time of the National Assembly until the elections of June 1920. It was composed of the Social Democratic, Center, and Democratic parties.

Chapter VIII. The Genesis of the Prussian Bureaucracy and the Rechtsstaat

a. The Fugger and Welser banking houses, both situated in Augsburg, reached the peak of their influence in the sixteenth century, declining in pace with the decline of Habsburg fortunes in the century that followed.

b. Charles V was Holy Roman Emperor from 1519 to 1558.

c. Albrecht Wenzel Eusebius von Wallenstein (1583–1634) was the most successful of the commanders on the imperial side during the Thirty Years War. Remarkable for his ability to raise and support large armies, he was also brilliant in operations in the field. He was murdered on suspicion of treason at Eger in 1634. Schiller wrote a dramatic trilogy on his career.

d. The "ideological superstructure" was provided, Kehr appears to imply, by Romantic theorists like Karl Ludwig von Haller, Friedrich Schlegel, and F.A.L. von der Marwitz, who exalted tradition and celebrated legitimacy.

e. "Jena": The reference is to the defeat of the Prussian army by Napoleon at Jena and Auerstadt in 1806.

f. The 14th of October was the date of the battle of Jena.

g. The *Deutsche Staatspartei*, founded in July 1930, was the *dernière incarnation* of the German Democratic party of 1919.

h. Theodor von Schön played a conspicuous part in Prussian politics until the reign of Frederick William IV, particularly as *Oberpräsident* of East Prussia. Karl von Altenstein was to serve until the end of the 1830's, notably in the ministries of finance and education. Barthold Georg Niebuhr was to be a distinguished diplomat and historian. Staegemann became secretary to King Frederick William III. All four men were brought into the service by Stein, although Kehr gives another impression.

i. Karl Twesten, who first attained a measure of fame in 1861 when the Chief of the Military Cabinet, Edwin von Manteuffel, challenged him to a duel because he had published a pamphlet that attacked the Military Cabinet, was later, in 1866, one of the founders of the National Liberal party.

j. The policies followed by Frederick William I during his reign (1713–40), and particularly his insistence that the nobility perform military service, were designed to end the resistance of the Junkers to the Crown and establish the latter "like a rock of bronze."

k. The October Edict abolished serfdom.

l. See above, Chapter VI, note p.

m. In December 1789, the French National Assembly issued treasury notes bearing 5% interest as a means of meeting current obligations and redeeming the public debt. In April 1790 these were made legal tender and more were issued, although without interest. The result was inflation. By 1796 there were *assignats* to the face value of 36 billion pounds in circulation, but they were worth less than the cost of printing them. This experience, or something like it, had been repeated in Germany in 1922–23.

n. Literally, *Rechtsstaat* means the state of law, that is, the state whose very existence exemplifies the rule of law. The concept was central in theories of political liberty in Germany, much of the discussion turning on the question of how to reconcile traditional authority with the rights and liberties of citizens in a viable political form.

o. Karl Friedrich von Beyme (1765–1838) was a cabinet secretary in Frederick William III's government before Jena and later became minister. Stein believed that Beyme was one of those advisers whose lack of moral fiber had led to the disaster of 1806.

p. The economic measures mentioned by Kehr were legislated by the Reichstag in the 1870's when the National Liberals were the strongest party. On the political defeats—the Indemnity Act of September 1866 and the *Septennat*—see above, Chapter III, note f and Chapter I, note g.

q. The supersession of parliament and the unorthodox measures mentioned here were all part of Chancellor Heinrich Bruening's attempt, during 1930–32, to grapple with the problems of the depression by emergency decrees issued under the authority of Article 48 of the Weimar Constitution.

Chapter IX. The Dictatorship of the Bureaucracy

a. Eugen Richter was later the leader of the Progressive party.

b. Leopold von Ranke (1795–1886) was the founder of the objective or scientific school of history. See Chapter X.

c. During the great inflation of 1922–23, the lower middle class, the *rentiers,* and those with modest savings deposits were highly vulnerable, whereas, in some cases, representatives of the propertied class were deriving so much profit from the inflation that they were not anxious to see it stop.

d. Otto Braun, Prussian Social Democrat, was Minister President of Prussia from 1920 to 1932, with brief interruptions in 1921 and 1925. The Young Plan, negotiated at The Hague in 1929, instituted a new schedule of reparations payments, scaling down the Dawes Plan. It was challenged by rightist forces in Germany, and a referendum had to be held before it came into force.

e. The question of the constitutionality of Bruening's actions is controversial, and Kehr's argument is oversimplified.

f. On 20 July 1932, Chancellor Franz von Papen used an emergency decree to depose the Braun government in Prussia, on the grounds that it was incapable of preserving public order. He himself became Reich Commissioner and assumed command of the Prussian police forces.

Chapter X. Modern German Historiography

a. Friedrich Althoff was Prussian Minister of Education from 1897 to 1907 and head of its universities section for fifteen years before that. He was a capable but self-willed director of university affairs and never hesitant about violating academic freedom if it stood in his way.

b. On Laband and Treitschke, see Chapter VI.

c. Walter L. Dorn was professor of European history at Ohio State University. He was the author of a notable study of the Prussian bureaucracy in the eighteenth century.

d. Otto Hintze (1861-1940), professor of history at the University of Berlin from 1902 to 1920, when he retired for reasons of health, was an incisive analyst of the social and constitutional history of Prussia and a pioneer in the uses of comparative history.

e. The Moroccan crisis of 1905, which for a time seemed to threaten war between France and Germany, was resolved, to the great psychological disadvantage of the latter, at the Algeciras Conference of 1906, in which Germany found itself virtually isolated.

f. All three of these were political historians. Max Lenz (1850-1932) and Erich Marcks (1861-1938) were Bismarck scholars. Delbrück was a student of the reciprocal relationship between civil and military institutions.

g. Emil Ludwig (1881-1948) won world fame with his highly colored biographies. His subjects included Goethe, Napoleon, Bismarck, and Jesus.

h. Werner Beumelburg wrote highly nationalistic accounts of the war and a novel, *Gruppe Bosemüller: Der Roman des Frontsoldaten* (1930), which was immensely popular for the next fifteen years.

i. Charles Austin Beard (1874-1948) taught at Columbia University from 1904 to 1917, was one of the founders of the New School of Social Research, and was an active and prolific historian until his last days.

j. William Edward Dodd (1869-1940), historian of the American South and biographer of Woodrow Wilson, was professor of history at the University of Chicago from 1908 to 1933, when he became U.S. ambassador to Germany, serving in that post until December 1937.

k. Avery Odelle Craven, professor of history at the University of Chicago from 1928 until the 1960's, wrote extensively on the origins of the American Civil War.

l. Siegfried Kaehler (1885-1962) was professor of history at Göttingen and a close friend of Meinecke, whose views of the Humboldt book were as critical as Kehr's, but for different reasons.

m. Gerhard Masur (born 1901), a skillful biographer, also wrote an impressionistic history of Berlin during the Second Empire.

n. Hans Rothfels (1891-1976) edited the *Vierteljahreshefte für Zeitgeschichte,* which he founded after returning to Germany from the United States, where he taught at the University of Chicago during the Nazi years. His long list of publications include editions of the works and letters of Bismarck and Clausewitz and a history of the German resistance against Hitler.

Index